Contents

Introduction

This book has been written for child care and education students and practitioners with the intention of providing a guide to all aspects of early years care and education of children aged from birth to 8 years. The book relates particularly to the requirements of the National Vocational Qualifications (NVQs) in Early Years Care and Education at level 2. Students on any of the many other courses that require a knowledge and understanding of early years care and education will also find this book useful. Child care settings may find this book a valuable addition to their reference shelves and helpful in supporting in-service training.

The book is divided into units and each unit relates directly to a unit in the National Occupational Standards in Early Years Care and Education at level 2. Each unit is presented in a way that is appropriate for level 2 students. The book emphasises the role of the child care and education worker, and their responsibilities when caring for children. Practical examples help the reader to relate theoretical points to real-life situations.

In each unit, at the end of every element, there is a section about assessment, which includes information on direct observation by the assessor and preparing to be observed. There are questions at the end of each unit, which will help students recall their knowledge, develop understanding and may provide evidence.

The first section in the book is about the principles of good practice, which underpin everything that we do with children and their families. Sections follow on assessment, observation and development. These sections provide useful information that will support students' underpinning knowledge and understanding.

Throughout the book references have been made to national legislation and/or local regulations relating to the care and education of children. The four countries that make up the United Kingdom are England, Wales, Scotland and Northern Ireland. There are differences in legislation and regulations for each of the four countries. You will find references to these differences within the book. The appendix at the end of the book has further information.

Acknowledgements

The authors and publishers would like to thank their friends, colleagues and the following organisations for permission to reproduce materials and photographs in this book:

Corbis for the photo on page 142; Sally and Richard Greenhill for the photo on page 6.

Many thanks also to Neil and Caroline Mulvihill and their daughter, Molly and to Rick and Clare Jackman and their son, Tom.

Every effort has been made to contact copyright holders and we apologise if anyone has been overlooked.

Principles of good practice

Values and principles

Throughout each unit of your NVQ you must show you are committed to the values expressed in the Statement of Underlying Principles in the National Occupational Standards. The ones you must put into practice in particular are shown in a table at the beginning of each unit in your assessment handbook.

These include:

- The welfare of the child
- Keeping children safe
- Working in partnership with parents/families
- Children's learning and development
- Equality of opportunity
- Anti-discrimination
- Celebrating diversity
- Confidentiality
- Working with other professionals
- The reflective practitioner.

This book is based on these values and principles throughout. Some units are directly related to values concerning children's safety, working in partnership with parents, children's learning and development, confidentiality and working with other professionals.

The values and principles you must put into practice with respect to discrimination, promoting equality of opportunity and valuing diversity underpin each unit; this section explains these in greater detail.

This section includes:

- The rights and needs of children
- Discrimination
- Equality of opportunity
- Valuing diversity
- Creating a positive environment.

Providing a positive care and education environment for children depends on recognising the needs and rights of children and on having a professional approach to meeting these needs.

The rights and needs of children

The following ideas, based on 'Young Children in Group Day Care: Guidelines for Good Practice' by the Early Childhood Unit of the National Children's Bureau, apply equally well to any care or educational setting. They outline a set of beliefs about the needs and rights of young children. These are as follows:

- Children's well-being is paramount (of the greatest importance).
- Children are individuals in their own right. They have differing needs, abilities and potential. Therefore, any day care setting should be flexible and sensitive in responding to these needs.
- Since discrimination of all kinds is an everyday reality in the lives of many children, every effort must be made to ensure that services and practices do not reflect or reinforce it, but actively fight against it. Therefore, equality of opportunity for children, parents and staff should be made clear in the policies and practice of a day care setting.
- Working in partnership with parents is recognised as being of major value and importance.
- Good practice in day care for children can enhance their social, intellectual, emotional, physical and creative development.
- Young children learn and develop best through their own exploration and experience. Such opportunities for learning and development are based on stable, caring relationships, regular observation and ongoing assessment. This will result in reflective practitioners who use their observations to inform the learning experiences they offer.
- Regular and thorough evaluation of policies, procedures and practices helps the provision of high quality day care.

The Human Rights Act (1998)

The European Convention on Human Rights was a treaty ratified (agreed) by the UK in 1951, guaranteeing the various rights and freedoms in the United Nations Declaration on Human Rights, adopted in 1948. The Human Rights Act 1998, which came fully into force on 2 October 2000, gives people in the UK opportunities to enforce these rights directly in the British courts, rather than having to incur the cost and delay of taking a case to the European Court in Strasburg.

Discrimination

Attitudes

It is important to adopt positive attitudes when working with children and their families. Negative attitudes and assumptions based on stereotypical ideas about people can damage children's personal development and lead to discriminatory practices against them. These result in reduced chances and achievements in later life.

Attitudes are our opinions and ways of thinking. Our attitude to people affects the way we act and behave towards them. Attitudes can be positive or negative:

- A positive attitude towards a person based on knowledge, understanding and respect enables that person to feel good, valued and have high self-esteem.
- A negative attitude towards a person, based on poorly informed opinion and stereotypical assumptions, can lead to low self-esteem and feeling unwanted or rejected.

Positive attitudes are therefore very important when working with children and their families. Child care workers need to examine their attitudes to make sure that they are not based on any negative or stereotypical assumptions.

Assumptions

To assume is to believe something without evidence or proof. Making assumptions can be a very useful way of helping to understand the world around us. Assumptions enable us to predict what is going to happen and to feel secure. Children gain security from assuming many things. For example, if it is home time, a child will assume that a carer will be meeting them; if it is bedtime, they may assume that an adult will read them a story; if they are hurt, they will assume that an adult will be there to help them etc. Such assumptions give a positive frame-work to their lives.

Stereotyping, however, involves assuming that all the people who share one characteristic (e.g. the same gender, race or social origin) also share another set of characteristics (e.g. being less strong, less able). We give specific names to some forms of negative attitudes and assumptions:

- **racism** – when people of one race or culture believe they are superior to another
- **sexism** – when people of one gender believe they are superior to the other.

Negative attitudes are based on poorly informed and stereotypical images

Other forms of stereotyping have less specific names. They involve discrimination against people with disabilities, those in low socio-economic groups, those of differing sexual orientation and others. Negative stereotypical assumptions can be very harmful. They are assumptions based on incomplete knowledge and understanding, and on fixed and prejudiced attitudes.

Stereotyping can lead to:

- **discrimination** (i.e. unfavourable treatment of people based on prejudice)
- **oppression** (using power to dominate and reduce people's life chances).

When one group in society is more powerful than another group and holds stereotypical attitudes, they can block the progress of other members of society. This reduces that group's life chances and achievements.

Institutionalised discrimination

Discrimination occurs not only when one person behaves in an oppressive manner towards another. It can also occur when individual workers have positive attitudes, but the institution (e.g. school, nursery, college) is not organised to meet the needs of all the people within it, or even excludes some people from membership altogether. This can happen when, for example:

- children with impairments are not provided with the equipment they need to take a full part in the curriculum
- the needs of children from minority religious groups are not recognised
- activities are organised in a way that makes it difficult for some children to participate.

This is called institutionalised discrimination. While most child workers try to ensure that they have positive attitudes, they are sometimes less aware of institutionalised practices that discriminate against certain groups of children and parents.

Effects of discrimination

Discrimination can affect individuals and groups within any child care setting. These are some of the main groups affected:

- **Disabled children and their families** – Disabled children and their families are prone to many forms of obvious discrimination. Even in a caring environment, concern to meet their special needs can distract from meeting their ordinary needs and from seeing them as unique individuals. Enabling people with disabilities to take an effective part in the world is called empowerment.
- **Children from black and other minority ethnic groups** – In a predominantly white society, children from black and other minority ethnic groups often experience overt racist comments and treatment. It is difficult to learn in an environment where such practices are allowed to exist. Racism is sometimes covert and involves, for example, a lack of understanding of differences, a lack of positive images of black people, or an absence of equipment and resources that reflect a multicultural society. Racism discourages the growth of the individual and prevents children reaching their full potential.

- **Women** – There is evidence to show that women are still discriminated against. Most top job positions are filled by men; women are more often employed in low-status jobs. Much has been done to address gender bias in schools, but certain attitudes and assumptions continue to cause many women to under-achieve.

- **Children from lower socio-economic groups** – Children from lower socio-economic groups (lower social status and poorer families) continue to under-achieve academically. The introduction of comprehensive education has given opportunity to all individuals, but it has failed to address the causes of under-achievement linked to social and economic disadvantage.

Opposing discrimination

The best way to oppose discrimination is to provide an environment that encourages a positive view of the people of the world, celebrates difference and actively opposes any discriminatory practice. Opposing discrimination involves developing an understanding of the different practices that may lead to it. This includes being aware of vocabulary or jokes that are, or might be, abusive, and being sensitive and alert to unequal provision of resources and opportunities. Through this knowledge and awareness, child care workers can learn to take positive action and promote equality of opportunity.

Any obvious abuse or discrimination should be challenged. Not to do so would be to accept and condone it. Challenging abuse can be a difficult thing to do, especially for a young worker. It is, however, a skill that needs to be learned. The ability to deal with discriminatory practices may not be very well developed, especially at the beginning of a career. Child care workers should not feel they have failed if they have to take advice about what to do. If you witness overt discrimination involving adults or children, it may be sufficient initially to make your views known in a calm manner to the people involved. You could then seek advice about alternative strategies and future contact.

Supervisors should be able to give advice and support about the need for further action or what to do if the situation arises again. It may be their duty to take the matter further. Many establishments have an equal opportunities policy or code of practice, setting out the steps that should be taken.

Equality of opportunity

What is equality of opportunity?

Equality of opportunity is about recognising differences and enabling people to have the opportunity to participate in every area of life to the best of their abilities. It can be promoted at government level by the passing of laws, at institutional level through working practices and codes of conduct, and at a personal level through increased awareness and skills in meeting needs.

Equality of opportunity:

- is not about treating all people the same and ignoring differences

Equality of opportunity is about recognising differences and enabling children to have the opportunity to participate in every area of life to the best of their abilities

● is about recognising differences and providing for all people according to their needs. Ignoring differences can be the very reason that people are not given equality of opportunity – because their needs are not recognised.

For example, if three candidates are invited for a job interview on the first floor of a building that does not have a lift, and one candidate uses a wheelchair, that person would not have an equal opportunity to get the job.

Other examples of ignoring differences may be less obvious but the effects are no less detrimental. For example, not recognising that some families cannot afford to pay for school outings; that some religious groups have particular dress and dietary requirements; that one gender group may dominate particular activities or curriculum areas – all these failures to recognise differences would have a serious adverse effect on the people concerned.

People are not the same: they have many differences and their individual and particular needs should be recognised and accommodated. There is now a commitment at many levels of society to promote equality of opportunity and to combat oppression and discrimination by recognising differences.

Promoting equality of opportunity at government level

Promoting equality of opportunity means enabling people to have an equal chance of participating in life to the best of their abilities, whatever their gender, race, religion, disability or social background. This includes providing equal access to education, health, social services and jobs.

The promotion of equality of opportunity is possible at a number of different levels in society. At government level, laws have been passed in Parliament aimed at combating some forms of oppression and discrimination. Some people believe that passing laws does not stop discrimination, and that discrimination will still exist. This may be true, but a law does make a public statement about what is not acceptable in society and gives those in authority the power to penalise those who break it. Few people would want to make housebreaking legal just because the law does not stop it from happening.

Laws on disability

- **The Education Act 1944** placed a general duty on local education authorities (LEAs) to provide education for all children, including those with special needs.

- **The Education Act 1981** was the main piece of legislation about special education. It laid down specific procedures for the assessment and support of children with special educational needs.

- **The Education Reform Act 1988** requires LEAs to provide access to the National Curriculum for all children, including those with special needs.

- **The Education Act 1996** has now replaced, and included, the provisions of the previous education acts.

- **The Children Act 1989** defines the services that should be provided for 'children in need' including those who are disabled (see appendix).

- **The Special Needs and Disability Act 2001** requires LEAs to parents of children with special needs (SEN) with advice and information. It strengthens the rights of children with SEN to be educated in mainstream schools.

- **The Disability Discrimination Act 1995** requires any services offered to the general public to be accessible to people with disabilities. This is backed up by the Disability Rights Commission, which will support legal action in cases of discrimination against disabled people.

Laws on race

- **The Race Relations Act 1976** which has been strengthened by the **Race Relations (Amendment) Act 2000** imposes a duty on public authorities to eliminate unlawful discrimination and promote equality of opportunity.

Laws on gender, religion and belief

There are a series of laws to protect people from being discriminated against on the grounds of their gender, religion or belief. These include:

- **The Employment Rights Act 1996** which includes women's rights to equal pay for equal work and the rights to paid maternity leave.

- **Sex Discrimination (Gener Reassignment) Regulations 1999.**

- **Employment Equality (Sexual Orientation) Regulations 2003.**

- **Employment Equality (Religion or Belief) Regulations 2003.**

Promoting equality of opportunity at an institutional level

Many organisations now adopt a voluntary equal opportunities policy in their recruitment procedures. You will see a statement of this commitment on many job advertisements. Many also have a written code of practice, clearly stating that no child or adult will receive less favourable treatment on the grounds of gender, race, religion, disability or other factors. Within some establishments resources and staffing are provided to ensure greater equality of opportunity.

It is recognised by many institutions and establishments that there is a need to regularly review and evaluate provision and policy to ensure that practices are up to date and in line with current understanding of the issues.

Promoting equality of opportunity on a personal level

At a personal level people can make a commitment not to discriminate against people. They can:

- examine their own attitudes and practices
- increase their knowledge and understanding of people who are different from themselves
- undertake training and awareness-raising courses to increase their ability to provide for the needs of all
- always be looking for up-to-date information and resources.

Valuing diversity

Valuing family diversity

Understanding and acceptance of family diversity is essential for child care workers. All children can benefit from an environment that embraces cultural and linguistic diversity. Discrimination must be actively opposed. A positive working environment is achieved primarily through attitudes and behaviour, and enhanced by the provision of resources.

Acceptance of family diversity and the different child care practices it produces is essential for child care workers if they are to adopt an anti-discriminatory approach to their work. People tend to see the world from their own point of view. We begin with an awareness of ourselves and then come to understand others. For this reason we often think of ourselves and our immediate environment as 'normal', and things that are different and outside it as 'not quite normal'. This view is not always helpful or professional when working with children and their families.

There are many different types of family. They vary in their beliefs and ways of behaving, in their size, structure, wealth and physical resources. Different types of families can and do provide security for their children and foster their healthy development in different ways.

Families should be accepted, respected and valued for the care they give their children. Differences in style should not be judged as better or worse. Workers need to develop an understanding of different practices.

Difficulties in caring for children, or failure to meet their needs, and the disadvantages that some children experience as a result, are not caused by the obvious differences between families. They are more closely linked to the personal resources, abilities and attitudes that exist within a family group.

Valuing cultural diversity

All children can benefit from an environment that embraces cultural and linguistic diversity. Cultural differences are more likely to be valued and understood in a child care environment where difference is seen as a positive quality to be valued. Children in modern society come from a variety of cultural backgrounds. They are more likely to experience equality of opportunity and feel valued in a positive environment where their cultures are recognised and reflected in the provision of books and resources for their use.

In schools and nurseries where there is less diversity of background, the use of resources that reflect a multicultural society adds to the richness of provision for all children and prepares them for their adult lives in a multicultural society. We are part of a world where there are many different languages, accents and dialects. If children are only aware of their own language and ignorant of the existence of others, their experience is very limited. By promoting a positive atmosphere that celebrates language diversity we can enrich the experience of all children, while at the same time valuing the experiences of children who are bilingual.

Cultural differences are more likely to be valued and understood in a child care environment where difference is seen as a positive quality to be valued

Creating an inclusive environment

An inclusive envirnment is one in which all children and families are included and none are excluded. It is achieved through having sound policies and through the attitudes and behaviour of all members of the establishment. It can be enhanced by the provision of equipment and activities that promote inclusion, avoid cultural and gender bias and present positive images of all children, including those with disabilities. Such provision should permeate both the care and the curriculum that children receive.

Providing for good practice should include the following:

- sound policies that promote inclusion
- books, displays and pictorial resources should reflect a multicultural, multi-ability society
- resources for practical activities, including painting, should enable all children to participate fully and represent themselves and their culture
- the environment and activities should be adapted to enable children with individual and special needs to participate to their full ability
- boys and girls should be encouraged to participate in a full range of activities, and to be expressive, active, sensitive and responsive as is appropriate to any situation and not according to gender
- plans and provision should be sensitive to parents' different financial circumstances and no child should be excluded because of their parents' means
- celebrations and festivities should reflect a multicultural society
- wherever possible, carers should be drawn from a variety of backgrounds and include workers of different genders, race and physical abilities. This will encourage understanding, make a clear statement and enable different children to identify with them
- including parents in the care and education of their children.

Conclusion – values and principles

You must show, throughout each unit of this award, that you are committed to all the values expressed in the Statement of Underlying Principles in the National Occupational Standards. You should refer to them as you work through each unit and demonstrate that you are putting them into practice.

Assessment of National Vocational Qualifications

This section describes who and what is involved in National Vocational Qualifications (NVQ) assessment, the structure of an NVQ and types of evidence. It describes some of the features in this book that will help you with your assessment. This section includes:

- The assessment process
- Are you ready for assessment?

The assessment process

What is assessment?

Assessment involves making a judgement about whether a person has achieved a particular standard or not. A person's learning is judged against the standards set by an awarding body. An awarding body is an organisation that is able to award (or give) a certificate or diploma when a person successfully completes the required assessment.

One of the reasons for assessment is to ensure that everyone concerned knows what standard has been reached. It means that people know which jobs to apply for and an employer knows whether it is appropriate to consider an applicant for a job.

Assessment of National Vocational Qualifications

The NVQ2 in Early Years Care and Education is a National Vocational Qualification (NVQ) at level 2. To gain an NVQ a candidate is assessed on their practice. An assessor observes (looks at) what a candidate *does* and assesses that. The assessor also judges a candidate's knowledge and understanding by finding out if they know *why* they are doing things in a certain way.

Competence

In order to successfully complete an NVQ2 in Early Years Care and Education you must show that you can care for young children competently. This means providing for children's developmental needs, and keeping them safe and healthy. Competent performance means that your performance meets specific standards. The specific standards are those laid down in the National Occupational Standards for early years care and education.

Performance criteria

The National Occupational Standards are written by experienced professionals in the field of early years care and education. The standards consist of a large number of separate performance criteria. A performance criteria is a 'bite-size' description of a small piece of activity. They are all printed in your assessment handbook. Each performance criteria is labelled using a letter(s) and numbers.

Elements

Performance criteria are grouped together in elements. An element contains a number of performance criteria, linked by subject matter. There are usually 6 to 12 performance criteria in an element.

Each element is labelled with a letter, numbers and a title. For example:

Element letter and numbers	Element title
C1.1	Help children to toilet and wash hands (this element has 10 performance criteria)
E2.2	Maintain the supervision of children (this has 8 performance criteria)
M1.3	Element Monitor, store and prepare materials (this has 8 performance criteria)
P9.4	Element Work with parents in a group (this has 10 performance criteria)
CU10.1	Contribute to effective team working (this has 9 performance criteria)

The range

Each element also has a 'range'. The range has one or more categories. In each category there are a number of range statements. Range statements are described later in this section.

Units

Elements are grouped together in units; the elements are linked by a theme. There are between two and five elements in every unit. Each unit has a letter, a number and a title.

Examples of units are:

Unit C1 Support children's physical development (this has 4 elements)

Unit E2 Maintain the safety and security of children (this has 4 elements)

Unit M1 Monitor, store and prepare materials and equipment (this has 3 elements)

Unit P9 Work with parents in a group (this has 3 elements)

The unit letter stands for the area of work:

- *C stands for children*
- *E stands for environment*
- *M stands for management*
- *P stands for parents*
- *CU stands for common unit (a unit common to other NVQ awards).*

The National Vocational Qualification (NVQ) you are undertaking is called an NVQ in Early Years Care and Education at level 2. For this NVQ you must successfully complete 10 units to gain the whole award.

The labelling of units, elements and performance criteria

Every unit has a unit title, letter and number; every element has a number, each performance criteria has a further number.

Example of performance criteria:	C4.2.4	Description of performance criteria	Interventions in conflict situations are promptly and fairly conducted
C4.2.4 is in:	Unit C4	Title of unit:	Support children's social and emotional development
It is in the second element of unit C4:	This is called element C4.2	Title of element	Help children to relate to others
It is the fourth performance criteria in the second element of unit C4, element 2	This is called performance criteria C.4.2.4	Description of performance criteria	Interventions in conflict situations are promptly and fairly conducted

Mandatory units

Eight of the 10 units in this NVQ are MANDATORY. That is you have to do every one of them. These are Units C1, C4, C8, C9, E1, E2, M3 and P1.

Optional units

There are also five OPTIONAL units, but you only have to do **two** of these.

You must choose two units from the list of five optional units. The optional units are C12, C13, M1, P9 and CU10.

You should choose the two optional units that suit your setting and that you are best able to show you are competent in. You should discuss the choice with your assessor. For example, you can only choose an optional unit about the care of babies if you are working with babies.

NVQ levels

There is not an NVQ in Early Years Care and Education at level 1. There are some introductory or foundation courses but these are not NVQs. They do not give you a qualification to work with children but they can provide a good introduction to the work.

There is an NVQ in Early Years Care and Education level 2 and above it at levels 3 and 4. At level 2 you must show that you can competently help and support children and adults. At level 3 you must show that you can provide for children and at times lead others. Level 4 is for experienced and senior practitioners.

Registering with an awarding body

Every NVQ candidate must register with an awarding body. You do this by joining an assessment centre. Each assessment centre is linked to an awarding body. The assessment centre will give you forms to complete so that you can register with their awarding body.

You will be linked to an assessment centre whether you become a Modern Apprentice, a Further Education college student or enrol with a private training organisation.

When you register with an awarding body, they send you a registration number to identify you and all your evidence. Some awarding bodies call this registration number a Candidate Enrolment Number. You need a registration number in order to start being assessed and must speak to your assessor if you are not sure about yours. You should write your number on all the pieces of evidence that you collect.

The role of your assessor

Your assessor is a very important person to you. She or he (in this chapter an assessor will be referred to as she) will help you with the following things.

Building up a relationship

Every NVQ candidate must have a personal assessor. You should know their name and where to contact them. You and your assessor should meet regularly and build up a positive professional relationship.

Your assessor may either be:

- work-based and work in the same room as you most of the time
- work-based and work in the same setting, but only be in your room some of the time
- peripatetic; based somewhere else and travelling to see you at particular times.

Your assessor should regularly help you to plan how to collect evidence of your competence and make a record of this plan for your portfolio

Planning

Your assessor should regularly help you to plan how to collect evidence of your competence and make a record of this plan for your portfolio.

Observation

Your assessor must observe you while you are working in your setting; she should arrange to do this even if she works with you all the time.

Different types of evidence

Your assessor will help you to collect different types of evidence in addition to what she observes. These are described later.

Portfolio of evidence

You should collect your evidence and put it in a portfolio of evidence. This is a folder that you organise in a way that you agree with your assessor. It should contain:

- records of the direct observations made by your assessor
- the other different types of written and recorded evidence you collect.

Labelling evidence

You should write on each piece of evidence the letter and number of the units, elements and performance criteria that it is evidence for.

Each piece of evidence must be signed and dated by you. Your assessor will sign and date each piece of evidence when she judges that it is:

● valid – that it shows you have reached the right standard

● relevant – that it matches the performance criteria and knowledge referred to

● authentic – that it is your own work.

Assessment

Your assessor will look at the evidence collected in your portfolio. She will judge or assess whether you have sufficient evidence to decide that you are competent.

Sufficiency

Having sufficient evidence means having enough. You need only to present sufficient evidence to show you are competent. It is not necessary to produce large amounts of evidence, much of which may be similar. This is time consuming and costly. On the other hand it is important that there is enough evidence for your assessor to make a decision that you are competent.

Making a decision

Your assessor will make one of two possible decisions. These are that you are:

● competent or

● *not yet* competent.

If she decides that you are not yet competent, your assessor should help you to plan how to gain sufficient experience and evidence to show that you are competent.

Feedback

Your assessor should give you feedback on your performance and on your performance evidence. She will tell you if your evidence is valid and relevant and meets the National Standards. Feedback should always be constructive and the key points should be given to you in writing. Feedback should review your progress and give you positive suggestions about how to collect further evidence. Your assessor should make it clear when you have successfully completed the unit or units for which you are being assessed.

Internal verification

If you are competent your assessor will sign the units record sheets. She will then pass your units to the person at the next stage of the assessment process. This person is called the internal verifier. The internal verifier:

● is a qualified person appointed by the assessment centre

● decides whether the assessor has used the criteria for assessment correctly

● should not have been involved in your assessment.

What happens next?	
If the internal verifier agrees with the assessment:	they will sign the units, return them to the assessor who will give them back to you completed.
If the internal verifier does *not* agree with the assessment:	they will pass the units back to the assessor, who will then work with you to make the changes needed.

Your assessor should pass your units to the internal verifier as soon as they are completed. In this way any assessment issues can be addressed before you complete further units.

External verification

The external verifier is appointed by the awarding body to check that the standard of assessment is correct.

At some stage you may be asked to bring individual units or your complete portfolio to the assessment centre. This is so that an external verifier can check them. You will be advised by your centre regarding the retention of your portfolio after completion of the award.

Are you ready for assessment?

At the end of every element in this book you are asked 'Are you ready for assessment?' This book will help you to prepare to be observed.

The book suggests how you can:

- prepare for direct observation by your assessor
- provide evidence of your knowledge and understanding.

Direct observation by your assessor

The best type of evidence of competence is direct observation by your assessor while you are working.

An assessor may observe you when you carry out:

- a particular activity you have planned to carry out at a pre-arranged time
- an activity that occurs from time to time during a session
- a frequently occurring activity during your normal working day.

The National Standards make it clear which performance criteria in every element:

- *your assessor must observe*
- *might not* be observed by your assessor (that is she does not have to observe them).

Your assessor *can* observe all the performance criteria, but she does *not have to*.

In this book we remind you of the performance criteria that must be observed at the end of each element, after the heading 'Are you ready for assessment?'.

Inspection of the setting

Another form of direct observation is 'inspection of the setting'. This form of direct observation is when the assessor observes you when you are maintaining, designing, creating or monitoring aspects of the children's immediate environment.

This includes:

- health and safety features of the environment, including safe storage and guards
- use of space and accessibility of activities to the child
- selection and presentation of things in the environment, including displays and books
- comfort levels for children, including temperature, lighting and seating.

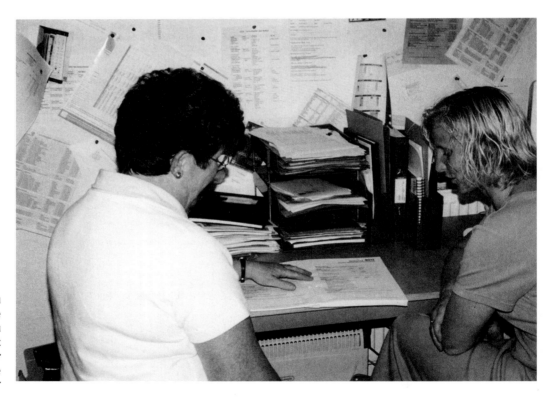

When you prepare to be observed you should plan what your assessor will observe

Preparing to be observed

When you prepare to be observed you should:

- plan what your assessor will observe
- read the performance criteria and range carefully beforehand

- make sure that you have the necessary skills and knowledge to perform competently
- aim to cover as much as you can during the observation
- plan to cover at least ONE aspect in each range category listed in an element.

The paragraph 'Preparing to be observed', at the end of each element, should help you to make the best of being observed. It describes all the things you should aim to do.

Other types of evidence

You may need to present different types of evidence in order to:

- cover criteria that do not need to be observed by your assessor
- cover other parts of the range
- show that you have the required knowledge, understanding and skills.

If all the performance criteria and range are not covered during your assessor's direct observations of you, you must use other types of indirect performance evidence for these criteria.

Below are descriptions of other types of evidence that you could collect. Remember to label them carefully to show which unit, element and performance criteria they give evidence for. Different types of evidence will be more suitable or appropriate for different elements. Suggestions about the most appropriate evidence are printed, in order of their relevance, in the introduction to each unit in the National Occupational Standards.

These are the main alternate types of performance evidence:

- reflective accounts
- log books and diaries of day-to-day practice
- witness statements/testimonies (authenticated statements from reliable sources)
- plans for activities and routines
- work products
- child observations and assessments of development
- simulations, role play or skills rehearsal
- case studies, assignments and projects
- evidence of skills transferable from other performance
- evidence from the past.

You may also use any of the above to provide evidence of your knowledge and understanding.

In addition your assessor can use:

- questions, either written or spoken, to assess your knowledge and understanding. All questions and answers must be recorded in some way.

Other types of evidence of performance

You can provide other types of evidence of your own performance in the workplace:

- Reflective accounts are a good example of this, especially if another professional, who has observed you in practice, signs them.
- Signed diaries, logs and witness statements also provide good evidence of what you have actually done.
- Activity plans, child observations and assessments, simulations, role play and skills rehearsal can also provide evidence of performance.
- Case studies, assignments and projects have a place in assessment, but they are usually of less value as they are more likely to reflect what you *would do* rather than what you *have done.*
- Evidence of skills transferable from other performance and evidence from the past can be used in some circumstances but never for whole units.

When planning your assessment you and your assessor should decide what kinds of additional evidence you need in order to cover the performance criteria, the range and to show knowledge and understanding.

Providing evidence of knowledge and understanding

It is good practice to provide evidence of your knowledge and understanding *at the same time* as you provide evidence of your performance. This encourages you to link practice to theory, rather than separating them. It will also help you to keep your portfolio to a manageable size!

For example, when you 'reflect' on your practice in a reflective account, you can link it to evidence of your knowledge and understanding. This is explained later.

Your assessor may also ask you questions after she has observed you. She will record your responses and these can be used as evidence of your knowledge and understanding.

You should get into the habit of putting the correct references to knowledge and understanding statements on your work as you write or record it.

Providing evidence to cover the range

Each element has a 'range'. The range is divided into a small number of categories and sometimes there is only one category. You should always read the range statements together with the title of the element. You have to show that you can perform each element of competence across the whole range. You must cover *every part* of the range while you are providing evidence of competence.

Each part of the range must be linked to at least ONE performance criteria; it can be linked to more, but it does not need to be linked to *every* performance criteria. In almost all circumstances you must be observed by your assessor performing at least ONE piece of the range from each category.

For example, for element C4.2 'Help children to relate to others':

Your assessor has to observe all the performance criteria except C4.2.4, C4.2.5, C4.2.7.

There are three range categories: <u>children</u>, <u>others</u>, <u>groups</u>

Your assessor has to see you perform one part from each category

She will do this for C4.2 if she observes you:

Providing <u>children,</u> who do not have difficulty relating to <u>other</u> children, with activities that encourage them to do things co-operatively in a small <u>group.</u>

You can then provide evidence of other parts of the range through different forms of evidence, linked to at least ONE performance criteria.

Reflective accounts

A reflective account is a description, in your own words (written, oral or recorded), of something you have done.

You should:

- describe the activity step by step
- link your description to the performance criteria in one or more elements and write down the references
- think about, or reflect on, what you have done
- describe any strengths in your performance and things you would do differently
- measure your performance against the performance criteria
- look at the knowledge statements that link to the performance criteria
- show, in your description, that you know why you did things in the way you did
- link your description to the knowledge statements and their reference numbers.

Reflective accounts can provide very good evidence of your competent performance. They are also a useful way of showing that you have covered parts of the range that your assessor has not been able to observe and that you have the appropriate knowledge and understanding.

Remember to include in your reflective account reference to the performance criteria, the parts of the range and KUS statements you have covered.

Log books and diaries of day-to-day practice

Log books and diaries are records of your practice in the work setting.

Diaries can be a very useful way of showing your assessor that you have covered performance criteria and parts of the range that she has not been able to observe.

You should write and use diaries carefully. It is not necessary to record daily activities over and over again. Remember, you only need sufficient evidence. It can be useful to write a log of a specific activity and describe it showing the different ways you have done it across the range.

For example, if your assessor has directly observed you selecting and 'using equipment and materials to stimulate role play' <u>indoors</u>, as part of a <u>planned</u> activity (C9.3), you might record in your diary/log occasions when you have used this equipment <u>outdoors</u> and <u>spontaneously</u> (to cover parts of range 2 and 3).

Witness statements/testimonies (authenticated statements from reliable sources)

Witness statements are reports or descriptions about what you have done from people who have seen you do it. You can ask employers, colleagues or parents to provide a witness statement. They should be signed and dated by the witness.

Witness statements:

- should contain factual descriptions of what you have done, not opinions
- should be linked to the National Standards
- are useful if they describe your consistent competent performance over a period of time.
- are useful if your assessor cannot see you do something because it is inappropriate for them to be there, or because it occurs rarely.

Witness statements:

- cannot be used to replace direct observation by an assessor, if this is required in the National Standards
- are not acceptable from people you are related to or are in a relationship with.

Plans for activities and routines

Work plans are plans for activities and routines that you carry out at work.

They can include:

- plans that you have written yourself
- activities you have planned as part of a team
- records of preparations you have made
- timetables or schedules of activities and routines you have been involved in planning.

You might use a format from your work setting to record plans. You should describe what happened when you carried the activity out; you could present this as a reflective account. As with other evidence you should always record what performance criteria, range, knowledge and understanding they give evidence for.

Work products

Work products are items that you produce for the workplace. It can be anything that is a result of your work in the setting.

They may include:

- games and other articles produced by you for children to use during an activity
- information for parents
- sets of papers you have copied
- equipment that you have prepared
- plans of the setting and safety rules
- records of incidents, accidents or injuries that you have completed
- procedures for many areas of the work setting (e.g. collection of children, child protection procedures).

Work products are something you have produced yourself as part of your work. You should describe what the product is and what it is for. You should ask someone in a position of responsibility to countersign that it is your work.

Some work products will not be your work but those of other people, for example, policies of the setting. You cannot use these as evidence of your own work, but:

- you may write something about these as part of an assignment including a description, in your own words, of what the policy or product is for and how you have used it in practice; or
- you may show a product to your assessor when she is observing/visiting you and answer questions about it and how you use it.

As with other evidence you should always record what performance criteria, range, knowledge and understanding it gives evidence of.

Child observations and assessments of development

Child observations and assessments are records, made by you, of aspects of a child's development. There are many different ways of recording your observations and assessments. They may provide some evidence of your competent performance. They will usually provide good evidence of your knowledge and understanding.

However, when using these records in your portfolio it is essential that strict confidentiality is maintained. It must not be possible to identify a child from anything that you write in an observation or assessment.

Simulations, role play or skills rehearsal

A role play should be a copy of conditions found in your normal workplace. You and other people act out what might happen. This can be useful when gaining evidence for working with parents. (P1 and P9.)

Simulations in early years care and education should not be used regularly. However, there are circumstances where they can be useful and of value. This is particularly so when confidentiality or safety are involved.

A skills rehearsal can be used when preparing bottles for a baby's feed (C12.1).

Case studies, assignments and projects

Case studies are descriptions of a situation that you are asked to give a response to. They can be set as an assignment. Recorded responses to a case study that describes an actual situation can count as performance evidence; responses to an imaginary situation can only be used as evidence of knowledge and understanding. Case studies may be used in situations where workplace assessment is difficult.

When using assignments and projects both candidate and assessor need to be clear about the aims and objectives of the work to be done, and the performance criteria and knowledge and understanding that will be covered.

Evidence of skills transferable from other performance

This is evidence that is taken from a parallel performance. It should not need to be used very often. A good example of this is if your assessor needs to see you listening to and comforting a child, who is upset because their parent has left them, but sees you comforting them when they are upset for a different reason.

Evidence from the past

Evidence that is accepted of your previous experience and learning is sometimes called accreditation of prior experience and learning (APEL). Your evidence needs to be signed by an appropriate person who can say it is yours. This might be used if:

- there are aspects of your practice that you do not cover in your present work but about which you can offer some evidence from your past performance
- you are experienced and competent and wish to present evidence of what you have done in the past.

However:

- it is not possible for candidates to complete a unit solely on the basis of performance evidence from past achievements
- evidence must not be so far in the past that it does not reflect current practices
- APEL is not a cheap or easy option and although it recognises the value of previous work, it is better used to strengthen other evidence, to cover the range and as evidence of consistently competent performance.

Principles of good practice

Throughout each unit you must show you are committed to the values expressed in the Statement of Underlying Principles in the National Occupational Standards described in the first section of this book.

Relationships between units

Many units are related to each other. They cover similar aspects of work. These links are referred to throughout this book.

Units also interlink. When your assessor is observing you carrying out what you think is a single task, she may be able to record evidence of your competence across more than one unit.

For example, while you are playing a game with children (C8.2):

- you may be supporting opportunities for children's exercise (C1.3);
- maintaining a safe environment (E2.1); and
- helping children to relate to others (C4.2).

When you are planning your assessment it is useful if you can make these links and cover as many performance criteria as you can. The more familiar you are with the performance criteria the easier it will be for you to demonstrate your competence across a number of units and elements while your assessor is observing you.

Conclusion

Providing evidence for NVQ assessment becomes easier as you become more familiar with the process of assessment and with the performance criteria, elements and units.

You may find it difficult and confusing to begin with. Don't give up. If you are a competent practitioner, with the help of your assessor and through the use of this book, you can and will succeed.

You may find it difficult and confusing to begin with. Don't give up. Providing evidence for NVQ assessment becomes easier as you become more familiar with the process

Development

The term development is used to refer to the ways in which children grow and change. Development occurs in an order or sequence, for example, babies sit before they walk. Developmental patterns are seen in all areas of growth and change. The charts in this section cover:

- physical development
- cognitive (or intellectual) development
- the development of play
- language development
- social and emotional development
- stages of development in children's behaviour.

Child care workers need to know about children's development

It is essential that people who work with children know about development sequences so that:

- expectations about what a child can do are realistic
- appropriate experiences and activities can be provided for the child
- experiences and activities can be offered that lead a child on to the next stage of development
- children's individual progress can be monitored against the developmental sequence.

The rate at which children develop will be different but the sequence will stay the same

The development of a child is an individual progression through the stages. All children are different and they have different life experiences. This means that they will develop at different rates. However, almost all children will progress in the same sequence.

Ages at which children are likely to have reached a stage are often given in developmental charts. These are usually average ages and many children will reach the stage before that age and many children will reach the stage after that age. This is absolutely normal. In a group of children who are the same age there will always be a range of developmental stages. While a child is within this range of development there is no cause for concern.

Physical development

Physical development is described in two areas, namely gross motor skills and fine motor skills.

Gross motor skills

The ability of humans to use two legs and walk involves the whole body. These whole-body movements are described as gross motor skills.

Examples of gross motor skills involved in the development of walking

Crawling

Sitting from lying down

Bear-walking

Walking with two hands held

Walking with one hand held

Walking alone

Fine motor skills

The use of the hands in co-ordination with the eyes allows human beings to perform very delicate procedures with their fingers. These manipulative aspects of physical development are called fine motor skills. They include aspects of vision and fine and delicate movements. The development of vision takes place along-side the development of fine motor skills.

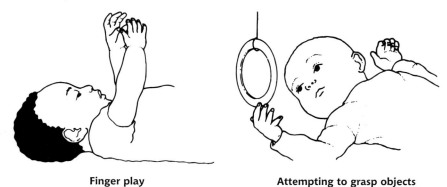

Examples of fine motor skills in the development of manipulation

Finger play

Attempting to grasp objects

Palmar grasp using whole hand

More delicate palmar grasp involving the thumb

Holding and exploring objects

Examples of fine motor skills in the development of manipulation

Inferior pincer grasp

Exploring with the index finger

Delicate/mature pincer grasp

The neonate

The newborn baby in the first month of life is often called the neonate, which means newly born.

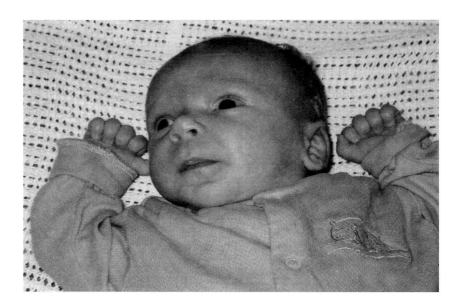

Fine motor development – fists are clenched

The chart below shows the main stages of physical development from 1 month to 7 years.

Age range	Gross motor skills	Fine motor skills and vision
1 month	*Prone (lying face down)* The baby lies with its head to one side but can now lift its head to change position. The legs are bent, no longer tucked under the body. *Supine (lying on the back)* The head is on one side. The arm and leg on the side the head is facing will stretch out. *Sitting* The back is a complete curve when the baby is held in sitting position.	The baby gazes attentively at carer's face while being fed, spoken to or during any caring routines. The baby grasps a finger or other object placed in the hand. The hands are usually closed.
3 months	*Prone* The baby can now lift up the head and chest supported on the elbows, forearms and hands. *Supine* The baby usually lies with the head in a central position. There are smooth, continuous movements of the arms and legs. The baby waves the arms symmetrically and brings hands together over the body. *Sitting* There should be little or no head lag. When held in a sitting position the back should be straight, except for a curve in the base of the spine. *Standing* The baby will sag at the knees when held in a standing position. The placing and walking reflexes should have disappeared.	Finger-play – the baby has discovered its hands and moves them around in front of the face, watching the movements and the pattern they make in the light. The baby holds a rattle or similar object for a short time if placed in the hand. Frequently hits itself in the face before dropping it! The baby is now very alert and aware of what is going on around. The baby moves its head to look around and follows adult movements.

Age range	Gross motor skills	Fine motor skills and vision
6 months	*Prone* Lifts the head and chest well clear of the floor by supporting on outstretched arms. The hands are flat on the floor. The baby can roll over from front to back. *Supine* The baby will lift its head to look at its feet. The baby may lift its arms, requesting to be lifted and may roll over from back to front. *Sitting* If pulled to sit, the baby can now grab the adult's hands and pull itself into a sitting position; the head is now fully controlled with strong neck muscles. The baby can sit for long periods with support. The back is straight. *Standing* Held standing the baby will enjoy weight bearing and bouncing up and down.	Bright and alert, looking around constantly to absorb all the visual information on offer. Fascinated by small toys within reaching distance, grabbing them with the whole hand, using a **palmar grasp.** Transfers toys from hand to hand.
9 months	*Prone* The baby may be able to support its body on knees and outstretched arms. May rock backwards and forwards and try to crawl. *Supine* The baby rolls from back to front and may crawl away. *Sitting* The baby is now a secure and stable sitter – may sit unsupported for 15 minutes or more. *Standing* The baby can pull itself to a standing position. When supported by an adult it will step forward on alternate feet. The baby supports its body in the standing position by holding on to a firm object and may begin to side-step around furniture.	Uses the inferior **pincer grasp** with index finger and thumb. Looks for fallen objects out of sight – is now beginning to realise that they have not disappeared for ever. Grasps objects, usually with one hand, inspects with the eyes and transfers to the other hand. May hold one object in each hand and bang them together. Uses the index finger to poke and point.

Age range	Gross motor skills	Fine motor skills and vision
12 months	*Sitting* Can sit alone indefinitely. Can get into sitting position from lying down. *Standing* Pulls itself to stand and walks around the furniture. Returns to sitting without falling. May stand alone for a short period.	Looks for objects hidden and out of sight. Uses a mature pincer grasp and releases objects. Throws toys deliberately and watches them fall. Likes to look at picture books and points at familiar objects. **Pincer grasp** using the thumb and first finger.
15 months	Walks alone, feet wide apart. Sits from standing. Crawls upstairs.	Points at pictures and familiar objects. Builds with two bricks. Enjoys books; turns several pages at once.
18 months	Walks confidently. Tries to kick a ball. Walks upstairs with hand held.	Uses delicate pincer grasp. Scribbles on paper. Builds a tower with three bricks.
2 years	Runs safely. Walks up and downstairs holding on. Rides a trike, pushing it along with the feet.	Holds a pencil and attempts to draw circles, lines and dots. Uses fine pincer grasp with both hands to do complicated tasks. Builds a tower of six bricks.
3 years	Can stand, walk and run on tiptoe. Walks upstairs one foot on each step. Rides a tricycle and uses the pedals.	Can thread large wooden beads onto a lace. Controls a pencil in the preferred hand. Builds a tower of nine bricks.

Age range	Gross motor skills	Fine motor skills and vision
4 years	Climbs play equipment. Walks up and downstairs, one foot on each step. Can stand, walk and run on tiptoe.	Builds a tower of 10 or more bricks. Grasps a pencil maturely. Beginning to do up buttons and fasten zips.
5 years	Can hop. Plays ball games well. Can walk along on the balancing beam.	Can draw a person with head, trunk, legs and eyes, nose and mouth. Can sew large stitches. Good control of pencils and paintbrushes.
6 years	Rides a two-wheeled bicycle. Kicks a football well. Makes running jumps.	Can catch a ball with one hand. Writing hold is similar to the adult.
7 years	Can climb and balance well on the apparatus. Hops easily on either foot, keeping well balanced.	Writes well. Can sew neatly with a large needle.

**From first steps
to managing the
apparatus**

Cognitive (or intellectual) development

12–15 months

- Infants explore objects using trial and error methods, and begin to treat objects in appropriate ways, e.g. talk into a telephone and cuddle a doll.
- They begin to point and follow when others point and to seek objects in the most likely places.

Children can follow a point

18 months to 2 years

- By this age infants can refer to themselves by name.
- They begin to understand the consequences of their actions, for example, spilling their juice makes a surface wet.
- They may show the beginnings of empathy, for example, by comforting a crying baby.

3 years

- Children can match primary colours. They can sort objects into categories, but usually only by one criterion at a time, for example, all the cars, but not all the red cars.
- They ask a lot of questions.

**Children can
sort and
match objects**

- They can recite the number words to 10 but are not yet able to count beyond two or three.
- They are beginning to understand the concept of time, talk about what has happened and look forward to what is going to happen.
- They can concentrate on an activity for a short period of time, leave it and then go back to it.
- They are beginning to understand the concept of quantity such as one, more, lots.

4 years

- At this age children can sort using more categories.
- They may solve simple problems, usually by trial and error, but are beginning to understand 'why'.
- They add to their knowledge by asking questions continually.
- Memory skills are developing, particularly around significant events like birthdays and holidays, and also of familiar songs and stories.
- They will confuse fantasy and reality, e.g. 'I had a tiger come to my house to tea too'.
- They can include representative detail in drawings, based on observation.
- They understand that writing carries meaning and use writing in play.

Children can incude representative detail in pictures

5 years

- By this age they have a good sense of past, present and future.
- They are becoming literate – most will recognise their own name and write it.

Most children will recognise and write their own name

- They will respond to books and are interested in reading.
- They demonstrate good observational skills in their drawings.
- They understand the one-to-one principle and can count reliably to 10.
- Concentration is developing. They can concentrate without being distracted for about 10 minutes at an appropriate task.

6 years

- Children are beginning to understand the mathematical concept of measuring – time, weight, length, capacity, volume.

Children are beginning to understand the mathematical concept of measuring

- They are interested in why things happen and can form and test a simple idea, for example, that seeds need water to grow.
- They begin to use symbols in their drawing and painting – a radial sun and strip sky appear now.
- Many children will begin to read independently, but there is a wide variation in this.

7 years

- Children are able to conserve number reliably and will recognise that a number of objects remains constant, however they are presented. They may be able to conserve mass and capacity.

- They begin to deal with number abstractly and can perform calculations involving simple addition and subtraction mentally.
- They may be able to tell the time from a watch or clock.
- They are developing an ability to reason and an understanding of cause and effect.

Children are able to conserve number reliably

Language development

12 months

- Vocabulary starts to develop. First spoken words appear (expressive language). Can respond to simple instructions.
- Children understand more than they can say (receptive language).

15 months

- Receptive language increases rapidly: active more limited.
- Points with single words.

18 months

- Expressive language increases – names of familiar things and people.
- Single words used, plus intonation to indicate meaning.
- Words and sentences repeated.

21 months

- Both receptive and expressive language increase – receptive still larger.
- Begin to name objects that are not there.

- Sentences begin as two-word phrases.
- Gesture important. Begin asking questions such as 'What?', 'Who?' and 'Where?'.

2 years

- Both receptive and expressive language continues to increase.
- Can generalise words. Use personal pronouns instead of names but not always correctly.
- Sentences become longer but still abbreviated.
- Questions asked frequently, particularly 'What?' and 'Why?'.

Reading with children is an excellent way to develop language skills

2 years, 6 months

- Vocabulary increases rapidly. Words used more specifically with less generalisation. Longer, more precise sentences, but still some abbreviation and incorrect word order.
- Use language to protect their rights. Show interest in listening to stories.

3 years

- Expressive language develops rapidly. New words picked up quickly.
- Sentences become longer and more adult-like. Children talk during play. Language is used for thinking and reporting on what is happening, to direct actions, express ideas and maintain friendships. Pronouns usually used correctly. Frequent questions are 'Why?', Who?' and 'What for?'. Rhymes are attractive.

3 years, 6 months

- A wide vocabulary develops. Word usage usually correct. Language can be used to report on past experiences. Incorrect word endings sometimes used.

Talking with others is necessary for children to pick up language and to adjust and refine their language skills

4 years

- Extensive vocabulary. New words added regularly. Longer, more complex sentences, some joined with 'because'. Able to narrate long stories, including sequences of events. Running commentaries during play. Fully intelligible speech with minor incorrect uses. Questioning at its peak, including 'When?'.

- Can usually use language to share, take turns, collaborate, argue, predict, justify behaviour, create situations in imaginative play, reflect on their and others' feelings.

5 years

- A wide vocabulary and can use it appropriately. Sentences usually correctly structured, may be some incorrect grammar. Pronouns may still be childish. Language continues to be developed.

- Questions and discussions are used for enquiry and information; questions become more precise as cognitive skills develop. Children offer opinions in discussion.

5–8 years

- Children practise, adapt and refine their language skills. Language is used for a wide range of purposes in relation to themselves and other people, including protecting themselves, directing others, reporting things, reasoning, predicting, projecting themselves into situations and imagining.

Children need opportunities to practise, adapt and refine their language skills

Social and emotional development

1–2 years

- Between 1 and 2 years children become aware of themselves as individuals and begin to assert their will, sometimes in defiant and negative ways. At this stage children are very egocentric. Their defiant and resistant behaviour can be seen as an attempt to protect their individuality.

15 months

- By this age toddlers use their main carer as a safe base from which to explore the world and are very curious about their environment. They are anxious about being physically separated from carers, have an interest in strangers but can be fearful of them.

- They tend to show off but do not react well to being told off, show interest but jealousy in other children, are emotionally changeable and unstable, throw toys when angry and resist changes in routine.

At 15 months, toddlers will hold a spoon and bring it to the mouth, spilling some food in the process

- Around this age children have a sense of 'me' and 'mine', begin to express themselves defiantly, and to distinguish between 'you' and 'me', and can point to members of the family in answer to questions.

- They may hold a cup and drink without assistance, hold a spoon and bring it to the mouth, help with dressing and undressing, and swing from dependence to wanting to be independent.

18 months

- At this age children tend to follow their carers around, be sociable and imitate them by helping with small household tasks, respond by stopping doing something when the word 'no' is used, imitate and mimic others during their play, and engage in solitary or parallel play, but like to do this near a familiar adult or sibling.

- They show some social emotions, for example, sympathy for someone who is hurt, but cannot cope with frustration, show intense curiosity, have intense mood swings, move from dependence to independence, eagerness to irritation, and co-operation to resistance.

- They try to establish themselves as members of the social group, begin to copy their values, are conscious of their family group.

- They are still very dependent on familiar carers and often return to a fear of strangers.

- They can use a cup and spoon well, and successfully get food into their mouth, take off some clothing and help with dressing themselves, and can make their carers aware of their toileting needs.

2–3 years

- Children are still emotionally and socially very dependent on familiar adult carers, although they are capable of self-directed behaviour. During this period extremes of mood are common. Children can change between aggressive and withdrawn behaviour, awkwardness and helpfulness very rapidly.

At 2 years

- By this age children can be sensitive to the feelings of others, display emotions such as sympathy and are capable of being loving and responsive.
- They demand their carer's attention and want their needs to be met immediately, and may have tantrums if crossed or frustrated, or if they have to share attention.
- They will ask for food but can sometimes respond to being asked to wait; they are possessive of their own toys and objects, have little idea of sharing, tend to play parallel to other children, and engage in role play, but are beginning to play interactive games. They tend to be easily distracted by an adult if they are frustrated or angry, join in when an adult sings or tells a simple story, and can point to parts of the body and other things when asked.
- At this age children do not always fully accept that their parent is a separate individual. They are sometimes self-contained and independent, at other times very dependent. They will feed themselves without spilling, lift a cup up and put it down, put some clothes on with supervision, say when they need the toilet, become dry in the daytime.

2 years, 6 months

- Around this age children develop their sense of self-identity; they know their name, their position in the family and their gender, play with other children, learn that different toys may be intended for girls and boys, and engage in 'pretend' play.
- They want to have anything they see and do anything that occurs to them, throw tantrums when stopped, are not so easy to distract, and are often in conflict with their carers.
- They have an awareness of some dangers and know they should avoid them (like stairs and hot stoves); they have the ability to use a spoon and some other tools to eat with well, to pour from one container to another and to get themselves a drink, dress with supervision, unzip zips, unbuckle and buckle, and unbutton and button clothing.
- They are toilet-trained during the day, and can be dry at night, especially if lifted (put on the toilet last thing at night).

3 years

- Around this age children can feel secure when in a strange place away from their main carers, can wait for their needs to be met, are less rebellious and use language rather than physical outbursts to express themselves, still respond to distraction as a method of controlling their behaviour, but are ready to respond to reasoning and bargaining, are beginning to learn the appropriate behaviour for a range of different social settings.
- They adopt the attitudes and moods of adults, want the approval of loved adults, can show affection for younger siblings, can share things and take turns, enjoy make-believe play, use dolls and toys to act out their experiences, and may have imaginary fears and anxieties.

**At 3 years, children can take themselves
to the toilet and wash their hands**

- They call themselves 'I' and have a set of feelings about themselves. They are still affected by the attitudes and behaviour of those around them. They see themselves as they think others see them.

- They may have the ability to use implements to eat with, toilet themselves during the day, may be dry at night, will wash their hands but may have difficulty drying them, and are learning to dress without supervision.

4 years

- By this age children can be very sociable and talkative to adults and children, enjoy 'silly' talk, and may have one particular friend. They can be confident and self-assured, but may be afraid of the dark and have other fears. They have taken the standards of behaviour of the adults to whom they are closest, and turn to adults for comfort when overtired, and ill or hurt.

- They play with groups of children, can take turns but not consistently, and are often very dramatic in their imaginative play. They are developing a strong sense of past and future, are able to cope with delay in having their needs

**Children will
gradually
become able to
dress themselves**

met, and show some control over their emotions. They can be dogmatic and argumentative, and may blame others, swear and use bad language.

- Most children have now developed a stable self-concept (i.e. a view of themselves that remains constant and fixed). Children who see themselves as likeable at this stage will not change this view of themselves when, from time to time, other children say that they do not like them.

- They may be able to feed themselves well, dress and undress, but may have difficulty with back buttons, ties and laces. They can wash and dry hands and face and clean teeth.

5 years

- Children usually enjoy brief separations from home and carers and show good overall control of emotions, but may argue with parents when they request something. They still respond to discipline based on bargaining, although they are not so easily distracted from their own anger as when they were younger.

- They often show the stress of conflict by being overactive, but may regain their balance by having 'time out'.

- They prefer games of rivalry to team games but enjoy co-operative group play, although they often need an adult to sort out conflicts. They may boast, show off and threaten.

- They are able to see a task through to the end, show a desire to do well, and can be purposeful and persistent.

- They develop a stable picture of themselves, are increasingly aware of differences between themselves and other people, including gender and status, and want the approval of adults. They show sensitivity to the needs of others and a desire for acceptance by other children, and are developing internal social rules and an inner conscience.

- They may use a knife and fork well, dress and undress, lace shoes and tie ties, wash and dry face and hands, but may need supervision to complete other washing.

At 5 years, children can dress and undress themselves

6 years

- At 6 years children have greater independence and maturity, have a wide range of appropriate emotional responses and are able to behave appropriately in a variety of social situations.

- They have all the basic skills needed for independence in eating, hygiene and toileting.

- However, they can be irritable and possessive about their own things, and have spells of being rebellious and aggressive.

7 to 7 years, 11 months

- At 7 years children become very self-critical about their work. They may be miserable and sulky, and give up trying for short periods, or so enthusiastic for life that carers have to guard against them becoming overtired.

- They are more aware of their gender group and more influenced by the peer group.
- Much of the child's personality is established by the end of this period. By the time they are 8 years old, children's experiences in their families and in their social and cultural environments will have led to the establishment of their personal identity, social and cultural identity, gender role, attitudes to life and skills for independence.

Disabled children

It is often by the age of 7 years that the differences of disabled children become more apparent. The development of sophisticated skills is the norm for children at this age; because of this the carers of a child who has a disability may be faced more starkly with their child's difference. They may struggle between a concern to see their child treated as 'normal' and acceptance of their child's disability and the need for support.

Children's behaviour

- At 1 year, children do not have a clear perception of themselves as individuals; they have a close attachment to, and are sociable with, adults they know; are anxious if separated from them and shy with strangers; are capable of varied and dramatic emotional responses; seek attention vocally and obey simple verbal instructions.
- At 15 months, children are more aware of themselves as individuals, but not of other people as separate from them; explore their environment indiscriminately (they are 'into everything'); are possessive of people they are attached to, and of objects they want ('It's mine!'); respond better to distraction than verbal reasoning or sharp discipline; may show off, throw toys in anger and have mood swings.

Pre-school-aged children are capable of loving, responsive behaviour

- At 18 months, children respond to the word 'No', but usually need the command to be reinforced or repeated; become more aware of themselves as separate individuals; are very self-centred (egocentric) in their awareness and behaviour, having only recently discovered themselves as separate individuals; are very curious about everything around them; are easily frustrated; can be defiant and resistant to adults; and may react by shouting and throwing things.

- At 2 years, children have a clear understanding of self but are still not fully aware of carers as separate individuals; are able to be self-contained for periods of time; are often possessive of toys and have little idea of sharing; want their demands to be met quickly but can wait if asked; may have tantrums if crossed or frustrated but can be distracted; have a wide range of feelings and are capable of loving, responsive behaviour; are aware of and able to respond to the feelings of others.

- At 3 years, children have developed a strong self-identity and a growing level of independence; show less anxiety about separation and strangers; often resist efforts by carers to limit their behaviour; have mood swings and extremes of behaviour; are impulsive and less easily distracted; can wait for their needs to be met; are less rebellious and use language rather than physical outbursts to express themselves; are ready to respond to reasoning and bargaining; are beginning to learn the appropriate behaviour for a range of different social settings; can understand when it is necessary to be quiet or noisy; adopt the attitudes and moods of adults; want the approval of loved adults.

- At 4 years, children have more physical and emotional self-control; have more settled feelings and are more balanced in their expression of them; are more independent of their main carers; are happier, more friendly and helpful; can respond to reason and bargaining as well as to distraction; are less rebellious and can learn the appropriate behaviour for a range of settings; are capable of playing with groups of children, tending to centre around an activity then dissolve and reform; can take turns but are not consistent about this; are often

Being argumentative is part of pre-school-aged children's behaviour

very dramatic in their play; engage in elaborate and prolonged imaginative play; are developing a strong sense of past and future; can be dogmatic and argumentative; may blame others when they misbehave; may even behave badly in order to get a reaction; may swear and use bad language.

- At 4–5 years, children are constantly trying to make sense of the world around them and their experiences in it; can be very sociable, talkative, confident, purposeful, persistent and self-assured; can take turns and wait for their needs to be met; may also be stubborn and sometimes aggressive and argumentative; still turn to adults for comfort, especially when tired, ill or hurt.

- At 5 years, children have achieved a greater level of independence and self-containment, generally show a well-developed level of control over their emotions; show a desire to do well and to gain the approval of adults; are developing a sense of shame if their behaviour is unacceptable to the adult; can also be argumentative, show off and be overactive at times of conflict; argue with parents when they request something; still respond to discipline based on bargaining; are not so easily distracted from their own anger as when they were younger; may regain their balance by having 'time out'; prefer games of rivalry to team games; enjoy co-operative group play, but often need an adult to arbitrate; boast and threaten; show a desire to excel and can be purposeful and persistent.

- At 6–7 years, children become increasingly mature and independent; develop a wide range of appropriate emotional and behavioural responses to different situations; are able to behave appropriately in a variety of social situations; can be self-confident, friendly and co-operative; may have spells of being irritable, rebellious and sulky.

By the age of 7, children can be self-confident, friendly and co-operative

Observing young children

Why do we observe children?

Observation is a vital professional tool for child care workers. We observe children so that we can:

- understand the pattern of children's development
- collect information to assess a child's progress in relation to normal development
- learn about the interests of a child or group of children
- identify any particular difficulties a child may have
- meet the specific needs of individuals or groups of children
- understand children as individuals and their likes and dislikes
- assess what the child has achieved and then plan for the next stage
- record and document any unusual behaviour or any that gives cause for concern
- provide information about the child to parents and to others who have an involvement with the child
- measure the progress and achievements of children against national targets
- evaluate the effectiveness of the provision made for children.

Different methods of observing children

Child care workers observe children and they act on these observations as part of their everyday practice, for example, seeing that a child has fallen over and offering comfort, noticing that the glue pot is empty and refilling it. There is also a place for child care workers to observe a child or children, perhaps at a chosen activity or with a particular focus, and to record this. Child care workers can then consider the needs of children and, importantly, plan to meet these needs.

What do you observe?

- Individual children during their play and other activities. You will get the best results from observing children in familiar, naturally occurring, everyday situations rather than those specially set up for the purpose of observation. All children will benefit from the attention of observation, not just those about whom you have a concern.
- Children in groups, to look at interaction and co-operation. Small groups will give you an opportunity to compare skills and responses.

- A particular activity or a piece of equipment to see how children respond to it.
- Children's choice of activities during a session. Do they join in with all the activities? Are some avoided?

Recording observations

- Try not to let children know that you are observing a particular child or group of children, as this might affect the way they behave.
- If you are not joining in the activity, place yourself where you can see the child but not within their personal space.
- Try not to make eye contact with the child as that may encourage the child to respond to you and make you lose your focus.
- Make notes while you are observing because you will not remember details later. A small notebook is better than a large folder.
- Write up your notes as soon as you can after your observation or you will forget what they mean.
- Sometimes preparation is necessary. For example, if you are observing the spread of children around the classroom, then you should make a sketch of the layout beforehand. Checklists can be used for many purposes and are straightforward to complete, particularly if you are with a group at an activity.
- If you want to observe children using their language skills, you could use a small tape recorder.
- You could use a video camera to record observations but filming will raise issues of confidentiality. Children often play to the camera too.

Different recording techniques

Child care workers use a variety of different techniques to record their observations of children. Some simple techniques are introduced below. Each method has advantages and disadvantages. With experience, you will be able to choose the method that is most suitable for the focus of your observation.

Checklist

This is a useful way of gaining a lot of information and recording it in a straight-forward way, usually by ticking against a chart. Published developmental scales and checklists can be used or you can devise your own, perhaps to assess a particular skill or stage of development. Checklists are also useful to compare different children. The main disadvantage of checklists is that they have a narrow focus and are not designed to enable you to record anything other than the skill or skills you have been looking for. The checklist below enables you to record and then compare the dressing skills of four 3 year olds.

Position yourself unobtrusively when you observe

A checklist observation

Aim: To observe children putting on their coats
Purpose: To see if they can manage unaided

Task	Child A	Child B	Child C	Child D
Find own coat?	√	√	√	√
Put it on the right way?	√	√	√	√ (turned it right way round)
Put it on unaided?	√	√	√	√
Zip it up?	X (needed help)	n/a	n/a	√
Fasten buttons?	n/a	√	√	n/a
Put on hat?	√	√	n/a	√
Put on gloves?	X	√	n/a	√ (but struggled with fingers)
KEY: √ Can do it X Cannot do it n/a Not applicable				

Narrative

This is a detailed account of everything that you see a child doing. It helps if you have a clear focus for your observation so that you can choose an appropriate activity to observe. For example, if you want to find out about how well a child gets on with others you would need to observe him in an activity with a group of children. Observing him, say, reading to himself would not give you a picture of his social skills. With this method, you should observe for a short time, about five minutes or so. It can be hard to observe so closely and write down everything that you see for any longer.

Here is an example of a narrative observation of a 6 year old at a computer activity, looking at her fine motor skills.

K sat down using her arms to hold the chair. She then placed her right hand tightly on the mouse and put her finger on the left button. She gripped the mouse with her fingers and palm but as she moved it around she held her middle finger up. She clicked on the paintbrush and picked a colour but her hand was wobbling. She clicked on a file and dragged the arrow over using the mouse. It took her quite a bit of time to do this. She then started to draw some flowers using the paintbrush. She filled in the sky by clicking on the paint tin at the side of the screen. She drew a sun and some grass, using different colours for each, by very slowly moving the mouse and keeping her finger pressed down all the time.

Time sampling

This method involves observing at regular intervals, say, every 15 minutes and noting down what the child is doing. It can be used for a number of purposes. Noting the range of activities chosen by a child would show whether a child was taking part in everything on offer. Recording children's interactions with others gives a picture of their social skills and friendship groups. A disadvantage of this method is that you have to be disciplined, recording only what happens during your watching slot and ignoring anything else.

The example of a time sample observation shown on page 53 provides a picture of E's ability to concentrate throughout a session.

Snapshot

This is a useful method for looking at the provision that you make for children. You can use it to show which activities are popular, where staff are located and demonstrate how space is used. The example on page 54 shows how the children were spread around the room during a session and shows where the adults were based to support activities.

AIM – to observe E throughout the session, for three minutes every 15 minutes.

PURPOSE – to identify any factors affecting his performance and to assess any need for support.

TIME/SETTING	OTHERS PRESENT	ACTIONS & REACTIONS	LANGUAGE
9.00 Classroom.	Whole class for register and assembly.	Sitting attentively. Hands up to face, starts to look around.	Answers "yes" to name. Body language, leaning across desk.
9.15 Classroom.	Whole class spelling test.	Gets ready with spelling book and pencil.	Waits quietly as teacher reads out spellings group by group.
9.30 Classroom.	Whole class.	E wanders round tables with spelling sheet. Should be in line to take new spellings to cloakroom.	Teacher asks E if he knows what he is supposed to be doing. He smiles at her, and says "yes". Teacher asks E to join the line of children.
9.45 Library, giving me instructions to work Roamer.	J and C.	E very interested, gave me precise instructions of how to use the Roamer.	E said, "To work the Roamer you switch on the button on the side, press CM, press one of the arrows, forward press a number and GO."
10.00 Craft table in area between library and classroom.	J and T.	Cutting paper and card for owl nest.	E said, "You give the paper a twist, on the floor of the nest is where the babies play", pointing, "that's their rattle".
10.15 Craft Area	J, P and T.	Standing to table making owls habitat. Stopped working to look at J and P making their nest. E was supposed to be working with T.	Staring at J and P working. Teacher walks through and asks E if he is helping T with their model. E nods his head.
10.30 Classroom milk time	Whole class and a teacher from another class.	Sits drinking juice from flask.	Does not enter any conversation with peers; concentrates on drinking.
10.45 Playtime	In line with whole class, standing between S and T.	Standing between S and T. Rocking backwards and forwards, knocking into them.	E smiles, nods head.

A time sampling observation

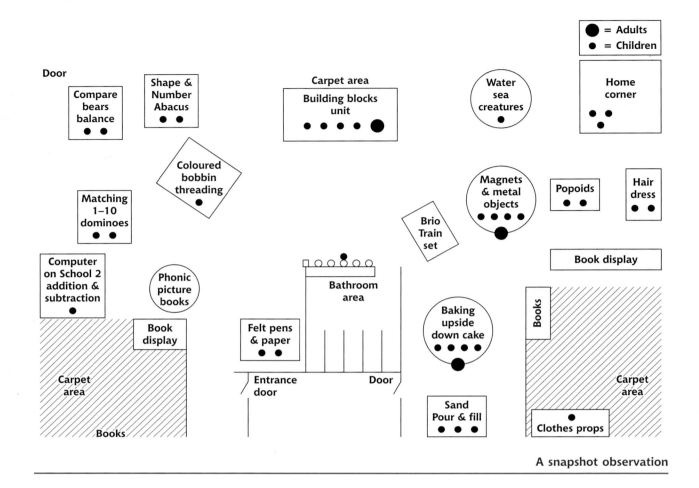

A snapshot observation

Policies and procedures relating to observation

Observing children will help you to understand children's development and is a very important professional skill. As a student, you must make sure that you follow any policies or procedures your placement has about observation.

Generally, the following will apply:

- Ask your supervisor's permission *before* you carry out an observation. (In most settings where students are trained, parents will have been told that their children will be observed and will have given their permission for this.)

- Show your observations to your supervisor *before* you take them away from your workplace. Sometimes parents like to have a copy too.

- Ask permission from both supervisor and parents before you take and use any photographs/videotapes of children in your observations.

- Maintain confidentiality and protect the child's identity by using an initial or changing the child's name and recording age as years and months, rather than date of birth. Do not identify the centre by name.

- Talk about what you have observed only with your supervisor and the child's parents.
- Tell your supervisor straightaway if you have any concerns about what you have observed.

Being objective

You must make sure that your observations of children are objective, that is, free of any personal feelings or thoughts. The way you see a child may be linked to:

- your previous experience of the child or other children
- your own attitudes and values
- any comments made by other people about that child.

If you approach a child or a situation with an idea of what you expect to find, then this will influence what you see. One way of making sure your observations are objective is to record exactly what you see without making any assumptions. For example:

- 'Jamie threw himself on to the floor screaming, kicking his feet and hammering the air with clenched fists' not 'Jamie was in a rage'
- 'Sarah snatched the doll from Nicola, kicked her and then bit her arm' not 'Sarah is an aggressive child'.

It will also help you to be objective if you *avoid*:

- jumping to conclusions, e.g. 'He is a naughty boy'
- making generalisations, e.g. 'All children cry when their mothers leave them'
- expressing personal opinions, e.g. 'She is a lovable child'
- labelling children, e.g. 'She is a bully'
- ascribing feelings to children, e.g. 'They were frightened'.

These examples give a subjective view. Describing exactly what you see will make your observations objective.

Using observation

Alex had been attending nursery for about six months. At this nursery staff make focused observations of individual children on a regular basis and discuss their findings at team meetings. The general feeling was that Alex had settled well and enjoyed most activities. The nursery nurse observed Alex for the whole of a morning session, focusing on his social interactions with other children and on the activities he chose. She found that although he appeared to be part of a group, for much of the time he was watching others play and was not able to take a real part in the activity. He chose a range of activities, but during that session avoided painting and craft. This observation was discussed at the team meeting with other staff. They had seen him enjoying painting and craft on other occasions and did not feel his missing those activities this time was significant. However, they felt that he did need a chance to break into group play and suggested that a member of staff play alongside Alex in a group and encourage him to be more assertive. At their next meeting, they would review the situation and decide whether there was still cause for concern.

➤ *Why was focused observation useful in this situation?*

➤ *What pre-conceived ideas might the staff have had about Alex?*

➤ *In your own placement or work setting, what use is made of observation?*

Check your knowledge

- Why is observation an important professional skill for child care workers?
- List three different methods of recording observations. Give an example of what you could observe using each method.
- Why should you discuss observation with your placement supervisor?
- How can you maintain confidentiality in your observations?
- Why is it important to be objective? How can you make sure that your observations are objective?

Support children's physical development needs

*T*his unit covers all aspects of care needed to support children's physical development needs. This includes supporting children's personal hygiene needs, eating and drinking, providing opportunities for exercise, rest and quieter activities.

This unit has links with units E1 and E2.

This unit contains four elements:

- **C1.1** Help children to toilet and wash hands

- **C1.2** Help children when eating and drinking

- **C1.3** Support opportunities for children's exercise

- **C1.4** Support children's quiet periods

Introduction

Personal hygiene

Personal hygiene is all about keeping clean and includes washing, bathing, hair washing and teeth cleaning. All children need adult help and supervision as they learn to keep themselves clean. Good standards of hygiene in childhood are important because they help to:

- prevent disease and the spread of infection

- prepare children for life by teaching them how to care for themselves and become independent.

Functions of the skin

The skin does the following things (functions):

- Protects the body by preventing germs entering.

- Feels sensations of hot, cold, soft, hard.

- Secretes an oily substance called sebum that keeps the skin supple and water-proof.

- Makes vitamin D when exposed to sunlight. (Vitamin D helps to make strong bones.)

- Makes sweat. Sweating helps to regulate the temperature when the body is hot.

Caring for the skin properly helps the skin to do all these things well.

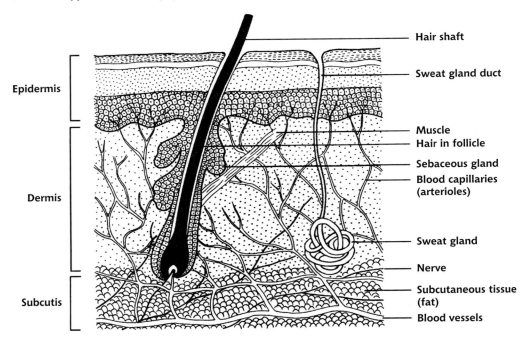

Epidermis

Dermis

Subcutis

The structure of
the skin

Hair shaft

Sweat gland duct

Muscle
Hair in follicle
Sebaceous gland
Blood capillaries
(arterioles)

Sweat gland

Nerve

Subcutaneous tissue
(fat)
Blood vessels

Eating and drinking

Eating and drinking the right things is essential to good health. Eating habits are formed at an early age and child care workers need to make sure that children establish healthy eating habits so they can grow normally.

Exercise and physical activities

Exercise is a necessary and natural part of life for everyone. It is especially important for young children who need to develop and practise their physical skills. Encouraging exercise from an early age will help children to develop healthy exercise habits. Many children do not get enough exercise and will be at increased risk of heart disease and other health problems later in life.

Rest and sleep

Children should exercise regularly but they must also be allowed to rest – this may be relaxation, sleep or just a change of occupation. One of the values of relaxing or quiet areas in early years' settings is that they provide children with the opportunity to rest and recharge their batteries. A book area, storytime, home play, soft cushions and other relaxing activities can be provided at nursery and at home. Children need not be stimulated all the time; it is sometimes useful for them to be given toys or activities that are easy to do.

Element **C1.1** *Help children to toilet and wash hands*

KUS
1, 8, 13,
14, 15, 20

Guidelines for good personal hygiene

- Wash the hands and face first thing in the morning.
- Wash hands after going to the toilet and after messy play.

- Wash hands before eating and drinking or helping to prepare food and drink.
- Keep the nails short by cutting them straight across. This will prevent dirt collecting under them.
- A daily bath or shower is necessary for young children who, while playing, may become dirty, hot and sweaty. Dry the skin thoroughly, especially between the toes and in the skin creases to prevent soreness and cracking.
- Observe the skin for rashes and soreness.
- Dry skin types need moisturising. Putting oil in the bath water and massaging oil or moisturisers into the skin afterwards helps to prevent dryness.
- If a daily bath is not possible, a thorough wash is good enough. Remember to encourage children to wash their bottoms *after* the face, neck, hands and feet.
- Hair usually needs to be washed two or three times a week. Can be more often if parents wish.
- Rinse shampoo out thoroughly in clean water. Conditioners may be useful for hair that is difficult to comb.
- Black curly hair may need hair oil applying daily to prevent dryness and hair breakage. Use a wide-toothed comb with rounded ends on the teeth. Take care to comb carefully without pulling.
- All skin types need protecting from the sun. Use a sun block or high factor sun cream and keep a close eye on the length of time children spend in the sun. Make sure that children wear a sun hat.

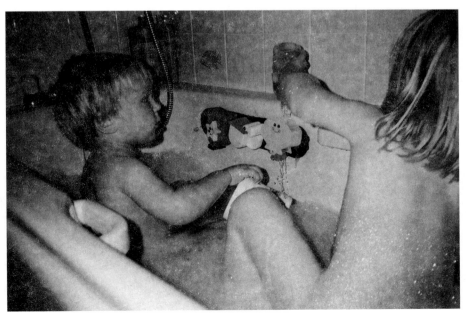

A daily bath is good for active toddlers

Normal development of bowel and bladder control (being able to be dry and clean)

Babies do not have control over their bladder or bowels and will just wet or dirty their nappies at any time, often after they have been fed. The ability to control the bladder and bowels, so that children become clean and dry, will develop gradually. This will happen when the messages received by the brain, that the bladder or bowel is full, can be understood. Most children will usually be reliably clean and dry by the age of about 3 years, but the age at which this happens will vary. There does not seem to be any point in rushing this. It is much easier if any 'training' is left until the child is at least 2 years old and is able to understand what is needed.

There are some general guidelines for deciding when a child is ready to be clean and dry:

- Wait until the child is ready; they may tell you they do not want to wear a nappy or show interest in other children using the potty or the toilet.
- The child must be aware of the need to use the toilet or potty and be able to tell that the bowel or bladder is full by recognising the feeling.
- Children must be able to tell their carer, verbally or with actions, that they need to go to the toilet.

How to help children become dry and clean:

- Be relaxed and give praise for success. As children become successful they will be more independent and they will feel pleased about their achievements, increasing their self-esteem. Do not show displeasure or disapproval about 'accidents', but just accept these. Do any cleaning and provide clean clothes without any fuss.
- Provide good role models. Seeing other children without nappies and being clean and dry will help children to understand the process.
- Children need to be given the opportunity to visit the toilet or use the potty regularly. They may need reminding if they are playing.
- Avoid sitting children on the potty for long periods of time.
- Remember that parents may have their own ideas about toileting. It is important that this is discussed so that you can follow a similar routine to the home one.

'Accidents'

It is not unusual for small children to wet or soil their pants. They have probably only learned to control their bladder and bowels not long before starting nursery or playgroup. Children will sometimes forget to go to the toilet or wait too long because they are really interested in what they are doing. The important thing is that this is dealt with quickly and without any fuss. Reassure the child and ensure that washing and changing takes place in private.

KUS
1, 8

Toilet training Terry

Cheryl is a nanny and cares for Terry, who is just two years old, while his parents are working. Terry is a happy little boy who is still wearing disposable nappies all the time. Terry's mother is very keen that he should become toilet trained and has asked Cheryl for her advice and help.

➤ *How will Cheryl know if Terry is ready to be trained?* **KUS 1**

➤ *How should she suggest that she and Terry's mother go about this?* **KUS 8**

Teeth

Teeth may appear at any time during the first two years of life. It is usually expected that they will begin to appear during the first year. They usually come through in the same order as shown in the illustration, but this may vary. The first 20 teeth are often called the milk teeth, and they will usually be complete by the age of 3 years. From 5–6 years, these teeth begin to fall out as the adult (permanent) teeth come through. There are 32 permanent teeth, and the care they are given in childhood will help them to last a lifetime.

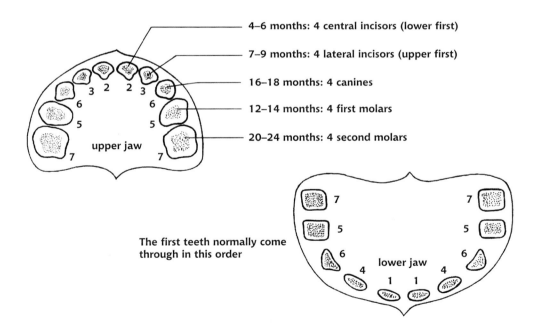

4–6 months: 4 central incisors (lower first)

7–9 months: 4 lateral incisors (upper first)

16–18 months: 4 canines

12–14 months: 4 first molars

20–24 months: 4 second molars

upper jaw

The first teeth normally come through in this order

lower jaw

Care of the teeth

Provide a soft toothbrush for a baby to use and become familiar with. Give them the opportunity to watch adults and other children clean their teeth. When the first tooth does appear, try to clean it gently with a small, soft brush. Ensure that cleaning the teeth becomes a habit: in the morning after breakfast and after the last drink or snack before bed. Cleaning the teeth after meals should be encouraged, but this may not always be possible.

Ensure that cleaning the teeth becomes a daily habit

Encourage healthy teeth and prevent tooth decay by providing a healthy diet that is high in calcium and vitamins and low in sugar. Avoid giving sweet drinks to babies and children, especially in a bottle, as this coats the gums and teeth in sugar and encourages decay. Sugar can also get into the gum and cause decay before the teeth come through. If you need to feed a child between meals, avoid sugary snacks. Provide food that needs to be chewed and improves the health of the gums and teeth, like apples, carrots and bread.

Visit the dentist regularly. Children attend with an adult, and then have their own appointments, will feel more confident about this. Prepare children for their dental appointments by explaining what will happen and introducing play visits to the dentist. Never pass on any adult feelings of worry about the dentist.

Encouraging independence in hygiene

Children need to be able to learn to keep themselves clean. There are several ways in which carers can encourage a child to develop independence in personal hygiene:

- Provide a good example yourself.
- Have routines that encourage cleanliness from early babyhood.

- Make bathtime fun: use toys in the bath, cups and containers, sinkers and floaters.
- Provide children with their own flannel, toothbrush, hairbrush etc. that they have chosen themselves.
- Encourage children to wash themselves and participate at bathtime. Let them brush their hair with a soft brush and comb with rounded teeth.
- Provide a step so that they can reach the basin to wash and clean teeth.
- Allow time for the children to complete the tasks without rushing.

Health education

Children need to learn about their bodies and why it is important to be clean and healthy. Children will need help as they carry out personal hygiene routines like bathing, hand washing, teeth cleaning. This gives you time to discuss why these activities are important to keep children healthy and safe from infection. This is also a good opportunity to talk about parts of the body and bodily functions with the children. How much you can talk about will depend on the age and development of the children.

Observation

Supporting children's personal hygiene routines will also give child care workers opportunities to observe the children for any signs of infection or abuse. Any sign of injury or infection, such as rashes, sore patches, bruising, blood in children's pants or knickers, should be reported promptly to your senior staff member. The accident/ incident book should be completed promptly and accurately.

Health and safety

In the bathroom/toilet area

All child care settings should have a procedure for ensuring health and safety in the toilet/bathroom area.

Make sure that:

- children are always supervised and help is given when needed
- the water in the hot tap is not too hot to be used safely
- steps are provided to help children reach the sink
- each child has sufficient time and privacy to use the toilet
- hand washing and drying is done thoroughly
- the area is checked regularly for cleanliness
- there is a supply of soap and towels, or hand dryers are in working order
- all waste is placed in a bin with a well-fitting lid
- protective clothing for the staff, e.g. aprons and gloves, is available.

Disposing of waste materials

All child care settings should have a health and safety policy that covers the disposal of hazardous waste. Care must be taken with all bodily waste (blood, faeces, urine and saliva) to prevent the spread of diseases.

When handling and disposing of waste materials:

- cover any cuts or grazes with a waterproof dressing
- wear disposable latex gloves when dealing with bodily waste
- cover blood with a 1% hypochlorite solution (such as bleach) before wiping up
- wash hands with an antiseptic soap
- dispose of nappies, dressings and used gloves in a sealed bag and place in a sealed bin for disposal
- provide designated areas with covered bins for different types of waste.

Are you ready for assessment?

Help children to toilet and wash hands

You need to show that you can competently help children to toilet and wash hands. You will need to be directly observed by your assessor and present other types of evidence.

Direct observation by your assessor

Your assessor will need to see you carry out these performance criteria (PCs):

C1.1 PCs 1, 2, 3, 4, 10

During these observations your assessor must see you cover at least ONE aspect in each range category listed in this element.

Remember the range categories for this element are:

1. Children
2. Responses

Preparing to be observed

Your assessor will need to see you taking children to the toilet so you will need to arrange to supervise that part of the routine, perhaps before snack or lunchtime. Make sure that you have checked the toilet area to make sure that it is clean and that there are enough towels and soap. Give help to the children if they need it and use the opportunity to talk to them about personal hygiene and why it is important. Avoid rushing the children but make sure that they wash and dry their hands thoroughly. Check that the area is left clean and tidy and that bins are properly covered.

Read the performance criteria and range carefully before your assessment. Try to cover as much as you can. ▶▶

Other types of evidence

You may need to present different types of evidence in order to:

- cover criteria not observed by your assessor
- show that you have the required knowledge, understanding and skills
- cover other parts of the range.

The amount and type of evidence you need to present will vary. You should plan this with your assessor.

Element C1.2 *Help children when eating and drinking*

KUS
2, 3, 4,
9, 15, 20

The requirements of a balanced diet

Nutrients are different kinds of food. To be healthy, the body needs a combination of different nutrients. These nutrients are:

- protein
- fat
- carbohydrate
- vitamins
- minerals
- water
- fibre.

Protein, fat, carbohydrates and water are present in the foods we eat and drink in large quantities. Vitamins and minerals are only present in small quantities, so it is much more common for those to be lacking in a child's diet.

Vitamins and minerals

Vitamins and minerals are only present in small quantities in the foods we eat, but they are essential for growth, development and normal functioning of the body.

The tables on pages 67–8 show the main vitamins and minerals, which foods contain them and what they do in the body.

Proteins provide material for:

- growth of the body
- repair of the body.

Types of proteins:

- **Animal** – first-class or complete proteins, supply all ten of the essential amino acids.
- **Vegetable** – second-class or incomplete proteins, supply some of the ten essential amino acids.

FOODS CONTAINING PROTEINS

Examples of protein foods include:

- **Animal proteins** – meat, fish, chicken, eggs, dairy foods.
- **Vegetable proteins** – nuts, seeds pulses, cereals.

Protein foods are made up of amino acids. There are ten essential amino acids.

Carbohydrates provide:

- energy
- warmth.

Types of carbohydrates:

- sugars
- starches.

FOODS CONTAINING CARBOHYDRATES

Examples of carbohydrate foods include:

- **Sugars** – fruit, honey, sweets, beet sugar, cane sugar.
- **Starches** – potatoes, cereals, beans, pasta.

Carbohydrates are broken down into glucose before the body can use them. **Sugars** are quickly converted and are a quick source of energy. **Starches** take longer to convert so they provide a longer-lasting supply of energy.

Fats:
- provide energy and warmth
- store fat-soluble vitamins
- make food pleasant to eat.

Types of fats:
- saturated
- unsaturated
- polyunsaturates.

Examples of foods containing fat include:
- **Saturated** – butter, cheese, meat, palm oil.
- **Unsaturated** – olive oil, peanut oil.
- **Polyunsaturated** – oily fish, corn oil, sunflower oil.

FOODS CONTAINING FAT

Saturated fats are solid at room temperature and come mainly from animal fats.
Unsaturated and polyunsaturated fats are liquid at room temperature and come mainly from vegetable and fish oils.

The main vitamins

Vitamin	Food Source	Function	Notes
A	Butter, cheese, eggs, carrots, tomatoes	Promotes healthy skin and good vision	Fat-soluble; can be stored in the liver. Deficiency causes skin infections, problems with vision. Avoid excess intake during pregnancy.
B	Fish, meat, liver, green vegetables, beans, eggs	Healthy working of muscles and nerves. Active in haemoglobin formation	Water-soluble, not stored in the body so a regular supply is needed. Deficiency results in muscle wasting, anaemia.
C	Fruits and fruit juices (especially orange and blackcurrant), green vegetables	Promotes healthy skin and tissue. Aids healing processes	Water-soluble, daily supply needed. Deficiency means less resistance to infection; extreme deficiency results in scurvy.
D	Oily fish, cod liver oil, egg yolk; added to margarines and to milk	Aids growth and maintenance of strong bones and teeth	Fat-soluble; can be stored by the body. Can be produced by the body by the action of sunlight on skin. Deficiency results in bones failing to harden and dental decay.
E	Vegetable oils, cereals, egg yolk, nuts and seeds	Promotes healing, aids blood clotting and fat metabolism	Fat-soluble; can be stored by the body.
K	Green vegetables, liver, whole grains	Needed for normal blood clotting, aids healing	Fat-soluble; can be stored by the body. Deficiency may result in delayed clotting, excessive bleeding.

The main minerals

Mineral	Food Source	Function	Notes
Calcium	Cheese, eggs, fish, pulses	Essential for growth of bones and teeth	Works with Vitamin D. Deficiency means that bones fail to harden (rickets) and leads to dental decay.
Fluoride	Occurs naturally in water or may be added to water, tooth-paste, drops and tablets	Makes tooth enamel more resistant to decay	There are arguments for and against adding fluoride to the water supply.
Iodine	Water, seafoods, vegetables, added to salt	Needed for proper working of the thyroid gland	Deficiency results in disturbance in the function of the thyroid gland.
Iron	Meat, green vegetables, eggs, liver, dried fruit, (esp. apricots, prunes, raisins)	Needed for the formation of haemoglobin in red blood cells	Vitamin C helps the absorption of iron. Deficiency results in anaemia, causing lack of energy.
Phosphorus	Fish, meat, eggs, fruit and vegetables	Formation of bones and teeth, helps absorption of carbohydrate	High intake is harmful to babies.
Potassium	Meat, milk, cereals, fruit and vegetables	Helps to maintain fluid balance	Deficiency is rare as potassium is found in a wide range of foods.
Sodium chloride	Table salt, fish, meat, bread, processed foods	Needed for fluid balance, formation of cell fluids, blood, sweat, tears	Salt should not be added to food prepared for babies and young children.

Fibre

Fibre is found in plants and adds bulk, or roughage, to food and stimulates the muscles of the bowel. This encourages the body to pass out the waste products left after digestion of food.

Water

Water is a vital part of the diet. It contains some minerals, but its main role is to maintain fluid in the cells and bloodstream.

A well-balanced diet

A well-balanced diet means that the food eaten provides all the nutrients that the body needs, in the right quantities. To do this a variety of foods should be eaten every day so that there will be no deficiency of a particular nutrient. A balanced diet gives children the opportunity to choose foods that they like and to taste new foods.

Proportions of nutrients

Children are growing all the time, so they need large amounts of protein to help them grow. They are also using a lot of energy, so they need carbohydrates in the form of starches. In addition, they will need adequate supplies of vitamins and minerals.

Suggested daily intakes are as follows:

- Two portions (helpings) of meat, fish or other vegetable protein foods, such as nuts and pulses.
- Two portions of protein from dairy products such as milk, cheese and yoghurt (for vegans substitute two other protein foods from plant sources).
- Four portions of starchy carbohydrate foods, such as bread, pasta, potatoes, sweet potatoes and breakfast cereals.
- Five portions of fruit and vegetables.
- Six drinks of fluid, especially water.

Begin with small portions. The size of the portions will get bigger as the child grows and can eat more.

Select the best quality food that you can. For example, choose wholemeal bread rather than white, and select fresh fruit and vegetables.

Diets of different groups

Each region or country has developed its own local diet over many years. Diets are based on available foods, which in turn depend on climate, geography and agricultural patterns, as well as social factors such as religion, culture, class and lifestyle. Each diet contains a balance of essential nutrients.

Diet is a part of people's way of life and the importance of familiar food should never be overlooked.

Religious aspects of food

For some people, food has a spiritual significance. Certain foods may not be eaten. Respecting an individual's culture and religious choices is part of respecting that individual as a whole. Talking to parents and carers about food requirements is important for child care workers, especially when caring for a child from a cultural or religious background different from your own.

Religious restrictions may affect the diets of Hindus, Sikhs, Muslims, Jews, Rastafarians and Seventh Day Adventists. Members of other groups may also have dietary restrictions.

People are individuals and will vary in what they eat and what restrictions they observe; you should be aware of this when discussing diets with parents or carers.

It is not possible to make blanket statements here about the diets of different groups, only to suggest things that may be important and that child care workers may find useful to know.

Group	Dietary Principles
Hindus	Many devout Hindus are vegetarian. Hindus eat no beef and drink no alcohol.
Muslims	May not eat pork or pork products. Alcohol is not permitted.
Jews	May not eat pork or shellfish. All other meat must be Kosher. Milk and meat are not used together in cooking.
Rastafarians	Mainly vegetarian. Whole foods are preferred. No products of the vine are eaten.
Christians	May avoid eating meat at certain times. Some foods may be given up in Lent.

It is very important to take account of these points when preparing activities involving food. If you are setting up a baking activity, for example, it would be best to make sure that you use vegetable fats, as these are more widely acceptable. Many more people are moving towards a vegetarian diet or a diet that includes fewer animal products.

Food allergy and dietary deficiencies

Food allergy and food intolerance may be caused by a number of factors, including an allergic response or an enzyme deficiency such as coeliac disease or diabetes. These children will need a special diet.

Special diets

Condition	Diet
Coeliac disease	Restrict intake of gluten, which is found in wheat, barley, rye and oats
Cystic fibrosis	Provide a high protein, high calorie diet. Vitamin and enzyme supplements are given
Diabetes	Diet is controlled. Intake, especially of carbohydrates, must match the insulin given
Phenylketonuria (PKU)	The diet is very restricted and the amount of phenylalanine found in protein foods is carefully controlled

Children may be allergic to some foods, for example nuts or milk. It is very important that staff are fully informed about any allergies to food that children may have. **Always check before giving food and drinks to babies and children.** If children are not allowed certain foods or drinks this should be made clear to all staff; notices in the kitchen and in the room where the children are cared for should clearly display this information. Information about children's allergies to food or drink must be regularly updated, and this must be discussed with the parents when a child is admitted and regularly after this to keep staff fully informed about any changes.

Helping children when eating and drinking and ensuring their safety

Children can learn the skills of feeding independently. They can share with others and learn about appropriate behaviour at mealtimes. The children should be comfortably and appropriately seated in a high chair or at the tables so that they can reach their food without difficulty. Children should not be allowed to eat or drink while walking or running around, nor should they run around holding any feeding utensils. If the children are using adult-sized furniture they will need a booster seat on the chair. Safety harnesses should always be fastened. Protective clothing such as aprons and bibs will protect the children's own clothes and allow them to have a go at eating independently. If younger children are to manage to feed themselves they need to be able to practise the physical skills to enable them to do this. They should be provided with:

- suitable utensils such as cups with two handles
- small-sized cutlery and large-rimmed dishes
- help to cut up their food if they need it.

Older children should be given the opportunity to use adult utensils and to manage their own food.

Social interaction at mealtimes

Mealtimes are a good opportunity for families and other groups to tell each other their news and ideas as they eat together. It is important to create a relaxed atmosphere at mealtimes so that this kind of social interaction can take place. It is good if adults and children sit together at the table without other distractions, such as the television, which will stop the conversation. Adults can provide help and encourage acceptable behaviour by providing positive role models for the children.

Illness

Children who are not feeling well may not have much appetite and may refuse food, or not eat very much. This is quite usual and appetite will return when the child feels better. However, it is important that the child drinks plenty, so encourage drinking, preferably clear fluids, such as fruit juices diluted with water, and as much as the child will take. If you are caring for a child who has an illness that lasts for a longer time then it will be necessary to encourage eating to help recovery. Offer small portions of food, find out what the child likes best and offer this if possible. Not eating well will affect a child in other ways. They may not have much energy and may not want to join in with play and activities or they may prefer to do things that are easier. In this case it will be important to provide quieter, less demanding activities.

Food refusal

Refusing to eat food provided and making a fuss about food at mealtimes is common among children. It is important to check that the child is of normal body weight and height and that the doctor has identified no medical condition. It is important that mealtimes should not become a battleground so child care workers should:

- offer food at mealtimes only
- avoid snacks between meals
- encourage children to take part in family and group mealtimes
- allow the child to eat independently
- not fuss about any mess when children are learning to eat independently
- remove any remaining food without fuss
- make mealtimes a pleasant experience.

Allow children to eat independently

Food additives

Additives are added to foods to add colour, give flavour or preserve the food. Permitted food additives are given an E number and these are listed on the label. For some children different behaviour may be associated with additives in food.

To reduce additives in the diet:

- use fresh foods as often as you can
- make your own pies, cakes and soups
- look at the labels; the ingredients are listed.

KUS
2, 3

Looking at the labels on food

Marian is a childminder who looks after Laurie and Anna. Marian needs to give the children lunch and as she hasn't got time to shop she will be using food from the fridge and freezer. Laurie's family is vegetarian and Anna is allergic to food colourings. Marian finds some fish fingers in the freezer and some chocolate puddings in the fridge.

This is what the labels say:

Fish fingers	Nutritional information
Protein	3.9 g
Carbohydrate	4.0 g
Fat	2.2 g
Fibre	0.3 g
No artificial colouring or flavouring	

Chocolate pudding
Ingredients:
Skimmed milk
Sugar
Chocolate
Vegetable oil
Beef gelatine

➤ *Will Marian be able to give the food to Laurie?* **KUS 2, 3**
➤ *Will Marian be able to give the food to Anna?* **KUS 2, 3**

Explain the reasons for your answers.

Preparing food

Food must be handled and prepared hygienically. Always:

- wash your hands well before touching food
- cover any cuts with a waterproof dressing
- wear an apron and tie hair back when preparing food
- avoid touching your nose and mouth, or coughing and sneezing in the food preparation area
- disinfect and replace kitchen cloths and sponges often
- disinfect all work surfaces regularly and especially before preparing food
- teach children these rules.

Cooking

To keep food safe it is very important to cook it properly. Always:

- defrost frozen food thoroughly before cooking
- cook foods like chicken and meat thoroughly, making sure that it is cooked through to the middle
- prepare raw meat separately – use a separate board and knife for this
- ensure cooked food is cooled quickly and then refrigerated or frozen
- cover any food standing in the kitchen
- keep raw foods and cooked foods separate in the fridge
- thoroughly cook eggs before eating – for babies and small children, cook the eggs until the white and yolk are solid
- remember that cooked food should only be reheated once – reheat until very hot all the way through
- reheat cooked chilled meals all the way through.

It is important that children learn the basic rules about handling food. Always make sure that they wash their hands before eating. If children prepare food as part of a learning activity, the food safety rules should always be followed. Children need to understand why this is important, so explain why they need to follow these rules.

Element C1.2

Are you ready for assessment?

Help children when eating and drinking

You need to show that you can help children when eating and drinking. To do this you will need to be directly observed by your assessor and present other types of evidence.

Direct observation by your assessor

Your assessor will need to see you carry out these performance criteria (PCs)

C1.2 PCs 1, 2, 3, 4, 6, 8

During these observations your assessor must see you cover at least ONE aspect in each range category listed in this element.

Remember the range categories for this element are:

1. Food and drink
2. Eating and drinking
3. Responses

Preparing to be observed

You will need to arrange to help children when eating and drinking at a mealtime or snacktime. Ensure that you prepare the area where children will eat and drink by making sure that all the tables and utensils are clean, and that there are enough suitable aprons and bibs if needed. Provide enough chairs of a suitable size and height for the children to be seated comfortably. Make sure that suitable cups, plates and bowls are provided so that the children can feed and help themselves. Create a relaxed atmosphere so that this is an enjoyable time.

Read the performance criteria and range carefully before your assessment. Try to cover as much as you can.

Other types of evidence

You may need to present different types of evidence in order to:

• cover criteria not observed by your assessor
• show that you have the required knowledge, understanding and skills
• cover other parts of the range.

The amount and type of evidence you need to present will vary. You should plan this with your assessor.

Element C1.3 Support opportunities for children's exercise

KUS
1, 5, 6, 11,
12, 13, 16,
17, 18, 19

Exercise and physical activities

Children need to have the opportunity to exercise regularly each day. This may be planned exercise, such as physical activities at school or nursery, or naturally occurring opportunities, such as walking to nursery or school.

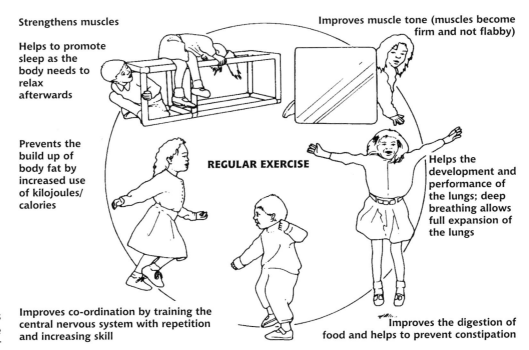

Strengthens muscles

Helps to promote sleep as the body needs to relax afterwards

Improves muscle tone (muscles become firm and not flabby)

Prevents the build up of body fat by increased use of kilojoules/ calories

REGULAR EXERCISE

Helps the development and performance of the lungs; deep breathing allows full expansion of the lungs

The benefits of exercise

Improves co-ordination by training the central nervous system with repetition and increasing skill

Improves the digestion of food and helps to prevent constipation

Physical development

Physical development is about the growth, development and control of the movement of the body. There is more information about this in the section on development on page 27.

Physical development, age 1–4

Many babies are mobile by the time they reach their first birthday. Babies have no idea of danger and need a watchful adult to ensure their safety until they can anticipate dangers. They need to explore and investigate the world in an environment that is safe. As the child gets older and their development progresses, they can run easily, sometimes falling, but less often now. Climbing stairs, jumping and riding a tricycle, gradually beginning to use the pedals are among their achievements.

When the child has achieved the basic skills of walking, running and climbing, their future physical development will depend on the opportunities they are given to practise and perfect these skills.

Physical development, age 4–7

The physical skills learned in the first four years will be practised and perfected. For example, children move from riding a tricycle by propelling it with the feet, to riding a bicycle without stabilisers, manoeuvring it around obstacles and using the brakes safely.

Physical development at nursery and infant school

All child care settings provide opportunities for physical exercise and activities. It is important that these are planned with the child's age, stage of development and safety in mind.

At nursery, outdoor play with tricycles, prams, trolleys, large building blocks, dens, tyres and climbing frames may create an environment for imaginative physical activity. Using music to encourage movement by using the body to interpret the sounds will improve co-ordination and balance. Group activities may encourage children who lack confidence.

At infant school, opportunities for exercise could include using the apparatus, dance, music and movement, football, team games, throwing and catching activities, and swimming.

Children will sometimes have separate clothing to wear when doing physical activities. However, during outdoor play at nursery the children will be wearing their own outdoor clothes. It is important to make sure that clothing does not get in the way or make play dangerous. It may be necessary to adjust long skirts or tie up trailing scarves to avoid accidents. Some children may need to keep their limbs and bodies covered for cultural reasons, so it is important to be aware of this and enable the child to take part in activities safely.

Supporting children's exercise

Developing gross motor skills

Physical play on large equipment helps children to develop:

- agility
- co-ordination
- balance
- confidence.

It allows children to get rid of surplus energy and to make noise. This is particularly important for children who spend a lot of time in smaller spaces. It is also important for children who are learning how to behave in a quiet, controlled indoor environment such as nursery or school.

The equipment provided should give opportunities for children to:

- climb
- slide
- bounce
- swing
- crawl
- move around.

Climbing

Equipment

- Match the size of equipment to the size of the children.
- Climbing up is often easier than climbing down – climbing frames with slides attached give children a safe way down.

Safety

- Climbing should always be closely supervised.
- Safety surfaces underneath the equipment are important – mats inside, safety surfaces outside.
- Equipment should be regularly checked for strength of joints, bolts etc.
- Care should be taken when moving large equipment – you could injure yourself or the children.

Climbing equipment

Sliding and bouncing

Equipment

- There is a huge range of slides in different materials and sizes. Before buying or using a slide think about who will be using it and where it will be put.
- Bouncing equipment includes trampolines, hoppers, bouncy castles etc.

Safety

- Children need to be taught basic safety rules when using this equipment, e.g. only one child at a time on the slide or trampoline.
- These activities should be supervised at all times. Children will be excited, which is good, but when they are excited they may need gently reminding of how to use the equipment safely.

Swings

Equipment

- There is a wide range available – what is used or bought needs to be matched to the physical development of the children in the group.
- Home-made swings are popular with older children – e.g. a tyre, a piece of wood on a rope or a large knot in a rope.

Safety

- Walking in front of swings is dangerous. Children need to be taught about this danger and reminded to be careful before playing outside.

Crawling

Equipment

- Rigid concrete tunnels can be installed outside.
- Collapsible plastic tunnels can be used outside and inside.

Tunnels can be used outside

- Other equipment such as climbing frames can be used for crawling through, under and over.

Safety

- Make sure that outside tunnels are kept clean; dogs and cats making a mess can be a problem.
- Make sure that the children know the rules about using the tunnels; for example, no jumping on to collapsible tunnels or rolling them around the floor.

Moving around

Equipment

- A variety of bikes, cars, trucks, trikes, carts and trailers will be needed to meet the range of abilities and needs.

Safety

- Wheeled toys need plenty of space to avoid collisions. It is sensible for these toys to be used in an area set aside for them.
- Regular maintenance will be necessary.

Wheeled toys need plenty of space

Avoiding stereotyping in physical play

It is important to make sure that all children can use the activities. The activities provided should be suitable for the range of abilities in the group and be managed by the staff to ensure that all children can join in. Activities should not be taken over by children who are physically very able. It may, therefore, be necessary to limit time on popular toys or at popular activities to make sure that everyone can have a go.

Adults should challenge any stereotyping linked to physical play; comments such as 'Girls can't run fast' or 'Cars are for boys' are unacceptable, as such remarks are likely to limit what children will try to do or play with. All children will then not have an equal opportunity to develop good physical skills.

Adults must also be aware of their own language and attitudes when supervising physical play. Comments or worries about whether certain children, for example girls or children with special educational needs, are capable of boisterous physical play, is likely to limit their physical play. Similar comments or a negative attitude towards less physically capable boys is not acceptable.

Outside play at the nursery

KUS
6, 11, 16, 18, 19

Staff had noticed that a number of children were reluctant to go outside to play. They decided to observe the play over a week to see how they could improve provision, so all children could take part happily in outdoor play. Each day a member of staff was given time to observe the play outside and to record what they saw. At the next staff meeting the staff were informed of the results of these observations. The staff had observed that a small group of boisterous children were taking over the space. They enjoyed playing on the bikes and would use the whole of the playground area in their game. This meant that the other children played at the edges of the playground and would sometimes be anxious about crossing the playground. Also, the boisterous children used the bikes all the time. They were the first children outside and raced to get to the bikes. Other children didn't get a chance to play on the bikes.

The staff discussed how they could improve the outdoor play. They decided to create areas in the playground for different activities. Their plans included the following:

• Marking out a section of the playground for the bikes with chalk marked roads, junctions etc.

• Sometimes selecting the quieter children to go on the bikes first.

• Creating an area with hoops, skipping ropes, juggling balls and stilts.

• Creating an area with large construction activities.

• Creating a pretend play area.

• Looking into acquiring or buying small benches and tables for outdoor tabletop activities.

The staff's observations and the changes that they made ensured that all the children were able to participate in all activities. It means that all children had an equal opportunity to develop the necessary skills and concepts. The boisterous children became involved in a wider range of activities and the other children were able to use the bikes and to play outside happily.

➤ *Why did the staff decide to observe the outdoor play before making changes?* **KUS 11**

➤ *Why was it important to allow the quieter children sometimes to go on the bikes first?* **KUS 11, 16, 19**

➤ *Why was it important to have a range of both boisterous and quieter activities planned for outdoors?* **KUS 6, 11, 18, 19**

Children with disabilities

When caring for children with disabilities, it is important to remember that every child is an individual with specific needs. Some children may not achieve the level of physical ability expected for their age group, so they may need an individual programme that will help them to progress at their own pace. They may spend longer at each stage of development before moving on to the next. Special/ individual needs should be viewed positively, and each achievement should be encouraged and praised.

Fresh air

All children need regular exposure to fresh air and preferably an opportunity to play outside. The indoor play area should be well ventilated to provide fresh air. Fresh air provides oxygen and helps to prevent infections being spread.

Safety

When supporting children's exercise it is very important to pay close attention to the safety of the children. Every setting will have health and safety procedures and you should make sure that you follow these in your work with the children. All settings that care for children outside their own home are regularly inspected to ensure that positive steps are taken to promote safety within the setting. Look at unit E2 for more information.

Before the children start any indoor exercise or outdoor play the area and equipment should be thoroughly checked for any hazards. Equipment should always be carefully and correctly assembled following the manufacturer's instructions. Any safety mats should be in place.

Children must always be carefully supervised to ensure their safety. However, it is also important to let the children develop their physical skills by joining in with more challenging activities or using more advanced equipment. Good supervision will mean that you are there to support them and to make sure that what they are trying to do is realistic. Give help where needed to support these attempts and to help the children achieve their goals.

Accidents

Any accidents should be promptly dealt with. Look at unit E2 for more information on first aid. Always follow the procedure of your setting. Seek help from a senior member of staff and remember to complete the accident forms or book carefully.

Element C1.3 Are you ready for assessment?

Support opportunities for children's exercise

You need to show that you can competently support opportunities for children's exercise. To do this you will need to be directly observed by your assessor and present other types of evidence.

Direct observation by your assessor

Your assessor will need to see you carry out these performance criteria (PCs)

C1.3 PCs 1, 3, 5, 6, 7, 8, 10, 13

During these observations your assessor must see you cover at least ONE aspect in each range category listed in this element.

Remember the range categories for this element are:

1. Children
2. Activities
3. Responses

Preparing to be observed

You will need to arrange to take part in indoor and outdoor activities that provide opportunities for children's physical exercise. It will help with your assessment if you write a plan for the physical play session beforehand so that you know what equipment you will need to provide and what you will be doing during the session. Drawing a plan of the equipment and where it will be placed may also help you. Make sure that the equipment and activities you select are suitable for the ages of the children involved. Check and set out any equipment carefully, and make sure

▶▶

Babies & Young Children

you use the space you have effectively. For example, you may wish to restrict the wheeled toys to a certain area well away from any ball games. During the session you should supervise the children carefully. This is usually a team effort but make sure that you know what your responsibilities are. Support and encourage the children so that they get maximum benefit from the session, and that they move on and develop their skills. For example, a child using the balancing beam for the first time may well need help or for you to be nearby, but after a few successful attempts may feel confident enough to try by herself.

Read the performance criteria and range carefully before your assessment. Try to cover as much as you can.

Other types of evidence

You may need to present different types of evidence in order to:

- cover criteria not observed by your assessor
- show that you have the required knowledge, understanding and skills
- cover other parts of the range.

The amount and type of evidence you need to present will vary. You should plan this with your assessor.

Support children's quiet periods

Element C1.4

KUS
1, 7, 15, 21

Rest and sleep

Children often have very busy lives and their days are filled with activity. However, although children will be able to join in with stimulating activities for a period of time, they must be allowed to rest. Whether the rest periods involve sleeping or just more restful and less demanding, quieter activities will depend on the age and stage of development of the child. It may also be important to take into account the parents' wishes, especially where daytime sleeping is concerned. When planning for the children child care workers should provide opportunities for rest and/or sleep as part of the routine of the day.

Restful activities

Restful activities should be planned and a suitable area chosen where the children can relax. Quiet activities could include:

- storytime in a suitable area, perhaps in a curtained off section of a bigger nursery or playgroup, with some soft cushions to sit on

- a quiet time to look at books
- quiet conversation
- listening to suitable music in a quiet area
- play with small world toys in a quiet area.

Children need not be stimulated all the time; it is sometimes useful for them to be given toys or activities that are relaxing and relatively easy to do.

Storytime should be an opportunity for quiet relaxation

Sleep

Everyone needs sleep but everyone has different requirements. Children need different amounts of sleep depending on their age and stage of development, and the amount of exercise taken.

Sleep routines

Babies and children need varying amounts of sleep. Some babies may just sleep and feed for the first few months, while others sleep very little. Toddlers vary too. Some need a nap morning and afternoon; others need one of these or neither.

Everyone needs sleep

Some children wake often at night, even after settling late. There is little that can be done apart from following a sensible routine:

- be patient
- plan a sensible bedtime routine and stick to it
- don't stimulate the child just before bedtime
- encourage daily exercise
- reduce stress or worries
- ensure that the bedroom is comfortable
- avoid loud noises.

Daytime sleeping

Younger children may need a daytime sleep. It is very important to discuss this with the child's parents so that you are following their home routine and their wishes. If children are sleeping at nursery it is important to provide a safe place for them to sleep. Cots, mats or beanbags may be provided. If children do not have their own cot to sleep in, then any sheets and covers should be changed for each child. The room should be properly ventilated and the temperature controlled so that the children do not become overheated. Dimming the lights will also help to provide a restful environment. Children should always be supervised when they are sleeping, so a member of staff should be with them all the time.

To prevent cot deaths current research recommends that all babies should sleep:

- on their backs
- without a pillow
- feet against the bottom of the cot
- using sheets and blankets NOT a duvet
- in a room temperature of 18°C (68°F).

Are you ready for assessment?

Support children's quiet periods

You need to show that you can competently support children's quiet periods. To do this you will need to be directly observed by your assessor and present other types of evidence.

Direct observation by your assessor

Your assessor will need to see you carry out these performance criteria (PCs)

C1.4 PCs 1, 2, 4, 6

During these observations your assessor must see you cover at least ONE aspect in each range category listed in this element.

Remember the range category for this element is:

1. quiet periods

Preparing to be observed

You will need to arrange to take part in organising and supporting children's quiet periods. Remember that this can include sleep times, rest times and quiet activities (look at range 1). These quiet periods are likely to be planned as part of the routine of the day or session. You will need to ensure that you can show your assessor how quiet periods are planned as part of the day, and show how they meet the children's developmental and physical needs. You should be aware of how your setting takes account of parents' wishes; find out if you don't already know. While you are supporting the children when they are sleeping or during quieter activities you will need to ensure that a relaxed atmosphere is maintained and keep distractions to a minimum. Check that any equipment you use is safe and that ventilation and temperature are correctly maintained.

Read the performance criteria and range carefully before your assessment. Try to cover as much as you can.

Other types of evidence

You may need to present different types of evidence in order to:

- cover criteria not observed by your assessor
- show that you have the required knowledge, understanding and skills
- cover other parts of the range.

The amount and type of evidence you need to present will vary. You should plan this with your assessor.

Check your knowledge

- What are the basic dietary requirements for good health? **KUS 2**
- How can adults help children to become more self-reliant? **KUS 8**
- Explain the importance of social interaction at mealtimes. **KUS 9**
- Describe a range of activities to promote physical development. **KUS 12**
- Describe the dietary principles of different groups of people. **KUS 3**

Support children's social and emotional development

*T*his unit focuses on the worker's role in supporting many aspects of the social and emotional development of children. It considers the needs on which the healthy social and emotional development of children depends. It looks at the wide variety of factors that may influence this development. While you are working through this unit, you will find it helpful to refer to the introductory section on children's development.

This unit has five elements:

C4.1 *Help children to adjust to new settings*

C4.2 *Help children to relate to others*

C4.3 *Help children to develop self-reliance and self-esteem*

C4.4 *Help children to recognise and deal with their feelings*

C4.5 *Assist children to develop positive aspects of their behaviour*

Introduction

In order to promote healthy social and emotional development adult carers must meet children's needs. Children need to feel loved and secure. The experience, in their early years, of a close, stable relationship with at least one caring adult enables children to feel loved and secure. Moving a child from one place of care to another (for example, from their home to a nursery) usually involves loss of a familiar carer and environment. Change and loss can make a child feel insecure. Adults should handle change carefully and sensitively so that it does not damage a child's sense of security and trust. Preparation for change and good substitute care help children to cope better with separation from the people to whom they are attached.

The experience of a close, stable relationship with at least one caring adult enables children to feel loved and secure

Attachments

The quality and character of children's early close relationships is very important for their social and emotional development. Children need to develop close, affectionate, two-way relationships with those who care for them. These relationships are called attachments. Good attachments help children to feel secure, happy and confident.

Infants will try to stay close to the adults to whom they are attached. They want to be cared for by them. By the end of their first year they show that they prefer to be with these adults. These adults may include people such as their grandparents, aunts and uncles, as well as their parents. Infants usually become unhappy if they are separated from them. They may show anxiety and cry if they are left with strangers. Infants need good preparation, understanding of their needs and good substitute care if they are to be cared for successfully by others, if, for example, their parents return to work.

How attachments are formed

Attachments build up over a period of time. Their quality depends on how a parent and infant relate to each other both before and after birth. Attachments develop best:

- if pregnancy and birth are a good experience
- if the child is wanted
- in a happy and secure family environment
- if there is good quality, close contact between infant and mother and other carers in the first three years of the child's life.

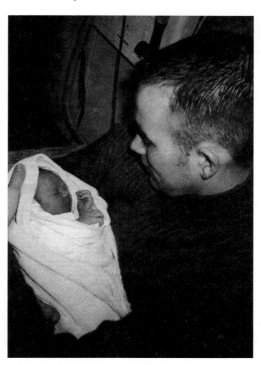

Attachments develop best if there is good quality, close contact between infant and carers

Meeting children's needs

Within their close relationships, children need the following:

- Love and affection. This means being loved for themselves and not what they do.
- A stable and secure environment. This is best provided by a small group of carers who are familiar to the child.
- Consistent care routines and guidelines for behaviour. Children need to be cared for in a happy environment that does not change from day to day.
- Praise and encouragement. Praise will make children feel they are valued and worth while.
- Gradual independence. As children mature physically their personal skills increase. They then become confident, independent and gradually learn to become responsible for themselves.

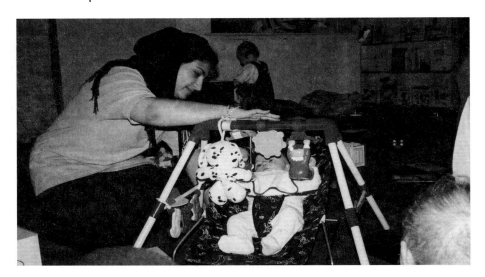

Children need to be cared for in a happy environment that does not change from day to day

Providing good quality care

Attachments develop if adults meet children's needs and give them good quality care. Good quality care includes a carer:

- playing with the infant
- cuddling them
- giving them individual attention
- having 'conversations' with them
- enjoying their company
- meeting their physical and emotional needs.

A child forms a stronger attachment with a person who plays and talks to them, than with someone who simply meets their physical needs.

Workers should therefore talk to and play with the young children in their care. In this way they will be able to relate closely to them. A key worker system is one where a worker is responsible for a particular child. This can help staff to form a special relationship with infants in their care. Key workers can also form a positive and helpful relationship with a child's parents/carers.

Good quality care includes giving individual attention

Disability

Parents of disabled children may feel disappointment and a sense of failure when they first learn their child has a disability. It may lead to difficulty or delay in forming an attachment with their child. Disabled children and carers have the same needs as other people. However, there may be different ways of meeting these needs. Children and carers with sight or hearing loss in particular need alternative or additional ways to help them to respond to one another.

Element C4.1 *Help children to adjust to new settings*

KUS
2, 3, 5, 17, 22

Change and separation

When a child starts nursery or school this usually involves:

- separation from their main, familiar carer
- a change of physical environment
- feelings of loss.

This loss can affect a child's feelings of stability, security and trust. In general, children react most strongly to separation between the ages of 6 months and 3 years.

Why support is needed

Children have to adapt to a new setting when they start at a day nursery, a play-group or school, or go to a childminder. They will need help to cope with separation from the people to whom they are attached. They may have feelings of loss, anxiety and stress caused by the changes. Adults need to help them to adjust to their new setting.

Preparing for change

Children are immature and vulnerable. Preparation before any change can help children to adjust. Preparation has become part of the policy of most nurseries, childminders, pre-schools and hospitals.

Workers can advise parents to prepare their children by:

- being sensitive to their needs and stage of development
- talking and listening to them
- explaining things to them and reassuring them honestly
- reading books and watching certain videos with them
- providing imaginative and expressive play to help them to express their feelings
- going on introductory visits
- providing personal details about their child and their cultural background.

Ways to help children to adjust to new settings

Workers should take the child's age into account when providing care for any child in a new setting. We know that generally separation is more difficult between 6 months and 3 years of age. The younger the child the more they will benefit from a one-to-one relationship with a particular person. Some settings have a named key worker for each child. This is the person who makes a relationship with a particular child. When possible they greet the child on arrival, settle them in and attend to their needs. The key worker will also be responsible for observing the child, making records and sharing observations with parents. Child care workers should find out the particular needs and background of each child. They will then be able to respond better to their individual needs.

Starting at a new setting

When children start a new setting it is good practice for child care workers to do the following:

- Prepare the other children and adults in the setting to receive the newcomers. They should tell them when the new children will be coming and what their names are. If this is done then they can all be more sensitive to newcomers' needs and make them feel welcome.

- Welcome new children warmly when they arrive and call them by the name they prefer.

- Make sure that children's comfort objects are readily available to them if they are needed. This may mean keeping a blanket or a favourite toy in a particular place and knowing the policy of the setting on this. They should agree this with the parent.

- Show children around so that the physical layout is less strange and becomes more familiar. Give them a special coat peg with a picture or label of their own. Provide a drawer to keep personal objects and work in. These will all help to make them feel they belong.

- Introduce them to other workers in a relaxed way without rushing them.

- Reassure them and comfort them if they appear anxious or upset. It is important to observe children closely to be aware of any early signs of distress and respond to these.

- Be sympathetic. Help them to deal with routines and other things that are unfamiliar. Remember that even adults can find unfamiliar surroundings difficult.

- Provide new children with appropriate activities. These should include parallel and associative play and play that encourages the expression of feelings.

- Developing ways or strategies to encourage children to join in with activities. This may mean allowing them to play alongside an adult or other children for a while. It could mean letting them watch and gently encouraging them to join in with you or another child when they are ready.

Encourage a new child to join in with another child when they are ready

● Allowing them to adjust to the setting and the routines in their own way and in their own time. Children will vary in the time it will take them. This may depend on their previous experiences of change, and on their age and personality.

Links to unit E1.3.

Nursery policies

Nursery policies can also help children to adjust to their new setting. They can include an admission programme that staggers the intake of children. In this way not too many new children start at any one time.

Staff should support parents during this period of change. They should communicate clearly with them. They can provide an informative brochure in the parent's home language. Staff can create a welcoming environment for parents and their children.

KUS
2, 3, 5,
17, 22

Starting pre-school

Emily is 3 years old. She recently moved with her family to a new town. She enrolled at a pre-school playgroup towards the end of the summer term. Her mother took Emily to the pre-school and spent several mornings with her, playing with both her and the other children. A key worker welcomed Emily, showed her around and introduced her to other children and workers. In the last week of term Emily's mother left her for half-an-hour on two mornings, and Emily stayed and played happily. When she started again in September her mother stayed for a while each morning for the first week. During the second week Emily kissed her mother goodbye as she hung up her coat and ran to join her friends.

➤ *Why did Emily's mother stay with her at the pre-school at first?*
   KUS 2, 3
➤ *What did the key worker do and why?* **KUS 2, 3, 5, 22**
➤ *Why did Emily's mother also play with the other children?* **KUS 17**
➤ *Why did her mother stay with her again in September?* **KUS 2, 17**
➤ *How did Emily react to leaving her mother in the second week in September and why was this?* **KUS 2, 3, 17**

Element C4.1 Are you ready for assessment?

Help children to adjust to new settings

You need to show that you can competently help children to adjust to new settings. To do this you will need to be directly observed by your assessor and present other types of evidence.

Direct observation by your assessor

Your assessor will need to see you carry out these performance criteria (PCs)

C4.1 PCs 1, 3, 4, 5, 6, 7

During these observations your assessor must see you cover at least ONE aspect in each range category listed in this element.

Remember the range categories for this element are:

1. Children
2. Items and activities
3. Unfamiliar features

Preparing to be observed

You need to have had experience of helping children to adjust to a new setting. You should be confident about doing this. You should arrange with your manager to take care of one or two new children on the day that your assessor can observe you. This need not be the children's first day. You could work with a child who is recently new or who has not yet settled and needs further support.

You should welcome the child or children individually. You should use the names that they prefer to be called by. You should show the child around the setting or a part of it that they are unfamiliar with. There may, for example, be unfamiliar things that are set out differently inside or outside on that day. You should aim to introduce the child to an unfamiliar worker. Try to be sensitive to how the child is reacting. Respond to and support the child appropriately. You should ask for or accept help from your supervisor if you are unable to deal with the child, for example if there is an intense level of distress. You must demonstrate that you can help a child to deal with things that are unfamiliar, for example, their parent's absence or how to find the toilet. You should encourage the child to join in with activities appropriately. This will help the child to adjust to the setting in their own way and at a pace that they are happy with.

Read the performance criteria and range carefully before your assessment. Try to cover as much as you can.

▶▶

> ## Other types of evidence
>
> You may need to present different types of evidence in order to:
>
> • cover criteria not observed by your assessor
> • show that you have the required knowledge, understanding and skills
> • cover other parts of the range.
>
> The amount and type of evidence you need to present will vary. You should plan this with your assessor.

Element C4.2 *Help children to relate to others*

KUS
1, 2, 6, 12, 19, 23, 24

The role of play

It is important that child care workers frequently provide activities and experiences that encourage children to play and do things co-operatively and purposely with others. Play is very effective in helping children to relate to each other.

Between a year and 3 years of age children need increasing social contact with adults and children.

By the time they are 3 years old many children are capable of taking account of other people's actions and needs. They are able to co-operate with others by

Play is very effective in helping children to relate to each other

taking on a role in a group. Child care workers should know which activities, both indoors and outdoors, encourage children to play and do things co-operatively. They should encourage children by praising and rewarding them for positive behaviour. They need activities that promote the use of all their senses. They should have access to resources and equipment that stimulate every area of development.

These activities include the following:

- Imaginative play experiences. Sometimes in role play areas such as a home corner, shops, a hospital, vets or garden centre.
- Games that involve working in pairs or in a group. These help children to share and take turns. They include board, dice, card and computer games.
- Children helping to prepare activities. They can help to put resources out and clear them away. Prepare and share meals and snacks.
- Using resources co-operatively. For example, collage and making models, sand and water play, and using a computer.
- The exploration and investigation of objects and events in a group. This includes group discussions, looking at natural and made objects. Some of these may be brought from home.
- Opportunities for children to talk and listen to each other and to share their experiences. This includes having agreed codes of conduct when taking turns, speaking and listening to each other.

Games that involve working in a group help children to share and take turns

Dealing with conflict and anti-social behaviour

Sometimes children behave in ways that produce conflict between themselves and other children. Adults should allow children to resolve minor conflicts themselves. This helps them to develop and use the skills of negotiation and compromise.

Adult intervention is, however, sometimes essential. This is particularly so if children are being physically aggressive. In this case the adult should stop the child who is being aggressive and tell them that what they have done is wrong. They should support and comfort the child who has been hurt. They should also support the child who has been hurtful, discussing why the action was wrong.

Adult intervention is particularly important when children are aggressive to other children because they are of a different race or gender or they are disabled. Sometimes hurtful behaviour involves excluding a child from a group. Aggression may be verbal or physical or both. Adults should not ignore unwanted behaviour just because it is not physical. They should help a child to know that hurtful behaviour of any kind is wrong and that you, as an adult, will support them as they learn this.

Adults should also support the child who has been hurtful

Encouraging positive interaction

Workers can help children to relate to each other positively. They can also promote tolerance. To tolerate means to allow the existence of another person, to accept differences in the way that others behave, think and speak without interfering. Workers can promote tolerance by:

- encouraging children to have a positive view of their own social and cultural group
- encouraging children to have a positive view of the culture of others
- providing activities and resources that encourage them to be familiar with differences
- encouraging children to accept difference
- celebrating the differences between people, e.g. in the way they dress, eat or celebrate festivals
- providing positive images of different kinds of people in books, pictures and toys.

Workers should use play and learning experiences to develop understanding, respect and acceptance:

- between children as they play
- of people from varied social and cultural backgrounds
- of children with special educational needs.

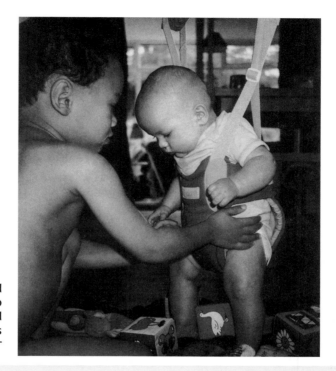

Workers should use play and learning experiences to develop children's understanding and acceptance of others

Are you ready for assessment?

Help children to relate to others

You need to show that you can competently help children to relate to others. To do this you will need to be directly observed by your assessor and present other types of evidence.

Direct observation by your assessor

Your assessor will need to see you carry out these performance criteria (PCs)

C4.2 PCs 1, 2, 3, 6

During these observations your assessor must see you cover at least ONE aspect in

each range category listed in this element.

Remember the range categories for this element are:

1. Children
2. Others
3. Groups

Preparing to be observed

Your assessor should see you help to provide activities and experiences that encourage children to relate positively to each other. You may be able to do this while you are being observed for another unit. You should show that you can help them to play and do things co-operatively and with a purpose in a group. You must demonstrate that you have realistic expectations of children's behaviour. You can do this by providing activities that are appropriate to their age and stage of development. It is important to allow children to resolve minor conflicts themselves amicably. The play and learning experiences you provide should encourage children and adults of various backgrounds to play together positively and develop mutual understanding and respect.

Read the performance criteria and range carefully before your assessment. Try to cover as much as you can.

Other types of evidence

You may need to present different types of evidence in order to:

- cover criteria not observed by your assessor
- show that you have the required knowledge, understanding and skills
- cover other parts of the range.

The amount and type of evidence you need to present will vary. You should plan this with your assessor.

Help children to develop self-reliance and self-esteem

Element C4.3

KUS
7, 12, 13, 21, 26, 27

Promoting self-reliance and self-esteem

As children grow and mature they need to develop the skills that will enable them to become self-reliant and independent. This includes learning the self-help skills they need to go to the toilet, wash, dress and undress. They also need to learn how to eat and drink independently with and without tools. The gradual development of children's physical and communication skills are essential to this process.

A child's self-image and identity is their view of who they are and what they are like. Children who think well of themselves have a positive self-image. This means that they will have high self-esteem. Having high self-esteem is not the same as being conceited. Conceit involves one person comparing him or herself to another. Having high self-esteem does not involve comparisons; it is having an assurance about yourself that you are good and worth while.

It is very healthy for children and adults to have high self-esteem. People with high self-esteem tend to:

- be happier and more successful in life
- make better and more secure relationships
- have better mental health
- be more able to cope with difficulties and frustrations in life.

High self-esteem is having an assurance about yourself that you are good and worth while

The role of the adult

Child care workers should help children to develop self-reliance and self-esteem. Adults should remember the following:

- Listen to children carefully. Encourage them to say what they need and help them to express their thoughts and ideas. Adults can talk with children about what they are doing and negotiate the ways they need help. They can encourage them gradually to increase their independence as their skills and confidence develop.
- Set goals at the right level for the child. Goals should challenge the child but allow the child to achieve them with as little help as possible.

- Praise children's efforts and achievements. This will increase their self-confidence and self-esteem. Praise and rewards are very effective. They can be the words that adults use, looks such as smiles and nods, gestures including touching a child gently or material rewards.

- Give children assistance when it is needed to overcome difficulties. This should not be in a way that undermines their growing confidence and skills.

- Be aware that children's level of confidence and their skills may vary from one day to another. A child may regress at times to a former level when tired, unwell or unhappy.

- Provide activities and routines that recognise the child as an individual. Children should be treated with care and respect. They should not be hurried beyond their capabilities or feel inadequate if they cannot achieve a task without assistance.

- Have expectations that are appropriate to their age and stage of development.

- Avoid assuming that a child is or is not capable of something because of stereotypical assumptions about children's capabilities. These assumptions may be based on their gender, family or cultural background or disability.

- Be aware that parents differ in their expectations of children. Some will expect them to be independent in their personal skills at a younger age than others. Accommodate parents' expressed wishes when possible.

- Show that they value what children do.

- Ensure that the children's safety is maintained at all times.

These positive responses towards children are likely to encourage them to develop appropriate levels of self-reliance and high self-esteem.

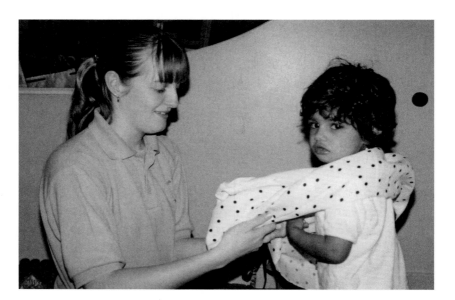

Give children assistance when it is needed to overcome difficulties

Practical Example

Promoting independence

KUS
7, 12,
26, 27

Leroy was the older of two boys. Before he started primary school Leroy's parents were trying to encourage him to go to the toilet independently and to wash his hands. Leroy was resisting this, insisting his mother or father stayed with him to help him to dress and wash. His parents agreed a plan. They encouraged him gradually to do a little more himself each day while they helped him a little less. They praised his efforts and rewarded him with a hug and smile each time he did a little more for himself. A month later Leroy was happy to use the toilet and wash independently.

➤ *Why do you think Leroy might be resisting doing things for himself?*
  KUS 7

➤ *What plan did Leroy's parents carry out?* **KUS 12, 26**

➤ *How did they encourage him?* **KUS 27**

Encouraging independence

Children naturally wish to do things for themselves and become independent. Child care workers should encourage the development of independence within safe limits. Children do not acquire skills straight away – they need time to experiment and practise in a positive environment where each achievement is recognised.

Children's development in all areas follows a path towards maturity and independence. Achieving independence involves the development of skills that gradually lead to less reliance on other people for help or support.

Physical skills

Age 1–4

As we have already seen in unit C1, becoming mobile and able to move around independently is central to the development of independence for babies. Many babies are mobile by the age of 1. They have no concept of danger and need to be supervised carefully while they explore the world in an environment that has been made safe. As the child's gross motor development progresses, they learn to run, climb stairs, jump, ride a tricycle and begin to use the pedals.

Age 4–7

Physical skills learned in the first four years of life will be perfected and adults need to make sure that children are given opportunities to practise. For example, children progress from a tricycle to a bicycle without stabilisers. Also, the refinement of fine motor skills enables the development of self-help skills such as feeding and dressing independently.

Children with disabilities

When caring for disabled children, it is important to remember that every child is an individual with specific needs. Some children may not achieve the level of physical competence expected for their age group, so emphasis must be on an individual programme that will enable the child to progress at their own pace within the usual sequence of development. They may spend longer at each stage before progressing to the next. Special/individual needs should be viewed positively and each achievement should be encouraged and praised.

When caring for disabled children, it is important to remember that every child is an individual with specific needs

Toilet-training

Most children will usually be reliably clean and dry by the age of about 3 years, but there is a wide variation as to when this happens. There does not seem to be any point in rushing this. It is much easier if any training is left until the child is at least 2 years old. Children need to be given the opportunity to visit the toilet or use the potty regularly. They may need reminding if they are engrossed in their play. Be relaxed, give praise for success and do not show displeasure or disapproval about accidents.

Eating

Once children have developed the necessary physical skills they will gradually begin to feed themselves in a manner that is socially acceptable to their own culture if they are given the opportunity to practise. Babies normally finger-feed from 6 months onwards, gradually using implements – e.g. a spoon and cup – from about 12 months onwards. Some children may continue to use their fingers before progressing to a spoon and fork and then, from 3–4 years, a knife and fork.

Eating together around a table in groups makes mealtimes more interesting and allows a good example to be demonstrated by other children

For children to become self-reliant feeders they need opportunities to practise and make a mess. Carers should praise and encourage their efforts. Eating together around a table in groups of children with an adult makes mealtimes more interesting and allows a good example to be demonstrated by other children and the adults.

Dressing

Children will gradually be able to dress and undress themselves as their physical development progresses. Carers should give them time to do this in an unhurried atmosphere. Encouraging parents to provide clothing with easy fasteners will help.

Children will gradually be able to dress and undress themselves as their physical development progresses

Children find it easier to take off and put on shoes if the fasteners are easy to manage. For example, velcro and buckles are easier than laces. Children may not be able to tie shoelaces until they are 6–7 years of age.

Washing

Having a step by the washbasin at home, or child-height sinks in child care establishments will enable children to achieve independence. Care should be taken that the hot water does not reach high temperatures and suitable supervision is required to give help and encouragement where needed.

Having child-height sinks will enable children to achieve independence

Working with difference

Emotional and social development, including the development of self-reliance and self-esteem, is strongly affected by things going on in the world surrounding the child. These include:

- the type of family background the child has
- issues concerning gender, disability and ethnicity
- the presence of abuse or neglect.

Child care workers should provide play activities and use planned ways to promote self-reliance and self-esteem. When they do this they must take into account that children come from various social and cultural backgrounds, are of different genders and some have special needs.

Social background

All children need a stable, secure family environment within which they are loved and nurtured. They need an environment within which adults make a priority of meeting their needs.

Some children come from a disadvantaged social background that includes poverty, domestic violence, drug abuse and social exclusion. Parenting can be more difficult if these exist. Parents who are coping with stress may not make their children's needs a priority.

All children need a stable, secure family environment within which they are loved and nurtured

Child care workers should:

- provide a safe, secure nurturing environment
- try to be aware of the difficulties faced by some children
- work in partnership with parents
- work with other professionals to help children and their families.

Gender issues

All children need an environment that nurtures them as individuals and promotes equality of opportunity. Adults sometimes emphasise gender differences unnecessarily. Girls may be encouraged to feel weaker and less able, boys to feel powerful and tough.

All children need an environment that nurtures them as individuals and promotes equality of opportunity

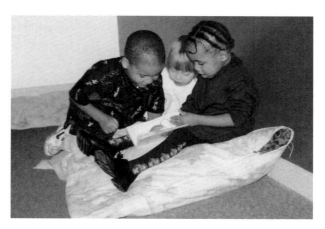

Child care workers should:

- never emphasise gender unnecessarily
- promote positive images of both genders
- ensure equal participation in activities.

Disability

All children, whatever their special needs, require an environment that nurtures them as individuals, recognises and values difference, and promotes equality of access. Children with a disability may feel different, inferior and less able to do things for themselves.

Child care workers should:

- try to enhance similarities
- work to accommodate the disability so that the child's experiences are not impaired. They should do this by good planning and the provision of equipment and access
- increase the child's positive self-image by praise and recognition of effort and achievement
- provide positive images of disabled people
- see the child before they see the disability.

Ethnicity and culture

Children, whatever their ethnic and cultural background, need an environment that nurtures them as individuals, recognises and values difference and promotes equality of opportunity. Children from a minority ethnic or cultural group, who may or may not have English as an additional language, may feel different and possibly inferior.

Child care workers should:

- try to provide resources and activities that reflect varied backgrounds
- be positive about differences
- celebrate difference.

Abuse and neglect

All children need a home in which they are well cared for, loved and their needs are met. Abuse and neglect not only damage a child physically but also emotionally and socially. Children will not develop high self-esteem if they receive messages that they are worthless. They are less likely to trust others. As a result they may have difficulty forming stable relationships.

Child care workers should:

- give unconditional affection, care and attention
- work to improve the child's self-esteem, using care, praise and encouragement
- make a child feel a person of worth

Abuse and neglect not only damage a child physically but also emotionally and socially

- accept and nurture the child
- be aware and make allowances for the fact that abused children may encourage rejection by their difficult behaviour.

Element C4.3 — Are you ready for assessment?

Help children to develop self-reliance and self-esteem

You need to show that you can competently help children to develop self-reliance and self-esteem. To do this you will need to be directly observed by your assessor and present other types of evidence.

Direct observation by your assessor

Your assessor will need to see you carry out these performance criteria (PCs)

C4.3 PCs 1, 3, 4, 6

During these observations your assessor

must see you cover at least ONE aspect in each range category listed in this element.

Remember the range categories listed for this element are:

1. Children
2. Self-help skills

►►

Preparing to be observed

Your assessor will need to see you working directly with children and communicating with them. She or he may be able to assess this element while assessing another unit, for example, units C8 and C9. Whatever the activity you are helping to provide, whether planned or unplanned, you must listen to the children carefully. You should be warm in your manner and encourage them to describe their thoughts, ideas, opinions and any needs they may have. You should make sure that you encourage children to make their own decisions. They might decide what they are going to do, make or play with next, what books they want to read or songs they wish to sing. You must also discuss the possible results of anything they decide. This will help them to feel responsible for their decisions. This might, for example, include helping them to understand they can decide not to make a model but if they do they will not have one to take home later. Or, it might be that you help them to understand that if they decide to spend a long time at one activity there will be less time at another.

While your assessor is observing you, you should ensure that you use any opportunities during the daily routine to help children to develop their self-help skills. This may include getting equipment out or putting it away, putting on their coat to go out, or eating and drinking a snack independently. Whenever you are with children you should make sure that you praise and encourage them for their efforts and achievements whenever it is appropriate.

Read the performance criteria and range carefully before your assessment. Try to cover as much as you can.

Other types of evidence

You may need to present different types of evidence in order to:

- cover criteria not observed by your assessor
- show that you have the required knowledge, understanding and skills
- cover other parts of the range.

The amount and type of evidence you need to present will vary. You should plan this with your assessor.

Help children to recognise and deal with their feelings

Element **C4.4**

KUS
1, 4, 8, 9,
11, 15, 16

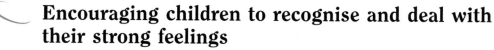

Encouraging children to recognise and deal with their strong feelings

Understanding and dealing with feelings is an important part of a child's emotional and social development. Most children feel things powerfully but they have to learn:

- to recognise what they are feeling
- to express their feelings in acceptable ways.

We can help children to deal with their strong feelings and express them appropriately. They can express their feelings in words, actions and through play. In order to help children we should remember what we know about children's normal behaviour at each stage of development.

Helping children to recognise, name and deal with their feelings

As infants develop, the range of feelings that they experience and express becomes more varied, subtle and complex. Adults should help children to express themselves by meeting their changing needs as they mature.

Babies

Babies' feelings appear to be linked to their experience of hunger, discomfort and need for contact.

As a result babies express feelings of anger, happiness and contentment according to whether their needs are met or not. By meeting a baby's needs as they express them, adults are helping the developing child to recognise and deal with their feelings.

Infants and young children

Young children gradually become capable of more complex feelings, including pride, excitement, sadness and guilt. By the age of 7 they are capable of complex feelings such as anxiety, sympathy and sensitivity to the needs of others. Adults can help children to name these feelings and to recognise that they are normal and that negative feelings are not bad.

The value of play

Child care workers must encourage children to understand and express their feelings safely and in a socially acceptable way. They should do this by providing a safe, secure and accepting environment in which children can play and that is appropriate to the child's developmental level.

Links to C8 and C9.

As infants develop, the range of feelings that they experience and express becomes more varied

Activities and experiences that encourage the expression of feelings

Activity	Its value	When this can be encouraged
Talking	Once children begin to use language they can be encouraged to put their thoughts and feelings into words	At circle time, storytime and while they are playing, both with other children and adults
Imaginative play	This gives many opportunities for children to act out their feelings in different pretend environments – they can pretend they are other people, imitate others and begin to understand what others are feeling and why they behave in certain ways	During play in varied imaginative play areas such as the home corner, shops, hospital; dressing-up; small-world play; outside play; and play with natural materials
Creative play and play with natural materials	This enables children to bring something into existence and express their thoughts and feelings freely – it involves children choosing from materials and using their skills and imagination to make something original and new	Children can use paint in varied ways; crayons and other drawing materials, collage and construction; play with water, sand, malleable materials such as dough and clay, and varied natural and made objects and materials
Physical play	This allows children to learn control, co-ordination and independence – they can express their feelings physically. It can be used as an effective outlet for their strong feelings. Use of equipment can promote imaginative expression and encourage co-operation in a group	Large equipment for climbing and balancing, wheeled toys; smaller equipment for throwing and catching; visual, audio and oral stimuli can promote self-expression during physical play and when dancing

Play gives
children
opportunities to
express their
feelings

Dealing with outbursts

Adults, rightly, do not expect young children to be in control of their feelings or always to express them in ways that are acceptable. Workers need to know what is normal at different stages of development and respond appropriately. In general, the younger the child, the more allowances adults need to make for any uncontrolled outbursts. It is normal and acceptable for a very young baby to cry loudly to be fed when they are hungry, but a normal 7 year old who cried loudly for

**Adults, rightly, do not expect
young children to be in
control of their feelings**

meals would need help in controlling and talking about their feelings. Giving attention and using rewards is an effective way of promoting acceptable behaviour. Physical punishment for unwanted behaviour is not acceptable; although physical restraint or time out may be necessary to protect a child or others.

Keeping calm

Around the age of 2, when children are gaining a clearer idea of who they are in relation to other people, they are more prone to outbursts of temper and frustration. At this age it is important that adults:

- accept this as a stage of development
- deal with the behaviour in a calm and reassuring way
- do not make a child feel they are bad
- make it clear that it is the behaviour that is unacceptable, not the child
- limit children's behaviour and impulses if the child's or another's safety is threatened
- give clear guidelines for acceptable behaviour.

An older child, who frequently has temper tantrums for very little reason, needs particular attention and help in dealing with and controlling their outbursts. Adults should stay calm. This is the best way to help a child, keep them safe and to prevent other children from becoming upset and disturbed by an outburst.

Using routines

Workers can also use opportunities that arise in daily routines. These can be used to help children to understand their feelings and develop good social relationships with other children and adults in their environment. You can use opportunities

Around the age of 2, children are more prone to outbursts of temper and frustration

effectively when children arrive at the setting, during group times, when they are sharing snacks, at mealtimes, during hygiene routines, as they prepare for activities and also as they move from one activity or room to another.

Acting as a good role model

Children often imitate those around them. Adults can set a good example by behaving appropriately when they themselves are happy, excited, or even upset or cross.

Disabled children and those from minority groups need to be able to model themselves on adults who are like them, rather than always seeing themselves as different from the significant adults in their world.

It is important that children have adult role models with whom they can identify

Predicting and recognising common fears and signs of distress in a child

It is common for babies and young children to develop fears and anxieties. The nature of these fears and anxieties changes as they grow older.

Around the age of 6 months, when babies are developing strong attachments to those around them, they show that they prefer to be with their main carers and they begin to develop and show fear of strangers that can last through infancy:

- Babies can also develop fears of specific objects, particularly if they have been startled by something moving quickly or making a loud noise.
- Between the ages of 1 and 2 they may become frightened of the bath and cry when they see it, having previously enjoyed it.
- By 3 or 4 years of age children begin to be able to put themselves in the position of others and picture dangers that they have not actually experienced.

It is common for young children to begin to develop imaginary fears and worries linked to their growing awareness of the world around them. These may include fear of the dark, of dogs or other animals, or of ambulances and fire engines.

Children express distress in different ways. They may express it by:

- crying
- becoming very quiet and withdrawn
- being aggressive to others
- destructive of objects such as toys
- showing a lack concentration
- developing sleeping difficulties or eating disorders
- regressing, or going back, to younger behaviour such as wetting, sucking and rocking.

Adults need to recognise and understand children's fears and distress. They need to accept the child and be reassuring when handling them. They should never force a child to confront fears unwillingly, but work towards overcoming them gradually, with their co-operation, and as the child matures.

KUS
1, 9,
11, 16

Common fears

Daisy had always enjoyed bathtime, including sitting in the 'big' bath with her older sister when their parents bathed them. At the age of 13 months, without warning, Daisy refused to be lifted into the bath. She cried and pulled away. Her parents decided not to worry. They returned to bathing her alone in a baby bath, putting in a small amount of water to do this. Gradually Daisy lost her nervousness and regained her pleasure in water play so that a few months later she was willing to sit in the adult bath again and play with her sister.

➤ Why were Daisy's parents right not to worry about her refusal to go in the bath? **KUS 1, 9, 11**
➤ Why did they go back to using the baby bath? **KUS 1, 9, 11**
➤ Was this an effective way to deal with Daisy and why? **KUS 11, 16**

Sharing concerns about children

It is important that workers share their concerns about children's behaviour with their colleagues. They should also share them with parents and when necessary with other professionals. Workers should meet regularly to discuss their concerns. They should agree on a way of handling a particular child. This may include:

- praising the child for particular behaviour

- supporting them individually during the day
- gradually encouraging them to take part in certain activities
- reassuring them if there are early signs of distress.

They may decide to ask for the advice or support of another professional, such as a speech or play therapist or a child psychologist. Workers should only share their concerns about children when necessary and maintain professional confidentiality.

Workers should share their concerns about children's behaviour with colleagues and parents

Are you ready for assessment?

Help children to recognise and deal with their feelings

You need to show that you can competently help children to recognise and deal with their feelings. To do this you will need to be directly observed by your assessor and present other types of evidence.

Direct observation by your assessor

Your assessor will need to see you carry out these performance criteria (PCs)

C4.4 PCs 1, 2, 5, 7

During these observations your assessor must see you cover at least ONE aspect in each range category listed in this element.

Remember the range categories for this element are:

1. Children
2. Feelings
3. Others

▶▶

Preparing to be observed

C4.4.1, C4.4.2

Your assessor will need to see you working with children as they play. This might be while you are supporting children who are playing freely, for example in a pretend play area or where they are taking part in an activity you have planned and organised.

C4.4.5

Your assessor will also need to see you using learning opportunities that arise during a daily routine to help children to understand their feelings and develop social relationships. This might be for example during snacktime, while hand washing or when putting on coats to go out.

C4.4.7

While observing you your assessor will need to see you providing a good role model for children. That is, they should see you express and deal with your own feelings effectively.

Read the performance criteria and range carefully before your assessment. Try to cover as much as you can.

Assist children to develop positive aspects of their behaviour

Element C4.5

KUS
1, 4, 10,
14, 18, 20

Activities for children

The role of a worker in any setting is to provide for all the developmental needs of the children in their care. C4 focuses on particular aspects of supporting children's social and emotional development. Workers also support social and emotional development while they are providing children with a range of activities and experiences that promote their development in other areas.

All activities for children should be planned so that they are appropriate to children's developmental levels. They should be attractive and varied so that children do not become bored or frustrated. They should include the following:

- *Activities for the development of language and communication skills.* Workers should focus on the quality of their interactions with children. They may include music sessions, talking and listening activities and role play. Children can also use books, stories and rhymes. Links to unit C9.

- *Activities for sensory and intellectual development.* Workers can provide these activities within an overall curriculum plan. They may include playing games and cooking activities. Children can also examine objects of interest. They will enjoy manipulative and creative play activities. Links to unit C8.

● *Opportunities for children's exercise.* These can be indoors and outdoors. Activities can be with and without equipment. These activities can help to promote children's self-confidence as well as their physical development. Workers should encourage children to participate in and enjoy physical activities. Links to unit C1.3.

Understanding young children's behaviour

Behaviour is:

● almost all the things we do and say
● the way we act and react towards other people and our environment
● both the acceptable and unacceptable things we do.

During their childhood children develop:

● a wide range of emotions and responses to different situations
● increasing independence and control over their feelings and behaviour
● an understanding of their own feelings and behaviour
● an increasing understanding of the feelings and behaviour of other people
● less need for other people to control their behaviour.

Children learn their behaviour by:

● becoming aware of what their family and other carers expect of them
● being immersed in the customs of their social and cultural group
● copying and imitating other people
● being rewarded for certain behaviour
● carers applying sanctions for other behaviour
● identifying with their peer group.

During their childhood children develop a wide range of emotions and responses to different situations

Promoting and reinforcing positive behaviour

Most children develop acceptable patterns of behaviour if adults:

- are consistent, loving and fair in their expectations
- are good role models
- set a clear framework for their behaviour.

A framework for behaviour is made up of goals and boundaries:

- *Goals* are the aspects of behaviour that adults want to encourage; they can cover social, physical and verbal behaviour. Goals include aims for positive behaviour including playing co-operatively, helping others, sharing, taking turns, concentrating on what they are doing, doing what they are asked, contributing creative ideas and expressing themselves effectively. Expectations of children's behaviour must be realistic and achievable in relation to children's age and stage of development. All children in a group must be able to understand them.
- *Boundaries* are the limits of what is considered to be acceptable behaviour. Children need to know that if they cross the boundary of acceptable behaviour they will be sanctioned (punished). Boundaries usually exclude physical aggression, verbal abuse and throwing or destroying equipment.

Goals and boundaries can safeguard the emotional and physical well-being of all others in the setting.

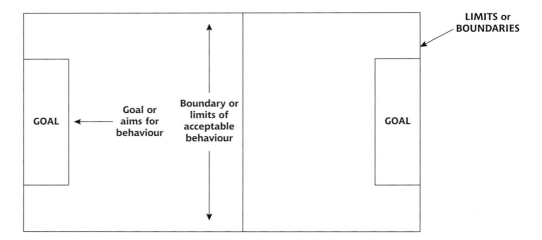

A framework for behaviour is made up of goals and boundaries

Providing goals and boundaries

Goal!!

- A goal is an aim for children's behaviour, e.g. being kind and helpful to others.

Over the line!!

- Behaviour outside the boundary is behaviour that is beyond the limit of what is acceptable and must be discouraged, e.g. aggressive behaviour towards others.

On side and in play!!

- Children may display acceptable behaviour for their age, within the boundary, but not yet have achieved the goal for their behaviour, e.g. a young child watching another child who is distressed but not helping them.

Values and norms

A framework for children's behaviour should be based on a set of values and norms that can be understood by all.

- A value is a shared idea of what a group of people believe is important and worth while.
- Norms are rules or customs of actual behaviour. These are based on values and beliefs.
- Many social and cultural groups share similar values and beliefs about what is acceptable or unacceptable behaviour.
- Groups of people have differing values or beliefs and therefore different rules and customs.
- The behaviour children learn at home is based on the values and norms of their social and cultural group.
- There may be some differences between values and norms at home and a child's nursery or school. This can result in some difficulties when dealing with children's behaviour.

Behaviour modification

Behaviour modification is the name given to techniques used to influence children's behaviour. It works by:

- promoting and rewarding positive aspects of children's behaviour
- managing and discouraging unwanted aspects of children's behaviour.

It is a useful tool for child care and education workers to use when managing children's behaviour.

Behaviour modification involves the following techniques.

1 Identifying behaviour

The first aim of behaviour modification is to identify different types of behaviour. This is both the positive behaviour that the adult wishes to encourage, including:

- playing co-operatively and sharing toys
- being considerate and helpful
- working well and completing a task
- complying with the requests of carers
- contributing ideas
- expressing themselves effectively.

This is also the unwanted behaviour that the adult wishes to discourage, including:

- aggressive, abusive or challenging behaviour
- behaviour that is disruptive, destructive or damaging to people or property
- self-damaging behaviour.

2 Rewarding positive behaviour

The second aim is to reward positive behaviour by promoting and reinforcing it. This can be done by giving a child:

- positive attention through words of praise or encouragement
- positive attention through non-verbal attention such as smiles, nods or hugs
- treats valued by the child such as stickers, badges or toys, more time at an activity or time with an adult (individual children value these things differently)
- the opportunity to share rewards. Workers can, for example, record each child's positive behaviour on a chart (see page 123), so that the 'points' gradually accumulate and the whole group gets a reward when the chart is full. This involves all children and helps them to understand the social impact of their behaviour.

3 Discouraging negative behaviour

The third aim is to discourage negative behaviour. This can be done by:

- having a clear policy in the setting
- showing disapproval of the behaviour but *not* of the child
- ignoring the behaviour
- remaining calm and in control of your reactions
- directing attention to another child who is behaving acceptably
- removing the child to a different, unrewarding situation
- showing disapproval verbally or non-verbally
- applying the sanctions agreed by the setting, e.g. loss of privileges (things they want to do)
- using physical restraint. You should seek guidance within your setting about the use of restraint. You should always follow the setting's guidelines for its use. This is to protect children and also to protect you from accusations of misconduct. Physical restraint should only be used if it is in the interests of the safety of the child or others. It should be very carefully administered.

Physical punishment is illegal and should never be used in a child care setting.

A behaviour management policy

Behaviour modification can be very effective. However, all adults caring for a child need to use behaviour modification consistently (regularly and in the same way). This can be difficult and needs close co-operation between many people. Everyone must have a clear idea of the behaviour they are trying to modify. They must agree when and how to apply sanctions. A child care setting should write and adopt a behaviour management policy in order to achieve this.

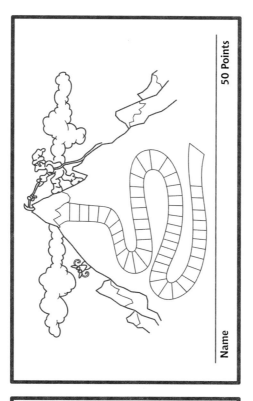

50 Points

Name

50 Points

Name

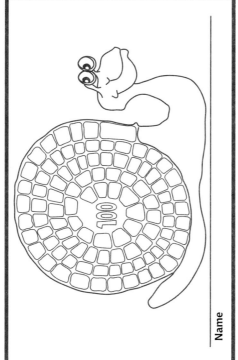

Name

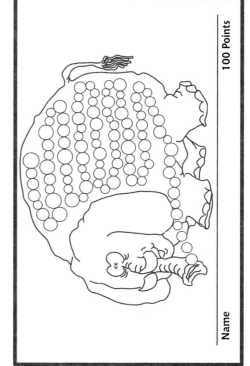

100 Points

Name

Merit charts displayed on walls around the setting can encourage positive behaviour

Managing persistent unwanted behaviour

Managing persistent unwanted behaviour can be difficult. Settings need a clear behaviour management policy and a team approach.

Workers should respond to directly challenging behaviour calmly, using the methods described above.

Unwanted behaviour:

- is usually attention-seeking
- may be self-destructive
- is often the result of a child being given attention only when they misbehave.

An effective method of changing unwanted behaviour is to:

- give the child positive attention consistently
- praise them when they behave acceptably
- ignore attention-seeking behaviour when possible (provided it is not too destructive or placing anyone in danger)
- help the child to learn that they get attention when they behave acceptably and not when they behave unacceptably.

Why does difficult and negative behaviour occur?

Most children want to be approved by adults and others. They therefore wish to behave in an appropriate way. Most children develop acceptable patterns of behaviour if adults are loving, fair and consistent, set clear boundaries and are positive role models.

Behaviour is not 'naughty' just because it does not conform to adult standards of behaviour. Children need to learn which behaviour is acceptable and which is unacceptable.

There is often a reason why behaviour occurs. This reason may be hidden, unconscious or in the past. The reasons are not always straightforward or obvious. Some behaviour is well established and it is difficult to understand why it occurs. These are some of the possible reasons for a behaviour occurring.

Cause	Explanation for behaviour
Feelings	Behaviour can often be caused by how a child is feeling. We must accept that feelings are real. It is the behaviour that results from the feeling that is either acceptable or not acceptable. You must never reject a child's feelings, only their behaviour. Similar feelings in children can lead to very different behaviour. For example, feelings of anger may result in one child being physically or verbally aggressive but another child being withdrawn.
Curiosity	A child learns by being active and curious about their environment. There may be a clash between the child's curiosity and the adult's wish for the child to be safe.

Imitation	Children often imitate what they see others doing. Sometimes what they imitate may be acceptable behaviour for an adult or an older child, but not for a young child.
Developing independence	Children need ways of showing their growing independence. This may result in them trying to influence others in unacceptable ways.
Attention-seeking	Human beings need and want attention from other people. Children's behaviour can be a way of seeking attention. This means attracting the attention of other people. Some children learn that they only get attention if they misbehave.
Anger or frustration	A lack of experience of the world sometimes means that children have unrealistic expectations of what is and what is not possible. This may result in anger or frustration. Children may show frustration in their behaviour. For example, a child may have a tantrum when told that mummy cannot stop it raining so they can go to the park.
Anxiety or fear	Children have lack of experience and understanding of the world. They may become anxious and/or fearful when changes in familiar patterns and routines occur. This can affect their behaviour. Examples might be a change in nursery, starting school, changes in friendships, lack of sleep. The feelings are often short term and their behaviour usually settles down.
Emotional needs	Children have many emotional and social needs, for example, the need for love and affection, belonging, consistency, independence, achievement, social approval and to develop self-esteem. When these needs are not met, a child may show unwanted behaviour as they struggle to get what they need.
Short-term stress	There are likely to be times in all children's lives where they experience short-term stress caused by, for example, moving house, a new baby in the family or a short period of hospitalisation. If these situations are handled sensitively any behavioural difficulties are not likely to be long term.
Long-term stress	When a child's emotional needs are not met over a long period of time their behaviour can be badly affected, for example, during long-term separation or if the child is abused. Their distress is likely to be shown in their behaviour. This may be anything from extreme withdrawal to violent behaviour.

Managing behaviour effectively

**KUS
10, 14, 20**

Tom, aged 3, was normally quite a quiet and gentle child. However, he often became upset and difficult when activity time ended and the children came together for a story.

He wouldn't put his toys away and shouted at the staff that he didn't want to have a story. This was clearly upsetting to Tom and disruptive to the group.

The staff decided to observe Tom over a period of a week to try to learn the pattern of events that led up to this behaviour.

The staff noted many things:

- That Tom often became very involved in activities, especially construction activities.
- That he produced quite complicated structures with the equipment.

- That when the children were asked to clear up, he became worked up. He quickly tried to finish his construction. He became anxious that the other children were going to break it up.
- This behaviour only occurred when he was part-way through an activity at storytime.

The staff agreed the following behaviour management plan:

- Tom was told, 10 minutes before storytime, that the session was ending soon. This was to give him time to complete what he was doing.
- Completed models were kept until the following day, not taken to pieces straight away.
- If Tom didn't finish what he was doing, his partly finished model would be saved until the following day. Then he could choose either to finish it or to break it up himself.

➤ *What were the events that led to Tom's behaviour?* **KUS 10**

➤ *What unwanted behaviour did he show?* **KUS 10**

➤ *How did this behaviour affect others?* **KUS 14**

➤ *How did the staff find out what was causing his behaviour?* **KUS 20**

➤ *How did they plan to manage Tom's behaviour?* **KUS 14**

Reporting unwanted behaviour

- Persistent unwanted behaviour should be reported to parents promptly and accurately. Parents have rights and responsibilities, and workers must work in partnership with parents.
- It is important to share issues with colleagues and discuss the management of children's behaviour with them. The benefit of a team approach is that it provides support for colleagues and consistency in dealing with a particular child or group.
- Workers have two responsibilities. These are to adhere to the policies of the organisation in which they work and to respect the wishes of parents. Sometimes it may be difficult to do both.
- There can be long-term problems that need specialist help and guidance. There are a number of different ways of getting this. It will depend upon the situation. In education the Special Educational Needs Co-ordinator (SENCO), who will be a named member of staff, will usually obtain help. Once the child's needs have been identified an individual education plan (IEP) will be drawn up, which may eventually involve an educational psychologist.
- Health professionals (e.g. health visitors, GPs) or social services staff (e.g. staff in nursery/family centres, social workers) can all give help. Professionals, parents or family members seeking help, concerned friends and others can all contact these people direct.

Physical punishment

Staff should discuss and agree appropriate policies and responses so that everyone is working to the same goals.

- The use of physical punishment is not allowed in child care and education settings.
- Physical restraint to prevent injury or damage must be very carefully administered (see previous section on discouraging negative behaviour).
- Significant incidents should be recorded accurately and objectively. This means recording only what actually took place, not the reactions or opinions of workers. Such records can then be referred to by other colleagues and, if necessary, used as evidence.

Element C4.5 Are you ready for assessment?

Assist children to develop positive aspects of behaviour

You need to show that you can competently assist children to develop positive aspects of their behaviour. To do this you will need to be directly observed by your assessor and present other types of evidence.

Direct observation by your assessor

Your assessor will need to see you carry out these performance criteria (PCs)

C4.5 PCs 1, 2

During these observations your assessor must see you cover at least ONE aspect in each range category listed in this element.

Remember the range categories listed for this element are:

1. Golas and boundaries
2. Children

Preparing to be observed

For this element your assessor can observe you while you are providing activities for children. This can be at the same time as your assessor is observing you for evidence for C1.3, C8 and/or C9. You should ensure that the activities and experiences are appropriate. They should also be sufficiently attractive and varied so that children will not become easily bored or frustrated. During the activity you should show your assessor how you can reinforce children's positive behaviour. You should do this by recognising and praising children's efforts and achievements. You can do this by communicating with them either by looks such as smiling, or through words of encouragement and praise. You may possibly offer the child or group some kind of reward for their positive behaviour. This will show that you are aware of the goals of the setting and are safeguarding the well-being of all the children.

Read the performance criteria and range carefully before your assessment. Try to cover as much as you can. ▶▶

Other types of evidence

You may need to present different types of evidence in order to:

- cover criteria not observed by your assessor
- show that you have the required knowledge, understanding and skills
- cover other parts of the range.

The amount and type of evidence you need to present will vary. You should plan this with your assessor.

Check your knowledge

- What kind of relationship do children need to experience in the first three years of their life and why is this so important? **KUS 1, 2**
- Why can separation from their main carer be difficult for a young child? **KUS 3**
- What kind of play experiences will help children to learn to relate to others? **KUS 12, 19**
- Why is it important for children to develop high self-esteem? **KUS 7, 26**
- What are the most important things to remember when you are encouraging the development of self-reliance in a child? **KUS 7, 12, 26**
- How can an adult be a good role model to children when they are helping children to recognise and deal with their feelings? **KUS 16**
- What does 'age appropriate' behaviour mean? **KUS 1**
- What may cause changes to a child's behaviour? **KUS 10**

Implement planned activities for sensory and intellectual development

*T*his unit covers the implementation of the variety of activities provided in care and education settings to stimulate children's sensory and intellectual development. These include playing games, cooking activities, selecting and examining objects of interest, and providing opportunities for creative and manipulative play.

This unit has close links with unit C9.

This unit contains five elements:

- **C8.1** *Provide activities, equipment and materials for creative play*
- **C8.2** *Play games with children*
- **C8.3** *Assist children with cooking activities*
- **C8.4** *Provide opportunities and equipment for manipulative play*
- **C8.5** *Examine objects of interest with children*

While you are working through this unit, you will find it helpful to refer to the introductory section on children's development.

Introduction

KUS
2, 7,
11, 20

All elements of this unit require an understanding of the importance of play in promoting children's sensory and intellectual development. Play is the most appropriate medium to approach and provide for all aspects of young children's learning and development.

Why is play important?

- Play occurs naturally in young children. It is a way for children to acquire and practise knowledge, skills and concepts in situations that are open-ended and enjoyable.

- Play cannot be wrong. It therefore provides a safe situation for the child to try out new things without fear of failure. This is important in promoting positive self-esteem.

- Play provides the opportunity for repetition. One of the important ways that learning takes place is through repetition.

- Play provides an opportunity for extending learning. A carefully structured play environment allows for learning across a wide ability range. For example, exploring sand may provide a soothing sensory experience but can also provide an opportunity to learn about capacity and volume.

- Play is always at the child's own level, so the needs of all children within the group can be met.

The development of social play

How children play within the group follows a developmental pattern. As children learn and develop social skills these are taken into account in their play. It is difficult to link these stages directly with ages as progress through the stages will depend upon having the opportunity to play with other children.

- *Solitary play.* This is an early stage of play. Children play alone and take little notice of other children.
- *Parallel play.* A child plays side-by-side with another child but without interacting. They may share space, possibly equipment, but their play remains independent of each other.
- *Associative play.* Here play begins with other children. Children make intermittent interactions and/or are involved in the same activity although their play remains personal.
- *Co-operative play.* Here children are able to play together co-operatively. They are able to adopt a role within the group and to take account of others' needs and actions. At this stage, they will begin to understand and keep to simple rules.

The development of social play

Curriculum frameworks

Planning for play will need to take into account any statutory requirements for the curriculum. Any setting in England receiving public funding (nursery grant) for the education of 3 and 4 year olds must follow the Curriculum guidance for the foundation stage (QCA, 2000), which focuses on children's progress towards the Early Learning Goals. These goals are across six areas of learning:

- personal, social and emotional development
- communication, language and literacy
- mathematical development
- knowledge and understanding of the world
- physical development
- creative development.

(If you are working towards your NVQ in Wales you should consult 'The Desirable Outcomes for Children's Learning before Compulsory School Age' (2000), issued by the Qualifications, Curriculum and Assessment Authority for Wales. In Scotland, 'A Curriculum Framework for Children 3–5' (1999) is published by the Scottish Office. In Northern Ireland, the relevant authority is the Council for the Curriculum, Examinations and Assessment.)

In maintained schools in England, including maintained special schools, the National Curriculum must be followed. The foundation stage curriculum is applied in reception classes and, in years 1 and 2 of primary school, key stage 1 of the National Curriculum is followed. As with the pre-school curriculum, separate guidance applies to Wales, Scotland and Northern Ireland.

'Birth to 3 matters: A framework to support children in their earliest years' (Sure Start 2002) was published with the intention to inform and develop the practice of those who work with the youngest children. The framework focuses on four aspects as a way of approaching and understanding how to provide for the growth, learning and development of very young children. These aspects are:

- a strong child
- a skilful communicator
- a competent learner
- a healthy child.

Four broad stages of development that occur during the 0–3 age-group period are identified as follows:

- Heads Up, Lookers and Communicators (0–8 months)
- Sitters, Standers and Explorers (8–18 months)
- Movers, Shakers and Players (18–24 months)
- Walkers, Talkers and Pretenders (24–36 months).

The adult's role in play

Adults have an important role in children's play to ensure that the maximum benefit is gained from it. The adult needs to plan and set up the activities carefully, interact with the children during the activity and monitor what is happening through observation.

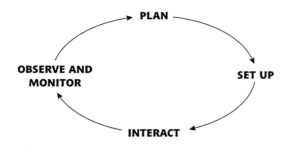

Think about:
- the needs of the children
- providing a range of activities
- the time available
- the space available
- staffing.

- Did the children enjoy it?
- Was it at the right level for the children?
- Could all the children participate?
- Was all the necessary equipment available?
- What did the children learn?
- Was there anything in particular that you noticed about an individual child that needs recording?

- Set up the activity attractively.
- Site the activity so that all the children can participate.
- Make sure all the necessary equipment is available.
- Consider any safety issues.
- Introduce the activity to the children – suggest ways they can play with it.

PLAN

OBSERVE AND MONITOR

SET UP

INTERACT

Different ways of interacting include:
- discussing what the child is doing
- asking open questions
- making suggestions
- playing alongside the child, saying what you are doing.

The adult's role in play

Things you need to do/think about	Why this is important
Plan	
• The needs of the children	• Different children will need different activities and experiences to help them learn. The activities provided must meet the needs of the children in the group.
• Providing a range of activities	• Children need to participate in many different activities to develop all the different skills/concepts and attitudes necessary. All activities and experiences will need to be repeated many times so that the children have the opportunity to practise and develop their emerging skills.
• Time available Space available Staffing	• For activities and experiences to be successful the appropriate time space and staffing needs to be considered. This will be different for each activity/experience. Children need a balance between free play and adult-directed play. ▶▶

The adult's role in play (cont.)

Things you need to do/think about	Why this is important
Setting up the activity	
• Set up the activity attractively	• Children are more likely to participate in an activity that looks inviting.
• Site the activity so that all children can participate	• All children should be able to participate in all activities. Careful consideration needs to be given to where and how activities are provided so that children who have particular needs can participate in the usual way.
• Make sure all the necessary equipment is available	• Children will need to be able to participate in the activity without searching for tools and equipment. They will learn more easily as concentration will be encouraged and they will feel satisfied at having completed a task if they are able to work without distractions. The equipment provided should also be of a good quality so that the children can use it successfully.
• Consider any safety issues	• Safety issues need to be considered before the children begin the activity. You are responsible for the children's health and safety.
• Introduce the activity to the children – suggest ways in which they can play with it	• Many activities will need some introduction. This will mean that the children are aware of different ways to play with the activity. They will also have been shown necessary skills to be successful at the activity.
Interaction during the activity Different ways that you can interact with the children include:	
• Discussing the activity with the children	• Discussing the activity will enable the children to think carefully about what they are doing. It will help them to express their ideas verbally. It will show that you are interested in what they are doing and it will give you an idea of what they are able to do and not do.
• Asking open-ended questions	• Open-ended questions are questions that require more than a yes or no answer. Questions like this encourage children to express their thoughts and ideas.
• Making suggestions of different ways to play with the activity	• Children need to play at the same thing over and over again. However, they will eventually need to move on to the next stage of learning.
• Playing alongside the children and describing what you are doing	• Joining in their play, and either making suggestions or playing alongside them showing them what to do, will encourage children to develop their skills and concepts further.

►►

The adult's role in play (cont.)

Things you need to do/think about	Why this is important
Observation and monitoring	
The activity	*The activity*
• Did the children enjoy it?	• It is important that the activities that are provided enable the children to practise their existing skills and develop new skills/concepts. Observing and monitoring exactly what children learned at an activity will mean that the activities planned are always appropriate for the children's level of understanding.
• Was it at the right level for the children? • Could all the children participate?	• Were there any reasons why certain children couldn't participate? It is vital that children who have particular needs are able to join in all the activities provided. This may mean very careful consideration of where and what to provide.
• Was all the necessary equipment available?	• Children will quickly lose interest if they have to keep stopping to find tools and equipment. So that they can concentrate and learn and develop all the necessary skills and concepts, things need to be readily available and in good condition.
The children	*The children*
• What did the children learn?	• It is important to know what individual children learned and also what the children learned from the activity (this may not be what you intended them to learn), so that future activities are appropriate for them. It is also important to monitor the progress that individual children are making.
• Could all the children participate?	• All children need to participate in a wide range of activities so that they have the experiences necessary to learn. Some children's needs may limit their ability to participate in certain activities, for example, physical or learning difficulties, lack of confidence. The staff in the setting must observe when this is happening and make sure that changes are made to enable all children equal access to the activities.
• Was there anything that you noticed about an individual child that needs recording?	• Individual children's learning needs to be noted and sometimes recorded so that further activities and experiences can move them on to the next step. Where there are issues around children's behaviour these too will need to be observed and perhaps recorded.

Provide activities, equipment and materials for creative play

Element C8.1

KUS
1, 3, 8, 19, 20, 21

The value of creative play in promoting learning

Being creative is a uniquely human characteristic involving the expression of ideas and feelings in a personal way. Children do not need to be taught to be creative but if we want to develop these abilities we must provide them with opportunities to explore and experiment with a wide range of materials, encouraging confidence to express ideas and respond in their own ways.

Creative play and development

- Creative play supports children's *emotional development*, giving them opportunities to express what they are thinking and feeling. It can help them to deal with negative as well as positive feelings. Their confidence and self-esteem will be encouraged by an approach that is not concerned with a 'right' or 'wrong' way.

- Creative play encourages children's *intellectual development* by introducing them to a wide range of materials. A 'hands-on' approach will enable them to discover the different properties of the materials they are using and encourage problem solving. This experiential learning stimulates the senses and the imagination.

Children work alongside one another, sharing equipment and space

- Using tools and other equipment promotes children's *physical skills*. Their fine motor skills are encouraged through handling brushes, glue spreaders, dough cutters etc. As these skills develop, more challenging tools and techniques should be introduced. Building with large 'junk' materials and moving buckets of water or sand provides opportunities to develop gross motor skills too.

- Children's *social development* is encouraged as they work alongside one another at creative play activities, sharing equipment and space. Older children will work as a group at an activity or collaborate on a project. Planning and completing a task will give children a sense of achievement and develop independence too.

- Creative play provides all kinds of opportunities for children's *language development.* They will talk with adults and with other children about what they are doing. Younger children, concentrating on a task, will often talk this through to themselves, accompanying their play with a commentary. As unfamiliar tools and materials are introduced into their play, children will learn the new vocabulary associated with these.

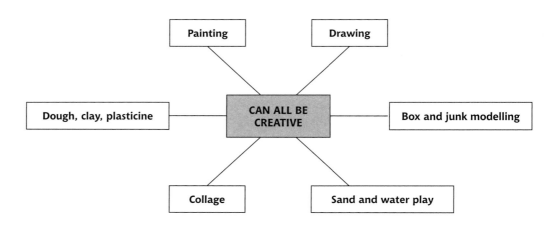

Some principles of providing for creativity

- To avoid frustration, children should be provided with materials and tools that are enjoyable to use and appropriate for their stage of development.

- Adults should support and encourage children's creative play but not dominate it.

- Something to take home is not so important to a child. For them, it is the process that is important, more so than the product.

- All children should have the opportunity to participate in creative play. Child care workers will need to consider the individual needs of any children in the group.

- Health and safety should always be a consideration but this need not stop children enjoying creative play.

Adults should support and encourage children's creative play

KUS
1, 3, 7

Stifling creativity

Luke, aged 3, had lots of drawing and painting experience before he went to nursery. He loved these activities and was eager to join in with them. Luke was looking forward to making a Mother's Day card for his mum. He was pleased when he'd finished his card and he took it proudly to his child care worker. She told him that he hadn't followed her instructions and that his mum wouldn't want a messy card like his. He would have to start again, this time copying her. He made another card, closely supervised, but didn't seem so pleased with it this time. Later, staff noticed that he didn't seem so eager to join in with sticking and painting any more, and was now constantly looking for reassurance that he was doing the right thing.

➤ *What effect do you think this had on Luke's confidence and enthusiasm? Why is it important for children to have their own attempts accepted and valued?*

➤ *How can you make it clear to children that you value their work for its own sake?*

Activities, equipment and materials for creative play

A wide range of activities and materials can be used to provide for children's creative play.

The chart below shows a range of materials, and some of the issues involved in using them.

Material	Positives	Issues
Water	Familiar, enjoyable, absorbing, cheap, readily available, therapeutic. Versatile – can be used with a range of equipment and additions.	Could irritate some skin conditions. Spillage can be hazardous. Clothing needs protection.
Sand	Inexpensive and available. Enjoyable, relaxing, therapeutic. Less familiar than some other materials. Can be used wet or dry in a variety of ways.	Not all types are suitable for play. Must be kept clean. Can get in eyes and hair. Floor becomes slippery if sand is spilt.
Malleable materials	Clay, dough and plasticine can be used many times, with different tools and implements. Materials are readily available, soothing, pleasurable.	Issues concerning freshness when stored. Should not be eaten. Protection of clothing.
Food	Peas, beans, lentils and pasta provide different textures, shapes and colours. Are easy to handle. Useful for collage.	Ethical issues over use of food, especially if not past 'sell-by' date. Possible allergies need consideration (esp. nuts). Choking could be an issue with very young children. Dried beans must not be eaten raw.
Plants and wood	Fresh or dried leaves, berries and flowers, wood and bark are readily available and children enjoy collecting them. Provides a stimulus for learning, particularly aesthetic awareness and an understanding of the natural world.	Care should be taken that poisonous plant material is not used. Storage needs care.
Paint	Can be used in many ways with fingers or tools. Helps manipulative skills, gives a sense of pride and achievement, valuable for self-expression, enjoyable.	Must be non-toxic, protection of clothing and surfaces required. Over-emphasis of outcomes to be avoided.
Pencils, crayons and drawing materials	Encourage concentration, experimentation and expression. Materials can be used in combination with each other. Provide range for different age groups. Inexpensive, easily stored and readily available for use.	Must be non-toxic. Any sharp points need supervision.
Collage and construction	Paper, magazines, fabric, wool, cards, boxes, food containers and other discarded materials are ideal for two- or three-dimensional play. Stimulates ideas, design and technology. Very enjoyable. Stimulates fine motor skills.	Hygiene might be an issue with recycled materials. Organised storage of a range of materials will be required. Use of scissors must be supervised closely. Children will become frustrated if tools are inadequate for the task.

Water is versatile and can be enjoyed in a variety of ways

Storing and using materials safely

The safe use and storage of any materials available to children for play must always be an important consideration for the child care worker. Some of these issues have been identified in the chart above. Whenever children have opportunities to play with water, they must always be closely supervised. Hygiene is an important consideration with sand, water and dough as contamination could present a risk with these materials.

Protection of surfaces and clothing

For some creative play activities it will be necessary to protect surfaces. If surfaces are not wipe-clean then covering will be needed for activities using glue, paint and malleable materials such as dough and clay. Some flooring, e.g. polished wood or parquet will need protecting if water or sand are used. (In some settings these activities may be prohibited inside as a condition of the lease and will need to be offered outside.) Plastic sheeting is useful for this purpose and old newspapers can also be used. Care will be needed to anchor securely if used on floors.

Children's clothing will need to be protected for some messy activities. They should be encouraged to select and put on aprons that are appropriate for the activity chosen. Aprons should be laundered regularly and fastenings checked so that they are easy for children to manage. Sand hats are provided in some settings to protect children's hair. Any policy regarding wearing aprons and hats should be discussed with the children and encouraged. Consideration should also be given to whether any of the materials provided are likely to provoke allergic reactions in children. Children with eczema may be sensitive to some materials; in this case it may be better to avoid the substance and provide an alternative to offer to all the children.

Painting is an absorbing activity

Element C8.1

Are you ready for assessment?

Provide activities, equipment and materials for creative play

You need to show that you can competently provide activities, equipment and materials for creative play. To do this you will need to be directly observed by your assessor and present other types of evidence.

Direct observation by your assessor

Your assessor will need to see you carry out these performance criteria (PCs)

C8.1 PCs 2, 3, 5, 6, 7, 9

During these observations your assessor must see you cover at least ONE aspect in each range category listed in this element.

Remember the range categories for this element are:

1. Equipment and materials
2. Locations
3. Protective coverings
4. Protective clothing

Preparing to be observed

You will need to ensure that your assessor sees you prepare and take part in creative activities in your area. You should be able to show how these are appropriate to the developmental needs of the children and fit in with any overall curriculum plan. You should be able to talk about what children will gain from the activities you have chosen. Think about where you locate the activities and how you support the children's learning, both in terms of provision of materials and equipment and in your interactions with them.

Read the performance criteria and range carefully before your assessment. Try to cover as much as you can.

Other types of evidence

You may need to present different types of evidence in order to:

- cover criteria not observed by your assessor
- show that you have the required knowledge, understanding and skills
- cover other parts of the range.

The amount and type of evidence you need to present will vary. You should plan this with your assessor.

Element C8.2 *Play games with children*

KUS
2, 18, 22,
23, 24, 26

Games can be of great value in stimulating children's development. Babies will soon learn and enjoy peek-a-boo and action rhymes such 'Round and Round the Garden', played one-to-one with a parent or carer. Later on, games with more structure provide an opportunity for older children to play together.

How games encourage development

Games encourage *social* development when children share equipment, take turns and show consideration for others in the group. Children playing table top games such as lotto and the pairs game, pelmanism, will usually play the game unselfishly, looking out for their friends as well as themselves.

Active games, for example, hide and seek, Simon/Sara says and ring games such as 'The Farmer's in the Den' and 'Oranges and Lemons' encourage the *physical* skills of movement and co-ordination and develop children's spatial awareness. It is important to remember that young children learn through their whole bodies. They need and enjoy regular physical activity and will benefit from games of this type.

Children's *intellectual* skills can be promoted through games such as lotto, snakes-and-ladders and snap that practise matching, sequencing and counting. All games require children to concentrate.

Playing games in a familiar environment, with adult support, allows children to learn how to cope *emotionally* with the experience of winning and losing. Games are also very enjoyable and exciting for young children.

While playing games, children will be commenting on what's happening, explaining the rules and predicting the next move. New vocabulary may be introduced as part of the game. All of this promotes children's *language* development.

Games encourage children's social development

When providing games, the age and stage of development of the child must be considered. Remember these points:

- Younger children may not be able to share, co-operate or take turns with other children and need games that they can play with an adult supervising, such as dominoes or other matching games.
- Some children may find it difficult to join in with a game or refuse to participate. Accept this, encourage them to watch or to take part in another activity and they will often join in when they feel comfortable.
- The ability to play games with other children comes gradually. From the age of 3 years onwards, children develop more social skills and become better at understanding the rules and the point of games. This enables them to play a range of games of increasing complexity.

Competitive games and their effects

Many games involve winning and losing. Some people might say that it is good for children to experience this early on in their lives as they are part of a society that is competitive. But most children find losing difficult, and the repeated experience of losing can be a blow to a child's fragile self-esteem. Children can be helped by discussion and by playing games where everyone has a chance of winning at some time. It is helpful if the child care worker emphasises to children the importance and enjoyment of taking part rather than winning. Non-competitive games that involve team co-operation and stress completing an activity, rather than winning, also help to reduce the negative effects of losing.

Children enjoy taking part in games

Avoiding stereotyping in children's games

As with everything we provide for children, it is important to be aware of the potential for stereotyping in children's games. Stereotyping means making assumptions that children will respond in a certain way because of their gender, their race or social background, or because they have a disability. This is limiting and can affect children's ability to achieve their potential. Be aware of the language and messages carried in some games and be prepared to counter these by adapting and changing them. Farmers are not always men and don't have to have wives! Select games, including ring games, that reflect the cultural diversity of the wider community and adapt so that children of all abilities can join in.

Devising and improvising children's games

Often a game can be an effective way of teaching and reinforcing a particular skill or concept. For example, snakes-and-ladders requires children to count and to go *up* ladders and *down* snakes. Other games reinforce concepts such as colour, shape or size, or encourage children to sort into categories. Games can also support and extend a current theme or topic. A wide range of good quality, commercially produced games designed to promote children's learning is readily available. However, it can be very worth while to devise games yourself, for groups of children or individuals, perhaps to teach a particular concept or to follow up on an interest.

Practical Example

Devising a game

**KUS
22, 23, 24**

Julie's placement was with the reception class. They had been working on number bonds to 5 but a small group of children were struggling with this. The class teacher asked Julie if she could think of a game to help this particular group of children. She made a game where she cut lots of cards in the shape of fish, each marked with a number from 0 to 5. The aim of the game was for each child to use the magnet fishing rods to make a 'catch' that added up to 5. She helped the children by making sure they could recognise the numbers and then encouraging them to count on. The game was a great success, with the children managing the task confidently. The game was later adapted to practise number bonds for 10 and then 20.

➤ *Why was it necessary for Julie to make this game?*

➤ *Why do you think this was a successful way for these children to learn?*

➤ *What was Julie's role while she was playing the game with the children?*

Adapting games to enable children with particular needs to participate

All children should have opportunities to join in with games. If there are any children with particular needs within the group then you should ensure that you can include them too. This might mean adapting the game, for example, including sound clues in a farmyard lotto game rather than visual ones, so that a child with partial sight can participate. Emphasising actions as well as words in a ring game would mean a child with a hearing impairment could join in. Consideration

Provide games for all abilities

must also be given to children with mobility or co-ordination problems when planning games involving physical activity. It is never acceptable to exclude children because they have a particular need and, with some forethought, most games can be adapted.

Element C8.2 — Are you ready for assessment?

Play games with children

You need to show that you can competently play games with children. To do this you will need to be directly observed by your assessor and present other types of evidence.

Direct observation by your assessor

Your assessor will need to see you carry out these performance criteria (PCs)

C8.2 PCs 1, 2, 3, 4, 5, 6, 7, 8, 9, 10

During these observations your assessor must see you cover at least ONE aspect in each range category listed in this element.

Remember the range categories for this element are:

1. Games
2. Group size
3. Location

Preparing to be observed

You need to plan for different types of games to be available during the session and ensure that you are familiar with them, so that you can play them with the children or help them to play them by themselves. Plan for outside games too so that part of the range can be covered. Make sure that you keep to any health and safety guide-lines, and be prepared to talk to your assessor about the purpose and reasons for selecting these games.

Read the performance criteria and range carefully before your assessment. Try to cover as much as you can.

Other types of evidence

You may need to present different types of evidence in order to:

- cover criteria not observed by your assessor
- show that you have the required knowledge, understanding and skills
- cover other parts of the range.

The amount and type of evidence you need to present will vary. You should plan this with your assessor.

C8.3 *Assist children with cooking activities*

KUS
4, 5, 9,
10, 16, 17

Cooking is always a popular choice of activity with young children and there is much that they can learn through these activities.

Learning from a cooking activity

Cooking promotes many aspects of children's *intellectual development*. It provides them with a complete sensory experience, including smell and taste. Cooking activities develop children's understanding of many aspects of mathematics as they weigh, measure and count ingredients, divide the mixture and watch the clock, waiting for the cooking time to finish. It is helpful to choose recipes that use non-standard measures such as cups and spoons with younger children so that they can count as they are added. Standard measures of grams and kilograms and the use of balance scales and weights should be introduced later as the children's understanding develops. They can learn about size and shape as part of activities, for example as they prepare a fruit salad. Cooking develops children's understanding of science too. They learn that food usually changes colour and texture when cooked. They will learn that some processes are reversible and others are not. For example, solid chocolate will melt to a liquid and then set back to a solid again, but if they try to unscramble eggs they will not succeed. They will find out about where ingredients come from and what grows where in the world.

For their *social and emotional development,* being involved in the preparation of food encourages children's independence skills and self-esteem. They will usually work in a small group sharing space and equipment. Contributing to the group activity and sharing out what they have made with others will give them a sense of achievement. Cooking activities also provide a good way for children to begin to explore and understand cultural diversity.

Children's *physical development* will be promoted as they handle tools and other equipment in cooking activities. Processes such as beating and whisking can be quite strenuous for small children and they may need to share these tasks with others. Cooking provides an ideal opportunity to talk with children about healthy eating and the need for a balanced diet and to try out recipes that emphasise this.

As they listen and talk as they cook, children's *language development* will be promoted. They will add to their vocabulary as they learn new words for the ingredients and processes. Older children can practise their literacy skills as they follow a recipe from a card.

Practical Example

Counting through baking

Darren was making rock buns in the cooking area. He had mixed the ingredients together and was dividing the mixture into the bun tin. There were 12 sections in the pan and he had already filled 5 of them.

KUS 5
PC 10

Nursery nurse: How many buns are you going to make?

Darren: (touching each space as he counts) Twelve.

Nursery nurse: Have you made some already?

Darren: Yes, five.

Nursery nurse: How many more do you have to make?

Darren: (counts empty spaces) Seven.

He continued to fill the spaces until the mixture was all gone. He noticed that some of the spaces contained lots of mixture while others contained very little.

Darren: No one will want those little ones.

He moved some of the mixture from the full to the less full spaces.

➤ *What did Darren show that he knew about counting and size?*
➤ *What was the role of the nursery nurse here?*

Opportunities for counting and calculation often occur in cooking activities

Hygiene and safety

When cooking with children, good practice in hygiene should be observed:

- ensure hands and fingernails are clean
- wear clean aprons, provided especially for cooking
- tie hair back
- make sure surfaces and utensils are clean
- store food at the correct temperature and in clean surroundings.

Safety must be an important consideration too:

- take care when children are around hot pans and ingredients
- choose recipes with a view to safety – avoid boiling sugar (e.g. toffee-making) and frying
- ensure that children do not sample mixtures containing raw eggs
- supervise children using sharp knives and tools
- wipe up spills straightaway to prevent slipping.

Cooking processes and choosing recipes

When choosing recipes to use with children, you should consider the following:

- The time that is available. It will be frustrating for the children if the session finishes but their biscuits are not baked.
- The skills the children will need to complete the recipe successfully. For example, very small children will struggle to whisk egg whites for meringues but will be able to mix eggs together for scrambling.
- The cost and availability of ingredients.
- Whether the recipe is suitable for all in the group, taking into account any dietary laws followed, preferences or allergies.
- What the children will learn from the cooking activity. You may be emphasising a process, for example, melting and setting, or selecting recipes to link with a theme or topic.
- If the children will be doing all (or most) of the cooking or whether they will just be watching you. If the latter is to be the case, choose something else.
- Whether any equipment the recipe requires is available.
- The size of the group and the level of adult supervision required. As a general rule, the younger the children, the smaller the group should be.

Often it is the simplest recipes, using familiar ingredients, that are the most successful. Whatever recipe you choose, you should always try it out for yourself first. This will allow you to identify any problems with the recipe and give you a chance to modify it. For example, you might find that the butter listed in a cake recipe is difficult to beat so you could replace it with soft margarine. As with all activities for young children, you should avoid over-emphasising the product. Children will usually be delighted with what they cook and will experience a real sense of achievement as they share it with others in the group.

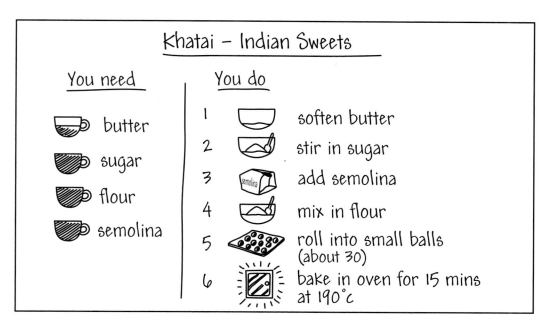

Simple recipe cards can be used with children

Cooking and cultural diversity

Cooking activities provide an ideal opportunity to introduce children to food that reflects the cultural diversity of Britain today. Many settings mark a range of different festivals and this presents an ideal opportunity for children to cook and taste the foods associated with these celebrations. Parents and other members of the community can be asked to contribute recipes and ideas, and some may be happy to cook with the children. There are other ways that cooking can help children to learn about cultural diversity. A topic on a particular food such as bread or rice could involve looking at the way the food is used in different communities, with cooking and tasting sessions. Harvest time can provide an opportunity to look at harvests around the world and at the range of dishes associated with this season.

It is always important to avoid making assumptions about the food preferences of different groups in the community. In Britain today, we have access to the very wide range of foods and cooking styles from all around the world and families will make their choice from these. For example, children from Caribbean families may eat a traditional dish of rice and peas at a family gathering, but they will also enjoy pizza and visits to fast food restaurants, as all children do.

Different types of cooking activities

Some settings may not have access to a cooker or microwave or a suitable area for children to use to cook. But there are still many worthwhile activities that involve preparing and making food that do not require special equipment. Most settings provide a snack for children at some time during the session and children will enjoy contributing to this. Here are some suggestions:

- Make sandwiches. Different types of bread and fillings can be used and children can put their own combinations together.

- Prepare salads. Children can be involved in the washing and drying of fruit and vegetables. Tools such as graters and peelers can be used (with care), and children can arrange the food on plates and dishes.
- Make drinks. Fruit such as oranges and lemons can be squeezed and diluted or mixed with other ingredients. Milk shakes can be made from soft fruits like bananas and strawberries mashed and whisked into milk. Some children might like to try 'sun tea', that is tea made with a tea bag in a screw-top glass jar and left out in the sun to brew.
- Jelly can be made without special equipment. It will take longer to dissolve in cold water and longer to set outside a refrigerator. (Make sure that it is covered and kept cool while setting though.)
- Children can whisk cold milk with an instant pudding mix to make a creamy dessert.
- Mix mashed soft fruit into plain yogurt. Children will enjoy changing the appearance and the taste of the yogurt.
- Ready-made biscuits can be decorated with a little icing and/or some sweets. They can be sandwiched together with cream cheese or chocolate spread.

Adapting cooking activities for children with particular needs

As with all other activities, cooking should be available to all children, including those with particular needs. Children can be involved in the entire process according to their age, development and needs. The choice of recipe and processes should be adapted to suit children with special needs so that they can participate as fully as possible. In some cases it might be necessary to modify recipes, use special tools or to provide one-to-one support so that children can participate.

Not all cookery requires special equipment

Are you ready for assessment?

Assist children with cooking activities

You need to show that you can competently assist children in cooking activities. To do this you will need to be directly observed by your assessor and present other types of evidence.

Direct observation by your assessor

Your assessor will need to see you carry out these performance criteria (PCs)

C8.3 PCs 1, 2, 3, 4, 5, 7, 9, 10, 12

During these observations your assessor must see you cover at least ONE aspect in each range category listed in this element.

Remember the range categories in this element are:

1. Cooking activities
2. Foods

Preparing to be observed

You will need to plan a cooking session that your assessor can observe. Make sure that you have everything organised, and that any ingredients, equipment and utensils are to hand. You must comply with hygiene and safety standards throughout the session.
A plan for your activity will be useful as this will show what you intend children to learn from the activity and how this fits in with the overall curriculum plan. A carefully chosen activity will enable you to cover much of the range. For example, preparing for a tea party could involve making cakes (cooking with heat, sweet foods) and preparing sandwiches (cold 'cooking', savoury foods).

Read the performance criteria and range carefully before your assessment. Try to cover as much as you can.

Other types of evidence

You may need to present different types of evidence in order to:

- cover criteria not observed by your assessor
- show that you have the required knowledge, understanding and skills
- cover other parts of the range.

The amount and type of evidence you need to present will vary. You should plan this with your assessor.

Element C8.4 *Provide opportunities and equipment for manipulative play*

KUS
4, 12,
21, 25

Manipulative play involves children using their hands. They need to develop both fine manipulative and gross motor skills:

- Fine manipulative skills – using and developing finger control, using the pincer grip (from about 12 months).
- Gross motor skills – using large movements alongside the fine movements, for example, pushing pieces of a construction set together to join them.

Children need a lot of practice to develop these skills. The range of activities and experiences offered should enable children to work at different levels and provide opportunity for increasingly effective use of tools and equipment.

Activities should provide opportunities for practising and refining these skills at all levels. For example, within a group of children there may be some who cannot yet build a tower of bricks, while others may be building complex structures. Any activity will need to provide an opportunity for practice while also providing an appropriate level of challenge.

Activities for developing manipulative skills include:

- threading
- jigsaws and puzzles
- large and small construction
- mark making
- painting
- using malleable materials such as clay and dough
- dressing and undressing (dolls and themselves).

Posting and threading activities help to develop fine manipulative skills

Equipment

It is important to choose materials and activities that are appropriate for the stage of development of the children. If they are too difficult the children will become frustrated and discouraged, but if they are too simple they will quickly lose interest. Remember, for manipulative play the smaller the hands the bigger the pieces need to be!

Guidelines when providing manipulative play materials

- Make sure that there is enough equipment for all the children to participate successfully.
- Ensure that you provide activities that are challenging and accessible to all children in the group, including those with special needs.
- Think carefully about where the equipment is put – table tops or carpet according to the type of play – this will mean that all children will be able to participate.
- Make sure that they provide sufficient challenge in the activities for the range of abilities in the group.
- Store equipment separately in labelled boxes. This will ensure that equipment is not lost and that children can quickly and easily put equipment away.
- Monitor all equipment regularly for hygiene, safety and completeness.
- Think about how children can record some of their work. Ideas could include drawings, photographs or video recording, written instructions or descriptions.

Suitable materials and activities for different age groups

Under 12 months	2 or 3 years
Activities such as rattles, activity centres and mats. Safe, everyday objects will also provide sensory stimulation. Babies will explore these through sucking, banging, rubbing, poking and dropping.	<ul><li>Simple construction kits, e.g. Duplo, sticklebrix etc. (safety – children of this age may still put things in their mouths and small pieces can be dangerous)</li></ul>
1 to 2 years	**3 to 5 years**
Suitable activities include:<ul><li>Simple cups/shapes fit inside one another</li><li>Simple posting boxes</li><li>Building blocks</li><li>Interlocking bricks – larger, simpler versions of construction equipment</li><li>Large crayons or pencils to experiment with mark-making</li></ul>	<ul><li>Provide equipment such as train sets, farms, garages etc.</li><li>Construction toys such as meccano and tool sets</li><li>Miniature play equipment (small world play), such as Playmobil, dinosaurs</li><li>Jigsaw puzzles – match level of difficulty to child's ability</li></ul>

Practical Example

Developing physical skills through manipulative play

KUS
1, 7

As part of their ongoing observation and assessment of children staff in the nursery noticed that, overall, the children in the group needed to work on their fine motor skills. The staff decided to work towards doing some sewing on fabric with each child. They planned a series of activities, linked to sewing, to develop the children's manipulative skills and their hand–eye co-ordination. Over a term, alongside all the other activities, the children were encouraged to:

• play with lacing boards and tiles

• thread beads, cotton reels and buttons

• play with peg boards

• do some weaving

• complete simple sewing boards, with laces and bodkin needles.

Finally, when the staff felt that they were likely to succeed, each child was introduced to sewing on fabric.

➤ *Why is sewing a good way to develop fine motor skills?*

➤ *Why did the staff plan activities linked to sewing for the children to attempt first?*

Element C8.4

Are you ready for assessment?

Provide opportunities and equipment for manipulative play

You need to show that you can competently provide opportunities and equipment for manipulative play. To do this you will need to be directly observed by your assessor and present other types of evidence.

Direct observation by your assessor

Your assessor will need to see you carry out these performance criteria (PCs)

C8.4 PCs 1, 2, 3, 4, 5, 6, 7, 8, 10

During these observations your assessor

must see you cover at least ONE aspect in each range category listed in this element.

Remember the range categories for this element are:

1. Equipment

2. Skills

Preparing to be observed

Your assessor will need to see you participating in a session where you have provided opportunities and equipment for manipulative play. If you plan the session carefully, you will be able to cover a large part of the range. Make sure that you have out small-scale construction toys such as Lego, other small blocks or perhaps construction straws. Provide some jigsaws or some shape sorting toys and include activities where children can use tools, perhaps crayons and pencils or cutters and shaping tools. Setting out some large-scale construction will give children an opportunity to use their gross motor skills too. Think carefully about what you choose and how you set the equipment out. You will need to consider the developmental level of your group. Do the activities allow the children to be successful while providing sufficient challenge to the more able? You will need to show that you have considered ease of access to activities and that you have complied with your setting's health and safety guidance.

Read the performance criteria and range carefully before your assessment. Try to cover as much as you can.

Other types of evidence

You may need to present different types of evidence in order to:

- cover criteria not observed by your assessor
- show that you have the required knowledge, understanding and skills
- cover other parts of the range.

The amount and type of evidence you need to present will vary. You should plan this with your assessor.

Element C8.5 *Examine objects of interest with children*

KUS
6, 5, 14,
15, 27, 28

Links to unit E1.2.

Children learn most effectively through first-hand experiences. They take in information through all of their senses; the younger the child, the more important it is to provide opportunities for sensory learning. Play with objects is known as heuristic play. This type of play is sometimes provided for babies and toddlers in treasure baskets containing a selection of interesting objects for the child to handle and explore. These would not be familiar toys but everyday items that the child could experiment with. Obviously safety must be considered when selecting these items, remembering that babies and toddlers explore with their mouths, as well as with their hands and their eyes. Appealing to all the senses should also

Exploring the washing basket

be a consideration. A good selection will offer the chance to explore interesting and contrasting textures, as well as including items that stimulate the senses of hearing and smell.

How handling objects of interest promotes development

Holding and handling objects will promote children's *physical* development. A range of differently sized and shaped objects should be provided. Fine manipulative skills and hand–eye co-ordination will be practised when picking up and holding, and also when opening and closing fastenings, for example on boxes, jewellery etc.

Introducing children to unfamiliar objects will provide them with an opportunity to develop their *language* skills. Naming the objects and describing their features will introduce new vocabulary in a meaningful way.

Giving children interesting objects to explore will promote their natural curiosity and widen their horizons. Older children will be able to think about where the object comes from, who owns it and what it might be for. This stimulates their *intellectual* development.

When children are encouraged to explore and investigate objects together as a group their *social* skills will be practised. They will learn to take turns and be considerate of others. Children can begin to learn about other people and cultures through examining and exploring objects. For example, handling a collection of

Giving children interesting objects to explore will promote their natural curiosity

special lamps (*divas*) would be a good starting point for children to find out about the Hindu and Sikh celebration of Diwali.

Handling beautiful and unusual objects will enable children to experience and show a range of feelings such as wonder, joy and fascination. This contributes to their *emotional* development. When children bring in items from home for others to examine and explore, this is likely to have a positive effect on their self-esteem.

Encouraging children to handle objects and cultural artefacts with care and respect

Small children will need to be shown how to handle objects that are fragile and delicate. It is part of the role of the child care worker to help children to handle objects with respect, showing them how to hold and touch. If you have borrowed objects for your circle time or interest table, it is likely that these are special or precious to someone. Children need to know about this. If children are examining living things, plants or small animals such as minibeasts in bug boxes, it is particularly important to ensure gentle handling.

Enabling children with particular needs to explore and examine objects

All children should be provided with opportunities to explore and examine objects. When planning an activity and selecting items, the child care worker must ensure that all children can participate fully. If there are any children with a visual impairment, objects that can be explored through the senses of touch, sound and smell as well as sight should be selected. Children who have a hearing loss will not appreciate the 'noisy' aspects of objects, but can explore with their other senses. Some children may have difficulty picking up and holding on to objects, so items that are easy to grasp should be included, perhaps on trays close to the child.

Choosing objects of interest and cultural artefacts for young children to explore safely

Many settings have interest tables where a selection of items, sometimes linked to a theme, are set out for children to handle. Circle time provides another, more structured, context for children to explore items. Children are naturally curious and will be interested in most items that are presented to them. However, care and thought needs to be given to choosing objects so that children's enjoyment and learning is maximised and their safety ensured.

Providing a range

The following are suggestions of general categories of items to offer to children:

- Natural materials with interesting features, e.g. pine cones, cork, bark, sponges, pumice, rocks and pebbles, fossils etc.
- Items associated with animals, e.g. feathers, nests and eggs (abandoned), a chrysalis, shells of all sorts, wool from sheep, fur etc.
- Manufactured items, particularly unfamiliar and unusual items, e.g. a sundial, barometer, metronome, chiming clocks, timers etc.
- Objects that reflect people and their culture, e.g. cooking utensils, music (tapes and instruments), fabrics, clothes, games and 'special' items such as candlesticks, prayer mats, statues.
- Things from the past, e.g. photographs, toys, household equipment, clothes and, for older children, printed material such as ration books, certificates, newspapers.

Where to find them

- Ask parents, friends and families but remember that items might be precious and you would need to be sure that you could look after them. Do not borrow anything that is irreplaceable.
- Make your own collection from car boot sales, your cupboards, your travels.
- Make contact with local community groups. They may have items to lend or can suggest sources.
- Many local museums have collections that can be borrowed for use with children.

Conservation

Remember to emphasise conservation. Children should be encouraged to care for and protect the natural environment. Wildlife must not be disturbed to provide objects for interest tables!

Safety

You must make sure that any objects are safe for the children to handle.

- Remember that babies and toddlers will explore by sucking and chewing, as well as in other ways. Check that objects are made of non-toxic materials, are clean and with no loose, small pieces.

- Older children can be warned about sharp edges or any other concerns. Make sure you look for possible hazards beforehand.

- Many plants have poisonous berries. As these are very attractive to small children you should make sure that children do not come into contact with them.

- If any of the children in the group are allergic to certain substances, for example, feathers or fur, you should avoid providing these.

Using the natural and local environment to promote children's learning

Children can learn a great deal from the outside environment. Most settings give children regular opportunities to play outside either on the premises or using facilities in the local environment. This experience can provide children with many relevant and worthwhile opportunities for learning. Here are some examples:

- Children can plant seeds and bulbs, and watch and measure growth. Caring for a pet can help children to understand about life cycles and develop a sense of caring and responsibility.

Children can learn a great deal from the outdoor environment

- Observing wildlife in its natural habitat can be very rewarding. Bird tables can be set up where children can see them easily. Minibeasts can be found and examined in a garden area, perhaps using magnifying glasses and bugboxes. Pond dipping can help children to understand a different type of habitat.

- Studying the weather can be fascinating for small children. They can watch puddles form and evaporate, measure rainfall and find out the direction of the wind. Children love to feel snow, to experience its texture as they build with it and to watch it melting away. Icy puddles and icicles provide interesting experiences too.

- On a walk in the neighbourhood, draw children's attention to street furniture such as signposts, letter boxes, lamp posts and shop and road signs. They can look for architectural features such as doorways, roofs and chimney pots too.

Element C8.5 Are you ready for assessment?

Examine objects of interest with children

You need to show that you can competently examine objects of interest with children. You will need to be directly observed by your assessor and present other types of evidence.

Direct observation by your assessor

Your assessor will need to see you carry out these performance criteria (PCs)

C8.5 PCs 1, 2, 4, 5, 6, 7, 8

During these observations your assessor must see you cover at least ONE aspect in each range category listed in this element.

Remember the range categories for this element are:

1. Objects
2. Location
3. Examinations

Preparing to be observed

Your assessor will need to see you participating in a session where children are examining objects of interest. You will also be able to refer to other opportunities you have provided, particularly if your previous displays or interest tables are still available. Make sure that you show that you have thought about the developmental level of the children you are working with in your selection of items. Your session will be more successful if you present items that engage children's attention and curiosity, perhaps linking with the current theme or as a way of introducing a new focus. Show how examining these objects is part of the overall plan for this group of children. Think about how you will present the items, ensuring that children have easy access to them and opportunities to handle them. Remember that children take in information through all their senses, so make sure that some items can be explored in a variety of ways. Selecting objects carefully will enable you to cover a significant part of the range.

As with all activities, you should show that you have considered and acted on health and safety guidance in your session.

Read the performance criteria and range carefully before your assessment. Try to cover as much as you can.

Other types of evidence

You may need to present different types of evidence in order to:

- cover criteria not observed by your assessor
- show that you have the required knowledge, understanding and skills
- cover other parts of the range.

The amount and type of evidence you need to present will vary. You should plan this with your assessor.

Check your knowledge

- Why is play so important to young children's development? **KUS 3**
- What is the role of the adult in supporting and providing for children's play? **KUS 7, 11**
- How can you provide activities that are inclusive and enable all children to participate, regardless of gender, ability or cultural background? **KUS 24, 25, 26, 27, 28**
- How can you encourage children who are reluctant or uncooperative to join in with activities? **KUS 11, 18**
- Why is it important to know about children's development when planning activities and experiences for them? **KUS 1, 2**

Implement planned activities for the development of language and communication skills

This unit covers working with children in ways that support their learning. The focus is the quality of interaction between workers and children, while talking, listening, playing and making music. The unit also covers choosing and presenting of materials and equipment in ways that are attractive and accessible to children.

This unit links closely with unit C8.

This unit contains five elements:

- **C9.1** *Implement music sessions*
- **C9.2** *Implement and participate in talking and listening activities*
- **C9.3** *Select and use equipment and materials to stimulate role play*
- **C9.4** *Select and display books*
- **C9.5** *Relate stories and rhymes*

Introduction

Language and communication are the basis of learning. Talking, listening and playing with children are therefore vital to their learning and development. The quality of interaction between workers and children has a direct effect on the quality of children's learning. It is therefore important that all workers know what is effective practice so that they can support children's learning and development.

While you are working through this unit you will find it helpful to refer to the introductory section on children's language development.

Element
C9.1 *Implement music sessions*

KUS
1, 4, 11, 13, 14, 17, 19

Children need many opportunities to listen and respond to music, and to make their own music. For most children the aim of these early musical experiences is to develop an interest in music and to become aware of music as a means of communication and self-expression.

Songs, rhymes and music for young children include:

- listening to music
- moving to music
- learning and enjoying songs and rhymes
- making music.

Listening

- Make listening to music part of every day. Introduce a wide range of musical styles to the children. Choose music that is culturally diverse, classical and contemporary. Encourage children to request music and to bring in music from home. Choose pieces that are not too long and repeat them often so that the children become familiar with them. Identify the characteristics of the music – pace, tone, pitch – and listen for repeated phrases.

- Provide a listening centre using cassette players. Again, provide a range of music for the children to listen to. Taped stories and poetry are also very enjoyable, and encourage careful listening.

- Invite people in to play musical instruments or to tell stories, maybe a parent or older child. Include a range of instruments and stories from different cultural and music traditions.

Give children an opportunity to make their own music

Moving to music

- Create a mood with music. Choose sad music, cheerful music, frightening music etc., and get the children to respond.

- Set a scene with music. A mixture of sounds and tunes can represent, for example, the sea or a rainforest.

- Use music to tell a story. Different pieces of music can be associated with characters and events in a story. Favourites include *Peter and the Wolf* (Prokofiev) and *The Carnival of the Animals* (Saint-Saëns).
- Give children an opportunity to respond physically to music. They need time and space to develop confidence in dance. Involve all children but be sensitive to less confident children.
- Introduce children to different styles of dance. Community dance groups will often perform for children.
- Make sure that your choice of music is from a range of cultural and music traditions.

Learning and enjoying songs and rhymes

- Teach children rhymes and songs.
- Include actions with the rhymes and songs. This will help the children to learn them.
- Choose many different types of rhymes and songs – traditional, funny, number, rhyming and not rhyming – from all over the world.
- During song time try to balance traditional songs and rhymes with newer ones. Leave time for requests so that the children can choose their favourites.
- Show children the rhythm in songs and rhymes through clapping and simple percussion accompaniment.
- Get children to use their voices musically, high and low voices, long and short, loud and soft.

Making music

- Encourage children to make simple instruments – to shake, pluck, blow and scrape. Provide a range of materials for the children to use so they can recreate the sounds they have heard instruments make.
- Provide commercially made instruments for the children to use alongside their home-made ones. Try to represent all musical traditions.
- Explore music made from body sounds – clapping, clicking, tapping – and listen carefully to different voice sounds.
- Provide opportunities for children to experiment and discover how to make sounds, and then to change them. For example, a bottle half filled with water will make a different sound when tapped to one that is half filled with sand.
- Use music to accompany stories – create a mood from music.
- Hold musical conversations where children respond to each other with instruments or clapping. Get them to repeat and then create musical patterns, taking turns, as in a conversation.
- Let children tape their music to listen to, play to parents or to use at storytime or in their play.

Practical Example

Chinese New Year

**KUS
4, 13, 14, 19**

Children in the nursery had been preparing for the Chinese New Year celebrations. Musicians from the Chinese community had been invited into school. The children had had a wonderful afternoon listening to some unfamiliar instruments and rhythms, and watching dancing. The musicians brought in many instruments. The children were encouraged to hold them and, when they felt ready, to join in with the music. The children were shown how to do simple dance steps and many of them joined in with the performance. Later that week the nursery held its own lion dance parade to celebrate the Chinese New Year. They used their own home-made instruments to tap out rhythms they had practised.

➤ *How did the children benefit from having the Chinese musicians visit their nursery?* **KUS 13, 19**

➤ *Why was it important that the children were able to join in the music session?* **KUS 4, 14**

➤ *How could these music activities be followed up in other activities in the nursery?* **KUS 19**

Element C9.1

Are you ready for assessment?

Implement music sessions

You need to show that you can competently implement music sessions. To do this you will need to be directly observed by your assessor and present other types of evidence.

Direct observation by your assessor

Your assessor will need to see you carry out these performance criteria (PCs)

C9.1 PCs 3, 4, 5, 6, 7

During these observations your assessor must see you cover at least ONE aspect in each range category listed in this element.

1. Songs and music
2. Group
3. Participation

Preparing to be observed

You will need to plan a music session that offers the children opportunities to participate in different musical activities. You will need to introduce a variety of songs, rhymes and music. This could include familiar and unfamiliar songs, music, action and counting songs/rhymes. Make sure that you include rhymes, songs and music from a variety of cultural and linguistic backgrounds. You will need to show that the songs, music and activities chosen and the length of the

▶▶

session are appropriate for the children in the group, allowing them to participate in and enjoy the session.

Think about how you will organise the children and about how you will introduce the songs and music to encourage children to listen and to participate. You will need to be flexible in implementing the session allowing, when appropriate, the children to follow their interests, choosing songs and exploring sound with the instruments.

Read the performance criteria and range carefully before assessment. Try to cover as much as you can.

Other types of evidence

You may need to present different types of evidence in order to:

- cover criteria not observed by your assessor
- show that you have the required knowledge, understanding and skills
- cover other parts of the range.

The amount and type of evidence you need to present will vary. You should plan this with your assessor.

Implement and participate in talking and listening activities
Element C9.2

KUS
1, 2, 5, 9, 10, 11, 14

Talking and listening to young children

The most important factor in children's language development is interaction with other people. It is important that people who work with young children adopt practices that contribute positively to children's language development. There is a recognised link between the quality of adult input and the quality of children's language. Listed below are some important points to remember when talking with children. However, these are only practical points. A sensitivity towards children's needs and knowledge of them as individuals form the basis of positive interaction.

The same guidelines apply when talking with children for whom English is an additional language to the language spoken at home. It is important to remember that many children who are learning English as an additional language are very proficient in their first language. This means that they are likely to have an understanding of the use and purposes of language, and have developed the skills involved in interaction with others.

When talking to children, remember the following:

The tone of your voice	Does it convey warmth and interest in the child?
How quickly you speak and the language that you use	Do you speak at a pace that is appropriate for the child or children you are talking with? Think carefully about the words that you use and the length and complexity of your sentences. These need matching to the children's developmental level and you need to remember that as the children's language develops your interaction must change to meet their needs.
Listening	How do you show the child that you are listening? Eye contact and getting down to the child's level, together with becoming involved in the conversation, indicate that you are listening and interested.
Waiting	Do you leave enough time for the child to respond? Young children may need time to formulate their response. Remember that pauses and silences are part of conversation too.
Questions	Do you ask too many questions? This may make the conversation feel like a question-and-answer session, especially if your response is 'That's right'. What type of questions do you ask? Closed questions require a one-word answer and do not give the child the opportunity to practise and develop their language skills. Open questions have a range of possible answers, and give the child the opportunity to practise and develop their language skills, and to develop their thinking.
Your personal contribution	Do you contribute your own experience and/or opinions to the conversation? Conversation is a two-way process. It involves both people sharing information. This should be the same with children. It is important that the choice of what to talk about is shared.
What do you talk about?	How much of what you say is management talk? How much is conversation and chatting? How much is explaining? How much is playful talk? Children need to be involved in a wide range of language experiences to enable them to practise and develop their own language.
Developing thought	Do you ask for and give reasons and explanations when talking with children? Do you encourage the child to make predictions in real and imaginary situations? Do you encourage the children to give accounts of what they are doing or have done? Children's language and cognitive skills can be developed in this way.
Whom do you talk to?	You must talk to all children within the group. All children need the opportunity to practise their language. There will be a range of developmental levels within every group of children and it is important that each child's needs are met.

Activities and experiences that encourage young children to talk

Talking and listening carefully are both learned skills. People who work with young children need to know how to encourage these skills.

Talking

To develop language successfully, young children need an environment with plenty of opportunities to practise talking. They need lots of time when they are using language in different ways and for different purposes. Children also need people who will provide good role models, and who will listen carefully and help them to adjust and refine their language. When children make mistakes the best practice is to reflect back the correction. For example:

Child: 'I wented to the park.'
Adult: 'You went to the park did you?'

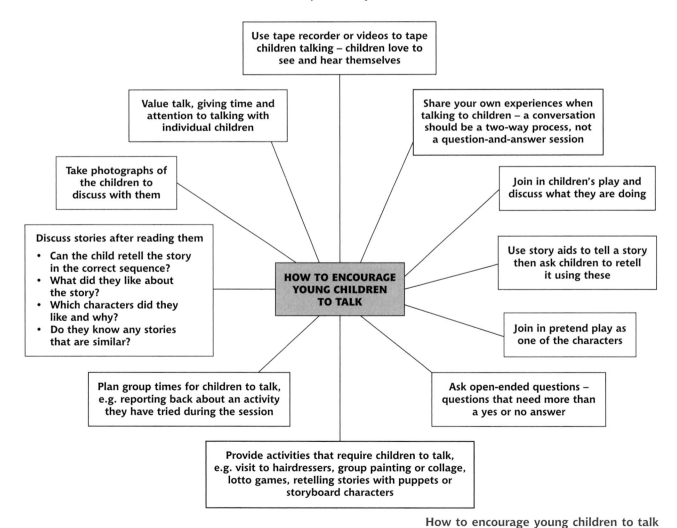

Use tape recorder or videos to tape children talking – children love to see and hear themselves

Value talk, giving time and attention to talking with individual children

Share your own experiences when talking to children – a conversation should be a two-way process, not a question-and-answer session

Take photographs of the children to discuss with them

Join in children's play and discuss what they are doing

Discuss stories after reading them
- **Can the child retell the story in the correct sequence?**
- **What did they like about the story?**
- **Which characters did they like and why?**
- **Do they know any stories that are similar?**

HOW TO ENCOURAGE YOUNG CHILDREN TO TALK

Use story aids to tell a story then ask children to retell it using these

Join in pretend play as one of the characters

Plan group times for children to talk, e.g. reporting back about an activity they have tried during the session

Ask open-ended questions – questions that need more than a yes or no answer

Provide activities that require children to talk, e.g. visit to hairdressers, group painting or collage, lotto games, retelling stories with puppets or storyboard characters

How to encourage young children to talk

Photo gallery

To encourage the children to talk in a group the staff took a series of photographs of outdoor play. They made sure that every child was in a photograph. They planned a number of activities\experiences using the photographs.

Initially they were put up as a gallery. Children were encouraged to look at them and find themselves.

The following week each key worker made a point of looking at, and discussing the photographs individually with the children in their group. The photographs were then used at group time and each child was encouraged to tell the group what they were doing in the picture.

Finally the photographs were put into a large book and each child's key worker, along with each child, wrote a sentence underneath the picture. The book was put in the book corner.

In this way the children were encouraged to talk. The subject was familiar and the children had time to consider what they would say before talking to the whole group. Making the photographs into a book meant that the children could continue to talk about the photographs.

➤ *Why was it important for all the children to be in the photographs?* **KUS 5**

➤ *How did the staff get the children to talk about the photographs at first?* **KUS 5, 9, 10**

➤ *Why did they make a book out of the photographs?* **KUS 1, 5, 9**

Listening

Listening is a complex skill. It involves selecting relevant information from all the information that we hear. To learn effectively young children need to be encouraged to listen carefully. This skill of active listening requires good powers of concentration. A child needs to be able to attend and to focus their attention on the task.

Go through a story after it has been read to the children:

- **Can the children recall the story?**
- **Ask the children to look out for a particular event or character**

Encourage children to play games with sounds and words:

- **Listening to rhyming poetry**
- **Rhyming words**
- **Rhyming lotto**
- **Sound bingo**
- **Tongue twisters**
- **Whispering games**

Go on sound walks

- **What can the children hear in the playground, or in the street?**

HOW TO ENCOURAGE LISTENING SKILLS

Tape the children and yourself talking and get the children to listen carefully:

- **Can they identify who is talking?**

Give simple instructions for children to follow:

- **Extend this to more complex instructions as the children improve**

Be a good listener yourself:

- **Give children your individual attention**
- **Maintain eye contact**
- **Physically get down to their level**
- **Reflect what the child has said in your comments and questions to show you've been listening**

How to encourage listening skills

Practical Example

Listening

KUS
1, 5, 9, 14

A playgroup planned to visit a farm park. Before they went they did a lot of work on identifying animals and the sounds they make. As part of this the playgroup leader made a sound lotto game for the children to play with. She made a tape of animal noises and a lotto set of animal pictures. The children had to listen to the tape and match the sound to each animal.

Before the activity was put out, the tape was played to the children at storytime. A number of different activities were introduced to encourage the children to focus their attention on the sounds.

They identified the animals and copied the sounds.

They imitated animal sounds for the others to identify.

They described an animal and the children had to make the appropriate noise.

In these ways the children achieved the aim of learning about animals and the sounds they make, and also they had been encouraged to listen in an active rather than a passive way.

➤ *Why is this a meaningful way for children to develop listening skills?*
  KUS 5, 14

➤ *How did the adult make this listening activity enjoyable for the children?* **KUS 5, 9**

➤ *How did listening carefully extend the children's learning?* **KUS 1, 5**

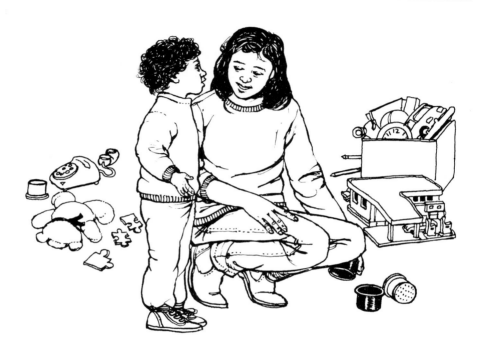

Adults can model careful listening

Common communication difficulties

Language is a learned skill. Some children have difficulties picking up and/or using speech and language. In a setting it is good practice to be aware of particular children's difficulties and to adapt the activities that are planned, so that all the children can participate together. Solving language and communication difficulties may need outside support as there are many ways to help children who have difficulties. People who work with young children need to be aware of the early signs of speech and language difficulties, so that advice and help can be sought if needed. Help and advice can be accessed in school and pre-school settings through the co-ordinator of special educational needs (often referred to as a SENCO – Special Educational Needs Co-ordinator), a general practitioner, a health visitor or a social worker.

There may be a problem if you notice any of the following:

● By age 1 an infant doesn't cry, babble or pay attention to other voices.

● By age 2 a child can't put some words together in speech.

● By age 3 a child's speech is difficult for those outside the family to understand.

- By age 4 a child doesn't have a growing vocabulary, speaks in very short sentences and cannot make most sounds – or a child points to things instead of talking.
- By age 5 a child can't carry on a simple conversation, stutters or sounds very different from playmates.

Assessment may be needed if a school-aged child:

- is difficult to understand
- uses and pronounces words incorrectly
- consistently uses incorrect grammar
- can't seem to hear or understand others well
- speaks too loudly most of the time.

Element C9.2 Are you ready for assessment?

Implement and participate in talking and listening activities

You will need to show that you can competently implement and participate in talking and listening activities. To do this you need to be directly observed by your assessor and present other types of evidence.

Direct observation by your assessor

Your assessor will need to see you carry out these performance criteria (PCs)

C9.2 PCs 2, 3, 4, 5, 6, 7, 8

During these observations your assessor must see you cover at least ONE aspect in each range category listed in this element.

Remember the range category for this element is:

1. Activities
2. Group
3. Children

Preparing to be observed

You will need to plan and implement activities with children during which you talk with, and listen and respond to the children. You will need to ensure that you use open questioning (questions that require more than a yes or no answer), so that the children have the opportunity to develop their knowledge and skills. Think about how you could adapt the ways that you interact with the children to ensure that they all are able to participate in the discussions. For example, how will you extend the fluent, confident children's language and understanding? How will you create opportunities for children with communication difficulties to be heard and listened to? How will you enable children who have English as an additional language to contribute to the session? How will you encourage the children to listen to one another? Your activities will need to extend the children's learning through discussion of familiar people and events. When planning your activities think carefully about the materials and equipment that you will use to encourage the children to participate in and enjoy the activity.

Read the performance criteria and range carefully before assessment. Try to cover as much as you can.

Other types of evidence

You may need to present different types of evidence in order to:

- cover criteria not observed by your assessor
- show that you have the required knowledge, understanding and skills
- cover other parts of the range.

The amount and type of evidence you need to present will vary. You should plan this with your assessor.

Element C9.3

Select and use equipment and materials to stimulate role play

KUS
1, 3, 9,
11, 12, 13,
18, 19, 22

Promoting learning through role play

Role play provides opportunities for children to practise and refine many skills and concepts. Children can do the following:

- Express creative and imaginative ideas.
- Express and experiment with many different feelings.
- Experience what it feels like to be somebody else.
- Experience playing in a group of children.
- Develop symbolic play – that is using one thing to represent another, for example, a box for a spaceship, a doll as a baby. This skill is important when learning to read and write. Think about words written down. They are only squiggles on a page that represent speech.
- Use reading and writing in a real way, for example, reading a menu in a cafe or writing it down, addressing an envelope in a post office.

Symbolic play – a doll is played with as if it is a baby

- Use numbers and counting in a real way, for example, putting five pieces of fruit in a bag for a customer in a fruit shop, working out how many plates will be needed when setting a table.
- Use gross motor skills to build and change areas.
- Use fine motor skills, for example, to set up play with small world activities, to dress and undress themselves and dolls.
- Learn and develop their ideas about the world that are beyond their own experience, for example, working on a farm or in a shop, sailing on a boat, camping.

Through role play, children have the opportunity to explore feelings that they have. They have the opportunity to experiment with responses to their feelings. Role play is a particularly good way for children to express positive feelings openly and begin to develop ways of expressing difficult feelings in acceptable ways. Children can experiment with being someone else, for example, a parent, a teacher, a powerful captain, a princess. They are in charge, in control, they can direct what happens. In this way children can begin to understand what it feels like to be someone other than a small child.

Play can also be a positive self-concept builder. Our self-concept is the way that we feel about ourselves and it has a large impact on all aspects of our lives. It is therefore important that children develop a positive self-esteem. Play is familiar and natural to them and so is not a threatening experience – play cannot be wrong. This is particularly true of role play. Children play at their own level and so the risk of constant failure is minimised. This familiar positive environment gives them the opportunity to develop a positive sense of their achievements and to begin to feel good about themselves. This in turn affects their later development.

Children can experiment with being someone else

Expressing and exploring emotions in role play

KUS
3, 12

Amelia's mummy had just had a new baby. Initially Amelia was excited and spoke a lot about the baby and what she did to help look after her. Once this initial excitement had died down, the staff noticed how she would role play being her mummy over and over again.

In the home corner, with a friend, Amelia would be the mummy and her friend became Amelia. They looked after the baby together. However, in role, Amelia would tell her friend that she was too tired to play and that they couldn't go to the park now because the baby needed to be fed. During this play, Amelia instructed her friend to cry when she was told that she couldn't do something that she wanted to do. Amelia responded by sighing a lot, putting her arm around her friend and kissing her, and sitting her on her knee to comfort her.

➤ *Why do you think Amelia wanted to play like this?* **KUS 3**
➤ *What are the benefits of this role play?* **KUS 12**

The role of the adult in role play

Things you need to do/think about	Why this is important
Plan • Is the activity suitable for the age and stage of development of the children?	• Different children will need different activities to help them learn. The activities provided must be planned for the particular children in the group.
• Can the activity be linked to the topic?	• Many settings plan around a topic. This needs to be considered when planning daily activities, e.g. if the topic is nursery rhymes, a role play activity could be planned where children build a wall from boxes and become Humpty Dumpty or the king's horses and men.
• What equipment will you need?	• The equipment that is required will need to be collected together before the children begin the activity. This will mean that the children can enjoy their play without getting frustrated that the things they need are not there.
• What safety issues are there?	• Careful thought needs to be given to equipment and activites that are provided.
• How can you make sure that the activity reflects all the children's experiences and all children are able to participate?	• Think about what will be needed to make sure that children with special needs can participate in the activity. Also, make sure that things like clothing, kitchen equipment and pictures show different ways of life. This will make all the children feel that different ways of living are valued by the setting.
Setting up the activity • Put all the necessary equipment out. Make sure that the children can get to the equipment easily	• Children need to be able to participate in the activity without having to search for tools and equipment. They will learn more easily, concentration will be encouraged and they will feel satisfied at having completed a task if they are able to work without distractions.
• Set the activity up in an attractive way	• Children are more likely to choose an activity that looks inviting. Ways of encouraging children to join in an activity include: – beginning the activity so there is an example of what the children can do – playing with the activity yourself and asking children to join you – making sure that the equipment is easy to see and to reach, e.g. the boxes for box modelling are in piles of different shapes, dressing clothes are hung up at the children's height, not flung in a box.
• Introduce the activity to the children. Suggest ways in which they can play with the equipment	• Many activities will need some introduction. This will mean that the children are aware of different ways to play with the equipment and also that they have the necessary skills to be successful at the activity, for example, showing children how to make a tent or den with blankets.

The role of the adult in role play (cont.)

Things you need to do/think about	Why this is important
Interacting with the children during the activity	
• You can play with the children	• Playing with children shows that you value what they are doing. It also means that you can observe the activity to see what the children are learning and how successful the activity is.
• You can play alongside the children at the same activity	• Playing alongside children means working at the activity on your own, perhaps talking with the children. You are demonstrating what the children can do at that activity. Children learn a lot by watching others to see what can be done and how to do it; for example, how to build a wall from large boxes.
• You can play with an activity and encourage children to join in the activity	• Children will often come and play with an activity when an adult is there. This is a useful way to make sure that all children play with all activities; for example, playing in the home corner and encouraging boys to come and join in.
• You can join in an activity to suggest different ways of playing with the activity	• Children will often play the same thing over and over again. This is important while they practise new skills. However, they will eventually need to develop these skills. Joining in their play and making suggestions about what and how to play helps to develop their skills; for example, encouraging children who are playing at hairdressers to write down an appointment in the appointment book or on an appointment card.
Observing and assessing the children and the activity	
• Was the activity at the right level for the children?	• Children will only learn and develop if they can play successfully with the activities provided. The activities planned must be at the right level for the children who are going to play with them. This will be different for each group of children.
• Was all the necessary equipment readily available for the children?	• Children will quickly lose interest if they have to keep stopping what they are doing to find tools and equipment. All necessary equipment needs to be readily available, so that they can concentrate and learn.
• Who played with the activity?	• All children need a wide variety of play activities to learn. Adults need to make sure that all children get the chance to join in all activities. This will mean that sometimes the adults need to encourage children to play with activities that they would not necessarily choose themselves; for example, boys to play in a clinic looking after babies, giving the girls and the quieter children time on the bikes, encouraging all the children to dress up in clothes that they do not usually wear.
• What did the children learn from doing the activity?	• It is important that the activities planned are right for the children in the group. Observing children at activities means that when the next plans are made, they can be based on what the children have already done and learned.

KUS
9, 11, 12,
13, 18

Practical Example

Creating a role play area

As part of a playgroup's topic on transport the staff decided to create a street in the playground to use with the bikes and trucks. The children had been out to look at the street outside and staff had made a note of all the different things that they had seen.

With boxes and tubing they made traffic signs including traffic lights, STOP signs and bus stops. They labelled the bikes and trucks as cars, buses, ambulances, fire engines and lorries. Finally, they drew the street markings on the playground with chalk, including roundabouts and junctions.

The staff introduced the area to all the children, pointing out simple driving rules. The children were then free to play.

The playground area set up as a street

➤ *Why did the staff involve the children in setting up the role play area?* **KUS 9, 18**

➤ *Why is it important that the staff encourage both girls and boys to play in this area?* **KUS13**

➤ *List the different ways in which the children could play with this area. Who could they pretend to be?* **KUS 12**

➤ *List other things that the staff could add to the play area to extend the play.* **KUS 9, 12, 18**

➤ *How did this role play area link with the topic plan? List other role play activities that could link with the transport topic plan.* **KUS 11**

Are you ready for assessment?

Select and use equipment and materials to stimulate role play

You need to show that you can competently select and use equipment and materials to stimulate role play. To do this you will need to be directly observed by your assessor and present other types of evidence.

Direct observation by your assessor

Your assessor will need to see you carry out these performance criteria (PCs)

C9.3 PCs 2, 3, 5, 6, 7

During these observations your assessor must see you cover at least ONE aspect in each range category.

Remember the range category for this element is:

1. Materials
2. Location
3. Role play

Preparing to be observed

You will need to plan and set up a role play activity. Before you begin consider the location of the activity ensuring that you offer a safe and accessible play area. You need to think carefully about the materials and equipment for the activity. Ensure that there is enough equipment for all children to participate fully and that items selected reflect the diversity within society. Think about how to present the materials and equipment in an attractive way to encourage children to join in the activity.

You need to consider how to introduce the activity to the children, demonstrating how to use unfamiliar equipment. Ensure that in your interaction during the role play activity you actively promote appropriate use of equipment and offer all children the opportunity to be involved in non-stereotypical ways.

Read the performance criteria and range carefully before your assessment. Try to cover as much as you can.

Other types of evidence

You may need to present different types of evidence in order to:

- cover criteria not observed by your assessor
- show that you have the required knowledge, understanding and skills
- cover other parts of the range.

The amount and type of evidence you need to present will vary. You should plan this with your assessor.

Select and display books

KUS
1, 7, 11,
20, 21, 22

Books are an important and integral part of the early years curriculum. They are provided in all nurseries and classrooms. Reading and storytime are part of each day. Some children also have books at home and read with parents and carers. This early experience of books is very important in establishing positive attitudes to books and to reading.

Why are books important?

Books and stories are an important part of children's development. Outlined below are some of the main skills that can be developed and nurtured. Books and stories can be introduced to very young children. Although the child may not fully understand the story, a quiet, intimate time reading with a parent or carer forms a positive association for the child. This in turn helps to establish a habit of reading and listening to stories that has many benefits for the child.

Language development

Language is learned: the more exposure a child has to different patterns in language, the richer their own language is likely to be. Initially this will be expressive (spoken) language, later read and written language. Listening to stories and talking about books enables young children to listen and respond to the sound and rhythm of spoken language. This is important to speech development at all levels. Initially children need to recognise the sounds and rhythms that occur in their language; once this has been established they need to practise and refine their use of spoken language.

Listening to stories can also extend a child's vocabulary. As long as most of the language in the text is familiar to the child, new, imaginative language can be introduced. The child will begin to understand these new words by their context, that is, how they are used and linked with the story line and the pictures.

Experience with books and storytelling is also an important part of a child's early understanding of symbols. A child who has contact with books begins to understand that the squiggles on the page represent speech. This is a vital skill in the development of reading and writing.

Emotional development

Books and stories are enjoyable. They give children the opportunity to express a whole range of positive emotions. They provide a rich, imaginative world that can be a source of great pleasure to the child, and through identification with the characters and the story line children can develop and practise their own responses to events, and experience situations and feelings that are beyond their own life experiences. This can be done in a safe environment where the child has an element of control over events.

Cognitive development

Books, if carefully chosen, can provide a rich source of imagination for a child. They can stimulate interesting and exciting thoughts and ideas. The development of imagination is an important part of being creative. Creative thoughts and ideas are an important part of the quality of life and necessary to the development of society.

Books can also introduce children to a wide range of concepts. Repetition and context enable children to develop their understanding of the world that they live in. Listening to stories, recalling and sequencing the events are also positive ways of extending young children's concentration span and memory.

Social development

Books and stories are more than just the presentation of a sequence of events; they carry in them a whole range of messages about how a society functions. This includes acceptable patterns of behaviour, expectations of groups within the society, and moral codes of right and wrong. Children pick up these messages. It is therefore vital that books for young children portray a positive view of society and the people within that society. This positive view of the world contributes towards young children developing a balanced and constructive outlook on life.

Group storytime and sharing books contribute to the development of social skills of sharing, turn taking and co-operating with others. Children begin to learn that they have to take other people's needs and wishes into account. Storytime can also provide children and adults with the opportunity to build and maintain relationships. If a cosy and comfortable environment is provided it offers a sense of closeness and intimacy for the children and adults involved.

Choosing children's books

It is important that children's books are chosen carefully. Children have different needs and interests at different stages of their development. The maximum benefit can be gained if the book chosen meets the child's needs. All children are individual, and will have different needs, likes and dislikes. This needs to be taken into account. There are, however, some general points to consider when choosing a book for a young child and these are listed below.

Setting up a book area

A book area needs to be a welcoming and attractive area to encourage children to use the books.

It should be set up in a quiet place, away from the bustle of other play activities. The space should be enclosed to limit noise and to make it feel cosy. There should be somewhere for the children to sit. Seats should be at child level, perhaps with

**Setting up a
book corner**

large cushions. The area needs to be well lit, if possible with natural light from a window. The children need to have easy access to the books. Shelving should be at child level and the books organised attractively, if possible displayed flat so the children can see the front covers.

The book area needs to be well maintained to make sure that it remains an attractive area that the children want to use. It should be tidy and the books should be kept in good condition. The wall and book displays should be changed frequently to maintain the children's interest. Included in planning should be some time for a member of staff to spend in the book area sharing books with the children.

Books are a powerful way of influencing children's views about the society they live in. Books for children must, therefore, reflect positive images of all people in both the text and the illustrations.

0–3 years

- Picture books are appropriate for this age range, especially for children under 1 year.
- Where there is text, it needs to be limited, especially for children aged 0–1.
- The pictures need to have bright colours and bold shapes.
- The pictures need little detail. They need to be simplified so that they are easily identified – the most obvious features stressed.
- Children enjoy familiar themes, for example, families, animals.
- The complexity of pictures and text can be increased for children aged 2+.
- The context of the storytime is as important as the book itself; the cosy, close and intimate time gives children a positive association with books and reading.

3–5 years

- Repetition is important – for language development and for the enjoyment of the sound and rhythm of language.
- Books need to be reasonably short, to match children's concentration span.
- Books need minimum language with plenty of pictures that relate to the text.
- Popular themes are still everyday objects and occurrences.

5–7 years

- A clearly identifiable story and setting are important.
- Children's wider interests, experiences and imagination should be reflected in themes.
- The characters can be developed through the story.
- Language can be richer – playing with rhyme and rhythm, the introduction of new vocabulary and the use of repetition for dramatic effect.

3–7 years

- Illustrations still need to be bold, bright and eye-catching, but can be more detailed and have more meaning than pure recognition.
- Sequenced stories become popular – with a beginning, middle and end.
- The story line needs to be easy to follow with a limited number of characters.
- Repetition is important so that the reader or listener can become involved in the text.
- Animated objects are popular – children can enter into the fantasy.
- Children enjoy humour in stories, but it needs to be obvious humour, not puns or sarcasm.

Element C9.4

Are you ready for assessment?

Select and display books

You need to show that you can competently select and display books. To do this you will need to be directly observed by your assessor and present other types of evidence.

Direct observation by your assessor

Your assessor will need to see you carry out these performance criteria (PCs)

C9.4 PCs 2, 3, 4, 5, 8

During these observations your assessor must see you cover at least ONE aspect in each range category listed in the element.

Remember the range categories for this element are:

1. Books
2. Books selected
3. Backgrounds and experiences

Preparing to be observed

You will need to select and display some books for children to use. You must select the books carefully, making sure that there are a variety of books for the children (check the range statements) and that they are at the correct level for the children to understand. Look carefully at the chart above, which describes how to select books for young children. Check the books to make sure that they are in good condition. Once you have selected the books, you need to think about how to display them so that the children want to come and use the books. Try to display some of the books so that children can see the front cover. Think about putting books on a similar topic or theme together in a labelled section or box. Make sure that there is enough light for the children to read and that any other health and safety issues have been considered – check with the setting's health and safety procedures.

Read the performance criteria and range carefully before assessment. Try to cover as much as you can.

Other types of evidence

You may need to present different types of evidence in order to:

* cover criteria not observed by your assessor
* show that you have the required knowledge, understanding and skills
* cover other parts of the range.

The amount and type of evidence you need to present will vary. You should plan this with your assessor.

Element C9.5 *Relate stories and rhymes*

KUS
4, 5, 6,
9, 8, 15,
16, 20

Storytime

Storytime needs to be considered as carefully as any other activity. The following are points to consider for storytime sessions with individuals and groups.

Preparing for storytime

* The choice of books needs to be matched to the child/children.
* Check that the illustrations and the story line have realistic but positive images of individuals and of different groups within society.
* If telling a story from memory make sure that you practise it – telling stories is not always as easy as it looks!

- Think about props that you could use to tell the story, for example, puppets, a treasure chest, a storyboard or music.
- Check that you know the story well enough to tell or read it fluently and dramatically, and to use props effectively.

Telling the story

Tracing the text with your finger demonstrates left-to-right and top-to-bottom orientation

- Make sure that the area is suitable for storytelling. Think about where you will sit, the children's seating, the light and the temperature.
- Check that any aids used by the children are in place, for example glasses and hearing aids. Make sure that children who need to sit close to the visual aids being used are able to do so.
- Settle the children before beginning the story. It is good practice not to begin until the children are listening.
- Ask the children to try to listen to the story all the way through without interruptions. This encourages concentration and allows the children to follow the storyline. Tell the children that they can discuss the story after they have listened to it. If children do interrupt quickly, remind them that they will have a chance to talk about it later and continue with the story. This pattern of storytelling may take a little while for the children to get used to, but if you do it every time you read a story the pattern will become established.
- Allow the children to see the pages as you read the story.
- Point to the words as you read them, demonstrating left-to-right tracking and individual words as you say them. This will help the children begin to develop early reading and writing skills.
- Tell the story enthusiastically. Children will pick up your enthusiasm. It is best to have read the story (or practised a story told from memory) beforehand, so that you can concentrate on fluent, dramatic storytelling.

As you read the story make sure that you are aware of how the children are responding. Which parts of the story did they enjoy? Which parts did they seem worried by? This will give you some ideas for discussing the book with the children. It will also help you to adapt the story next time that you read it. Perhaps you could make the exciting parts more dramatic or change the storyline to make it less worrying for some children.

Extending storytelling

Talk about the story when you have finished reading it through. After this you could:

- read or tell the story again, this time encouraging the children to comment
- retell the story, sequencing the events
- look closely at what happens in the story
- recognise similar things that have happened to them
- develop the story with 'What could happen next?' or 'What if?' questions
- join in rhymes, songs or poems that develop the themes introduced in the story
- retell the story using props and/or puppets.

Make sure that children's comments are received with enthusiasm and encouragement. Children need to feel that their contributions are valued and that storytime is an enjoyable activity.

Storytime

Using props to tell a story

A theatre group was going to visit the playgroup to do a performance of Goldilocks and the Three Bears. The theatre group wanted the children to be involved in the performance so the staff felt that it was important that the children were familiar with the story before the theatre group's visit.

KUS
4, 5, 9, 16

Initially a member of staff told the story to the whole group. The following day the staff member used a treasure chest to retell the story. In it she had put a wig, hats, bowls, spoons and a pillow. As she told the story she produced the props from the treasure chest, much to the delight of the children. She then retold the story, encouraging the children to select the right prop at the appropriate point in the story.

The props were then put in the role play area, which was set up as the three bears' house.

When the theatre group did their performance the children were able to become fully involved in the experience, as they were familiar with the story. This made the experience enjoyable, it formed positive associations with stories and theatre, and contributed to the development of the children's language and communication skills.

➤ *Why did the staff use props to tell this story?* **KUS 4, 16**

➤ *How did using props help the children to be fully involved in the theatre production?* **KUS 5, 9**

Are you ready for assessment?

Relate stories and rhymes

You will need show that you can competently relate stories and rhymes. To do this you will need to be directly observed by your assessor and present other types of evidence.

Direct observation by your assessor

Your assessor will need to see you carry out these performance criteria (PCs)

C9.5 PCs 2, 3, 4, 5, 6, 7, 9

During these observations your assessor must see you cover at least ONE aspect in each range category listed in this element.

Remember the range category for this element is:

1. Books
2. Group
3. Backgrounds and experiences
4. Methods

Preparing to be observed

A storytime session needs to be planned in advance just like other activities. Look carefully at the range when preparing to be observed and make sure that you cover one aspect in each range category. Before the storytime session you will need to think about which book or story you are going to read or tell, making sure that it is suitable for the child/children. Think about how you will extend the story with discussion and songs or rhymes. Choose where you will tell or read the story, making sure that the area is quiet enough and there is appropriate seating and light. Think carefully about how you will manage the children's behaviour. How will you settle them? How will you manage interruptions? How will you make sure that all the children are able to participate in the discussion? How will you encourage the children who are reluctant to join in? Before your assessor observes you it is a good idea for you to observe an experienced storyteller and see how they manage these issues.

Read the performance criteria and range carefully before assessment. Try to cover as much as you can.

Other types of evidence

You may need to present different types of evidence in order to:

- cover criteria not observed by your assessor
- show that you have the required knowledge, understanding and skills
- cover other parts of the range.

The amount and type of evidence you need to present will vary. You should plan this with your assessor.

Check your knowledge

- Why is it important to plan activities where children can play in different ways and at different levels? **KUS 9**
- How do you offer children a non-stereotypical view of the world in books and during activities? **KUS 13**
- How could you encourage children with different needs and abilities to talk during an activity? **KUS 5, 6**
- What do you need to know about a group of children before you can plan an activity or storytime? **KUS 1, 5, 6, 17, 20**
- How should materials and equipment be presented to encourage children to join in at an activity? **KUS 18, 19**

Maintain an attractive, stimulating and reassuring environment for children

UNIT E1

This unit covers all aspects of maintaining an attractive, stimulating and reassuring physical environment for children. The environment includes everyday living areas and play areas, indoors and outdoors.

This unit has close links with unit E2.

This unit contains three elements:

› **E1.1** *Maintain the physical environment*

› **E1.2** *Prepare and maintain displays*

› **E1.3** *Maintain a reassuring environment*

Introduction

There are many things involved in creating a stimulating and caring environment for children. These include:

- providing a range of equipment and resources
- giving careful consideration to the layout and decoration of a room
- good teaching skills
- a caring approach
- displays and interest tables.

National Standards

Standards and regulations relating to the care and education of children are laid down by each of the four countries in the United Kingdom: England, Wales, Scotland and Northern Ireland. The standards include aspects of child care such as safety and the physical environment. This includes heating, ventilation, hygiene and outside play spaces. Regulations also cover amount of space needed for each child and the number of adults required to care for the children. See appendix.

Element E1.1 *Maintain the physical environment*

KUS
3, 4, 5, 6,
7, 11, 12,
13, 14

Arranging the area

Child care settings may be in different kinds of accommodation. Some may be purpose-built, for example, a day nursery or nursery school. Others could include:

- a village hall, for a pre-school, playgroup or toddler group
- a family home where children are cared for by a childminder or nanny.

Choosing furniture and equipment and planning the layout is important to make any setting welcoming, safe, secure and reassuring for the children.

When deciding how to arrange the area, the following factors are important.

Provide a welcoming environment

Using the available space

The National Standards (see above) lay down the requirements for the minimum space that is to be provided for each child. In day care in England these requirements are as follows:

AGE SPACE

Under 2 years   3.5 square metres for each child
2 years   2.5 square metres for each child
3–7 years   2.3 square metres for each child

The environment needs to be organised so that there are different areas for different types of play and learning. There should be room to use large bricks, make bigger models, and to use road and rail layouts. These activities should be situated away from other quieter activities. Smaller, quieter areas should be provided for some types of activities, for example, sand, water, painting, imaginative play area and the book area. Messy activities like painting, sand and water may need to be placed where the flooring can be swept and washed. Messy activities also need to be near the sinks for hand washing and drying racks for the paintings.

Activities can be provided at small tables with the right number of chairs. This will encourage the children to concentrate more easily and to work with a partner or in small groups. A carpeted area is good for bringing the children together for registration, sharing news and at storytime. A larger area that can be used for drama and music and movement should be available. This may be outside the main room or perhaps shared with other groups.

Resources that are provided for activities should be where the children can reach them. This will help them to choose which materials they are going to use. In some settings, such as a nursery, the toys and equipment can be kept in cupboards and on shelves that are labelled with a picture as well as the written word. This will help the children to be tidy and to replace and care for the things they use. However, in some settings such as a playgroup, everything will need to be put into storage at the end of each session. In this case equipment may be put into large storage boxes at the end of each session before being locked away. However, it is still important that the children help with the packing up. In every setting there will be some areas where the children are not allowed to go, such as the kitchen or storerooms.

Acorn pre-school

KUS
4, 5

Acorn pre-school group uses a community hall. The hall is large and airy and has easy access to an outside play space. The child care workers provide a wide range of activities. They encourage the children to move freely between them. However, they noticed that very few of the children settled into the activities for any length of time. The room seemed very noisy and the children were frequently being reminded not to race around.

The child care workers decide to set up the hall in a different way and to make sure that each staff member had a particular role to play at each session, as well as generally supervising the children.

➤ *How would you arrange the hall? Say what activities you would have and how you would set about arranging the space. How does your new layout meet the children's needs?* **KUS 4**

➤ *What would you want the child care workers to do during the session? Think about safety and security.* **KUS 5**

Comfort

The temperature of the setting should be kept between 16–24°C (60–75°F). Ventilation should allow fresh air to circulate. Opening the windows can usually achieve this. Check that children cannot climb out. Lighting in each part of the setting should be adequate for the activities provided. Natural light from windows is always best, but on duller days or in dimmer areas additional lighting will be needed. From a safety point of view always use the main room lights rather than smaller table lamps that may get knocked or pulled over. A quiet area with books and comfortable seating will encourage children to pick up and look at books and engage in quieter activities. Where possible furniture should be child sized. Attractive curtains and soft furnishings will add to the general attractiveness and comfort of the setting. Any soft furnishings must meet the safety and fire regulations. There is more information about this in unit E2.

Involving the children

Children can be encouraged to help in putting equipment away and tidying areas of the setting. They should be encouraged to value and care for their environment. Time should be allowed as part of the routine of the setting for putting away all the equipment. Even the youngest children can take part by 'helping', even if this takes longer than doing it yourself. Check the equipment for any damage as you put it away so that the children can see that it is important to care for things. Remove anything damaged and report this so those repairs can be made or the item thrown away.

Ensuring accessibility

All activities and areas of the setting must be accessible to all children, although there will always be some areas where the children are not allowed, such as the kitchen.

- Children with a physical disability may need wider doorways, ramps and a larger toilet area. Ensure there is space to allow them to move around classroom furniture.

- Children with a sensory impairment may need additional equipment. For example, a deaf child may need a hearing aid. Is there a carer who can use British Sign Language?

- Children with a visual impairment will need the reading area to be well lit. Natural light is best but if the area does not get enough daylight then extra lights will be needed. Books with large print and clear pictures will be helpful. There should be extra space to help movement around classroom furniture. The floor must be kept clear of obstacles. Any changes to the physical environment should be planned and explained to the child in advance.

Playing outside

The outdoor play space should be safe and secure. The area and the toys and equipment should always be checked **before** the children use it. There is more information about this in unit E2. A variety of surfaces on the ground will provide for different types of play and learning, for example, hard surfaces such as concrete for the wheeled toys and bikes, and grassy areas or soft surfaces for sitting and running games. Also, it is very useful to have some outside play space that is covered for when the weather is wet, shady areas to provide cover on hot days and space to run around and use the wheeled toys safely. Trees and plants and an area to be used for planting and growing things will add to the children's learning experiences.

Provide a shady area outside

Safety in the environment

It is the responsibility of the adults to enable children to play and learn safely.

Health and safety policies

All child care settings should have a health and safety policy that includes:

- clear safety rules for children's behaviour
- safety equipment, e.g. safety catches on doors and windows, non-slip surfaces, safety glass, safe gym equipment
- procedures for using equipment
- policies for dealing with spills of bodily fluids
- procedures for staff to report potential hazards
- clear rules to ensure that staff practise safely, e.g. closing and fastening safety gates, reporting any damaged or defective equipment, keeping hot drinks away from children
- policies for collecting children.

There is more information about safety in unit E2.

Changes to the layout of the environment

Introducing changes to the layout will help to stimulate children's ideas and support creative play. Some of the most common changes made are in the imaginative play areas. For example, staff may set up a shop or hospital, often to support a current theme or topic. Changes of this kind should be discussed in advance with the children so that they can share ideas and contribute to the project. Changes to the outdoor area may be made because new equipment has been bought, changes in the weather or for safety reasons.

Feeling secure

Children need to know about the physical layout of their environment, for example, where the toilets are and where things are kept. They also need to know about the routine, for example, when snack time and storytime take place. This knowledge helps children to feel secure. It is important to discuss any proposed changes with the children before they happen. This will help them get used to the idea that changes are going to be made. Children who feel secure in their environment will make best use of the play and learning opportunities provided. They will usually separate happily from their parent, join in and participate well. They will progress in their development and in their ability to share and make relationships with other adults and children. Children who feel insecure may not like being left by their parent. They will be reluctant to join in with play and activities. They may cling to one particular carer at the setting and have difficulty in relating to the other children and adults.

There is more information about separation in unit C4.

Element E1.1 Are you ready for assessment?

Maintain the physical environment

You need to show that you can competently maintain the physical environment. To do this you will need to be directly observed by your assessor and present other types of evidence.

Direct observation by your assessor

Your assessor will need to see you carry out these performance criteria (PCs)

E1.1 PCs 1, 2, 3, 4, 5, 6

During these observations your assessor

must see you cover at least ONE aspect in each range category listed in this element.

Remember the range category for this element is:

1. Physical environment

Preparing to be observed

You will need to arrange to take part in the preparation and setting up of activities in your area. You should be able to show your assessor how the temperature, ventilation and lighting are controlled, and know the required room temperatures. You should familiarise yourself with the location of the exits and in particular the fire exits and be able to show that you know about the health and safety rules for your setting. You will need to show that responsibility for caring for the environment is shared with the children by, for example, encouraging them to be tidy, and to help put toys and equipment in their proper places. You could prepare for your assessment by drawing a floor plan of your setting, showing the indoor and outdoor play space. Mark the following on your plan:

- exits
- fire exits
- layout of the furniture
- where equipment and resources, that are accessible to the children, are placed
- activities.

Look at your plan and write about how the physical layout of the activities helps the children's learning.

Read the performance criteria and range carefully before your assessment. Try to cover as much as you can.

Other types of evidence

You may need to present different types of evidence in order to:
- cover criteria not observed by your assessor
- show that you have the required knowledge, understanding and skills
- cover other parts of the range.

The amount and type of evidence you need to present will vary. You should plan this with your assessor.

Prepare and maintain displays

Element E1.2

KUS
8, 15,
16, 17

Displaying children's work

Displays and interest tables are an effective way of creating a stimulating and attractive environment for children.

The values of display

Display has many values. It can:
- be used as a stimulus for learning

- encourage children to look, think, reflect, explore, investigate and discuss
- act as a sensory and imaginative stimulus
- encourage parental involvement in their children's learning, and reinforce links with home
- encourage self-esteem by showing appreciation of children's work
- encourage awareness of the wider community, reflect society and reinforce acceptance of difference
- make the environment attractive.

The length of time a display remains in place should be considered and planned. Any display that has become old or faded should be replaced.

Display encourages children's interest

Where to display

Displays should be placed where they can be seen easily, or touched if appropriate. It is worth an adult getting down to the child's eye level and viewing the surroundings from that position.

What to include in a display

Variety makes displays interesting. Displays can include:

- children's painting and other individual work
- children's co-operative efforts

- natural materials and plants
- objects of interest, photographs, pictures, collage, real objects
- use of different colours, textures and labelling.
- items that the children have brought in from home. This will make the display more personal to the children in the group. These can be familiar items or things that will show aspects of different cultural backgrounds, for example, different items of clothing or material.

All children should be able to contribute to the displays in their environment. When looking around their room, every child should have at least one piece of their work displayed, or have taken part in a group display. This will help the children to feel they are part of the setting and that their work is valued. Children should be involved in the choice of work that will be displayed. They should also help in the mounting of work and the creation of the display.

Displays that include people should reflect positive images of black people, women and people with disabilities. For example, show positive images of all types of people working as politicians, doctors or lawyers and taking part in sporting activities. Children should be given the opportunity to represent themselves accurately. Child care workers should provide mirrors, and paints and crayons of suitable colours. This will enable children to see and match their own skin tones.

The entrance to a setting gives the first impression that parents, children and visitors gain of your work. A welcoming entrance with displays of children's work will contribute to giving a positive impression.

Good planning and presentation are essential

Planning displays

It is important to plan displays, thinking everything through first. Think about the position, appropriate colours, backing, drapes and borders. Good presentation is essential. This includes good mounting, backing and well-produced lettering. Staples and adhesive materials should be used discreetly.

The use of colour should be carefully considered. There are no rules – bright colours can be effective, but black and white may also be appropriate.

Mounting

Mounting involves putting children's work on to a background of card or paper to provide a framework. This can be a single or a double framework, and can enhance children's work. When you do this it is important to make sure that you cut the mount accurately. A cutting machine will help to make sure that the edges are straight and level.

Mounting children's work provides a framework

Backing

The backing and borders around a display should complement the children's work. Choose the background colour carefully and avoid fancy borders that will detract from the children's own work.

Labels and captions

Any labels and captions must be clear, of an appropriate size. Lower case letters should be used except at the beginning of sentences and proper nouns (people's names or place names). Include the home languages of the children in the setting. If labels and captions are hand-written they should be carefully printed; it is important to practise printing using guidelines to help you until you are confident enough to print free hand.

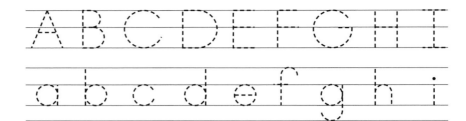

Practise printing using guidelines to help

What do you need to make a display?

It is always useful to keep all the things that are required to make a display altogether in a box. These items will be useful but can be added to:

- adhesive-tak (Blu-Tack or something similar)
- drawing pins (these must be used carefully to avoid accidents)
- craft knife (e.g. Stanley knife with a safety cap fitted)
- glue, glue sticks
- pencils
- rubbers (make sure they are of good quality)
- rulers and tape measures of different lengths
- a good selection of pens in different colours and sizes
- scissors, in a selection of different sizes
- tape, single and double sided
- spirit level.

Keep the toolbox out of the reach of the children.

Displaying work effectively

If the children are helping with the display, then rigorous supervision will be needed if they are using the tools.

Interest tables

Interest tables can be used to follow a theme, topic or to display work/collections from a recent outing. They should be at the child's height, and put in a quieter area of the setting. The table should be covered and any objects that are not intended to be touched should be placed in a protective container, such as a plastic tank.

Helping children to learn about the natural world is important. Seeing how things grow and develop is part of learning about the world. Children can collect and display natural objects such as leaves, plants and berries. Be aware of the dangers of poisonous plants. If you are in any doubt about anything you are going to use on a display use a good reference book to identify it. Put the items in a container that will prevent the children handling them. It is important to help the children to learn how to care for any plant or cut flowers and foliage. Regular watering and removing any dead leaves and flowers will ensure that the display remains fresh and attractive. Children should be supervised when examining plants and berries. They should be taught not to taste or put objects in their mouths. Reference books can be put out on the table. These will help children and adults find out more about the things on display.

Interest tables can be used to display collections

Adding interest to displays

Interest can be added by good use of:

- colour – a co-ordinated backing and border can be used to display the children's work to its best advantage
- texture – include things that are interesting to touch and contrast with each other, for example, smooth, shiny pebbles and rough sandpaper
- movement – consider hanging displays and objects that move
- sound – shakers and musical instruments made by the children
- familiar characters from books read at storytime
- people they have met on a trip or who have visited the setting.

Benefits to child development of display work

Creating work for displays and taking part in putting a display together will benefit all areas of the children's development and learning.

Area of development/learning	Skills
Physical, fine motor	Placing, cutting, sticking, drawing.
Physical, gross motor	Co-ordination, stretching, bending, balancing.
Cognitive	Thinking, problem solving, decision making, using memory.
Language and literacy	Discussion, negotiating, describing, communicating ideas, learning new vocabulary, developing writing.
Mathematics	Measuring, estimating, creating patterns, using shape, angles, working in three dimensions.
Personal, social and emotional	Team work, co-operation, sharing, concentration, pride in their environment, awareness of wider environment and society. Sense of achievement, increased self-esteem, appreciating an attractive environment.
Creative	Explore colour, shape and texture, use imagination, express ideas and use a variety of materials.

Element E1.2

Are you ready for assessment?

Prepare and maintain displays

You need to show that you can competently maintain a reassuring environment. To do this you will need to be directly observed by your assessor and present other types of evidence.

Direct observation by your assessor

Your assessor will need to see you carry out these performance criteria (PCs)

E1.2 PCs 1, 2, 3, 4, 5, 6, 8, 10

During these observations your assessor must see you cover at least ONE aspect of each range category listed in this element.

Remember the range categories for this element are:

1. Pictures and other visual displays
2. Positive images of people

Preparing to be observed

During your work with children you will be involved in preparing and maintaining displays, and it is important to keep a record of what you do as evidence. You could take a photograph of your displays or draw a diagram and write a description. Your assessor will need to see your display work and if possible see this in progress with the children involved in the preparation. Make sure that your displays use the children's work and that you display the work attractively. Labels should be neat, clear and suitable for the children's age and stage of development.

Read the performance criteria and range carefully before your assessment. Try to cover as much as you can.

Other types of evidence

You may need to present different types of evidence in order to:

- cover criteria not observed by your assessor
- show that you have the required knowledge, understanding and skills
- cover other parts of the range.

The amount and type of evidence you need to present will vary. You should plan this with your assessor.

Element E1.3 Maintain a reassuring environment

KUS
1, 2, 10

Feeling secure

Welcoming children into an attractive and thoughtfully arranged environment will help to reassure them and help them settle in. Child care settings should be geared to the needs of the children with child-sized equipment, attractive displays and a quiet, calm atmosphere. Cloakrooms, washbasins and lavatories should be easily accessible. If possible these fittings should be child-sized. This will promote security and growing independence. Providing a routine to the day will help children to feel secure. They will become familiar with the structure of the day and will become more confident, as they recognise familiar routines and begin to know where they fit in.

A sense of belonging

Children need to develop a sense of belonging. They will feel more at home in a setting that contains things that are personal, familiar to them and reflect their own experiences and culture.

Children will feel secure with familiar objects that reflect their own culture

- Each child should have a coat hook labelled with their name and perhaps a picture.

- Other equipment such as work trays, work books, bags and lunch boxes should be named.

- The imaginative play area should contain a range of equipment. A selection of different dolls should represent different facial features and skin tones, as well as male and female body parts. Cooking equipment and play food needs to reflect different cultural preferences.

- The dressing up clothes should be varied; hats, uniforms and different forms of dress should represent male, female and different cultures.

- The selection of books should show positive images of different races, cultures and sexes and reflect equality of opportunity.
- The displays should contain the children's work and reflect their interests.

Predicting and recognising common stages of fear and anxiety

It is common for babies and young children to develop fears and anxieties, and then change, as they grow older.

- Around the age of 6 months babies show a preference to be with their parent/ main carer and they begin to develop a fear of strangers.
- Babies can also develop fears of noisy objects, especially if they have been startled by them. Examples could include the vacuum cleaner or telephone.
- Between 1 and 2 years of age they may become frightened of things they previously enjoyed, for example, the bath or having their hair washed.
- By 3 or 4 years of age children begin to put themselves in the position of others. They can picture dangers that they have not actually experienced. It is common for young children to begin to develop imaginary fears and worries linked to their growing awareness of the world around them. These may include fear of the dark, dogs or other animals.

The effects of separation from their parent/ main carer on children's behaviour

Sudden change and separation, that is not handled well by adults, can have a powerful effect on children's behaviour.

- Babies and toddlers may protest by crying, screaming and other expressions of anger at being left. If their carer does not return they may become listless and refuse to play.
- Children aged 3–5 years may not want to play or explore their environment. They may become more demanding, unhappy and clingy.
- Children aged 5–7 years may go back (regress) in their behaviour to earlier, more childish behaviour. They may show stress by being overactive and unable to concentrate, or they may become quiet and withdraw.

Comforting children

Most children who are afraid will cry and seek comfort from a caring adult. Some fears are shown in more subtle ways and a child may show signs of being generally anxious. Children in an unfamiliar environment may react in a variety of ways. They may show their fears by crying, clinging to their parent/carer, being unwilling to try new experiences, loss of appetite and sleeping problems. As children cannot always tell the adult what is worrying them, the child care worker must try to identify the cause.

Dealing with the problem depends on the cause of the anxiety. Some children may need more reassurance than anticipated in certain situations, so it is important to know about any special methods for helping individual children. Listening to what parents and carers tell you about this will help. Generally children will respond positively to the following:

- A clear and honest explanation about what is going to happen. You may need to repeat these explanations, as young children may not remember or understand what you have said.
- A clear explanation of what has just happened, in the case of an unexpected incident.
- A reassuring cuddle – although some children may not appreciate physical comfort.
- Stress-reducing activities like playdough, looking at books and painting.
- Having their preferred comfort objects, such as a special blanket or soft toy. This is especially important for the under 2s. Young children should not be discouraged from having their preferred comfort objects as they help to bridge the gap between the home setting and the care environment. They also play an important part in helping children to become more confident and independent in new situations. Comfort objects should be readily available to children. It may be advisable to keep all comforters, labelled with the children's names, in a central place until they are needed. A list of comforters and particular remedies will be useful if this can be displayed where staff can see and readily refer to it.

Changes and unexpected events

Children can easily become unsettled and upset if there are changes to their routine or environment. This can be more upsetting if the changes are unexpected or not explained. It is important that children have advance warning of any changes that you know about. Child care workers can tell the children what is going to happen in simple and understandable terms. This will help to prevent anxiety. It is important that child care workers are positive and cheerful about any changes. This will be reassuring for the children. It will also be necessary to repeat and remind the children about what is going to happen.

One of the most upsetting changes for children can be when their child care worker leaves or is absent because of sickness or holiday. Whenever possible, children should be prepared for changes, but it is not possible to plan for unexpected events, so the children will need to be reassured and comforted if they become distressed.

Offering reassurance

Child care workers should be warm, caring and responsive. Children easily recognise those who value and appreciate their company, and those who have no real interest in them. The following points can help if you are not confident and will give positive messages to the children in your care.

- Be calm and try to speak softly.
- Maintain eye contact when speaking to children and try to get down to their eye level, sit with them or squat down to them if they are playing on the floor.
- Meet their needs quickly. Pick up the non-verbal clues and anticipate their needs. For example, the child hopping from one foot to another may need the toilet.
- Be ready to cuddle a young child who is unhappy or upset. On the other hand, never force physical comfort on a child who does not welcome it.
- Encourage conversation and give children time to speak. Ask open questions that will encourage a child to answer with more than a yes or no.

Are you ready for assessment?

Maintain a reassuring environment

You need to show that you can competently maintain a reassuring environment. To do this you will need to be directly observed by your assessor and present other types of evidence.

Direct observation by your assessor

Your assessor will need to see you carry out these performance criteria (PCs)

E1.3 PCs 4, 5, 6

During these observations your assessor must see you cover at least ONE aspect of each range category listed in this element.

Remember the range categories for this element are:

1. Environment
2. Children

Preparing to be observed

You will need to show your assessor that you know about any comfort objects that the children in your setting have and that they are readily available as appropriate to the child's stage of development and the parent's wishes. You should ensure that you provide items labelled for individual children, e.g. pegs, trays. Equipment and materials should reflect cultural diversity, so check the imaginative play area for different cooking utensils and the range of dressing up clothes. Use examples of other languages from the children's own backgrounds on displays and in the selection of books provided.

Read the performance criteria and range carefully before your assessment. Try to cover as much as you can. ▶▶

Other types of evidence

You may need to present different types of evidence in order to:

- cover criteria not observed by your assessor
- show that you have the required knowledge, understanding and skills
- cover other parts of the range.

The amount and type of evidence you need to present will vary. You should plan this with your assessor.

Check your knowledge

- What are the common stages of anxiety? **KUS 1**
- Describe the possible effects of separation on children's behaviour. **KUS 2**
- How can children be encouraged to take part in making decisions and taking responsibility? **KUS 6**
- Why is it important to arrange activities to meet the children's needs? **KUS 4**
- Why is it important to display children's work attractively? **KUS 15**

Maintain the safety and security of children

*T*his unit covers the important aspects of maintaining a safe and secure environment for children. It includes keeping children safe in the setting where they are cared for and also in some situations outside the setting, such as outings and visits. Candidates will need to show that they understand the importance of accident prevention and that they can meet the children's needs while keeping them safe. Candidates will also need to show that they understand the responsibility that adults have for keeping children safe and that they understand the role of the adult in helping the children to learn about safety. Dealing with accidents and injuries to children and keeping children safe from abuse is also part of this unit.

This unit contains five elements:

E2.1 Maintain a safe environment for children

E2.2 Maintain the supervision of children

E2.3 Carry out emergency procedures

E2.4 Cope with accidents and injuries to children

E2.5 Help protect children from abuse

E2.6 Maintain the safety of children on outings

Introduction

Child care workers should plan and create an environment that is caring, stimulating and safe. The resources and equipment provided should be suitable. Child care workers should be aware of possible dangers and always ensure the safety of the children.

Health and safety requirements

The Health and Safety at Work Act 1974

The Health and Safety at Work Act 1974 is the Act of Parliament that regulates health and safety in the workplace. Similar legislation is in force in Wales, Scotland and Northern Ireland.

National Standards for child care

National Standards and Regulations relating to the safety of children are included in legislation for England, Wales, Scotland and Northern Ireland. See appendix.

Maintain a safe environment for children

KUS
8, 9,
10, 11

Potential hazards

Potential hazards are possible dangers and threats to the children's safety. Many potential hazards are a normal part of everyday environments, for example, electric sockets and cleaning fluids. It is up to the child care worker to be aware of things that might be a danger to children and to know how to deal with them. For example, use socket covers and keep cleaning fluids well out of the children's reach, in a high or locked cupboard. The chart below gives other examples of how to cope with potential hazards.

Health and safety policies

All child care settings should have a health and safety policy that includes:

- clear safety rules for children's behaviour
- safety equipment, e.g. safety catches on doors and windows, non-slip surfaces, safety glass, safe gym equipment
- procedures for using equipment
- policies for dealing with spills of bodily fluids
- procedures for staff to report potential hazards
- clear rules to ensure that staff practise safely, for example, closing and fastening safety gates, reporting any damaged or defective equipment, keeping hot drinks away from children
- policies for collecting children.

Keeping children safe

Child care workers need to create a safe environment. They should identify potential hazards and take action to prevent accidents. Children are cared for in a range of settings and all of them have hazards. The chart on page 211 outlines some of the most common hazards that can be found in places where children are cared for.

Reporting hazards

There may be times when hazards should be reported to a supervisor or the health and safety officer. Unsafe or broken equipment should be immediately removed. Children should also be removed from any dangerous situation. It is important to check for any hazards in areas that are going to be used by the children, especially the outdoor play space. This is an area that may be used by other people who may create hazards for the children.

Area	Risk	Hazard	Prevention
Kitchen	Burns and scalds	Unguarded cooker Kettle left near the edge of the work-top Hot drinks and food	Use a cooker guard. Use a coiled kettle flex, push the kettle to the back of the work-top. Never leave a hot drink within a child's reach. Don't use a cloth on a kitchen table. Children may pull the cloth and hot food or drinks on to them.
	Cuts	Knives and scissors left out and within reach	Store knives and scissors in a drawer well out of reach.
	Poisoning	Medicines and cleaning fluids left where a child can reach them	Lock medicines in a cupboard. Store cleaning fluids in a high cupboard well out of reach.
	Choking	Small objects left where a baby can reach them. Babies feeding from a bottle or eating other food without supervision	Keep small objects away from babies. Always supervise mealtimes. Do not leave a baby with a bottle to feed herself. Ensure food is cut up appropriately for small children.
	Falls	Falls from baby chairs and high chairs	Never put baby chairs on a worktop. Always ensure that a proper harness is used for babies in high chairs.
Lounge / living areas	Burns	Fires left unguarded	Ensure that there is a properly fitted fireguard.
		Unattended cigarettes	Do not allow smoking in the same room as babies and children.
	Electrocution	Uncovered plug sockets, televisions, videos	Use socket covers, make sure televisions and videos are out of reach. Teach children not to touch.
	Cuts and falls	Glass in coffee tables. Glass in low windows or the bottom of doors	Remove glass-topped tables, cover any low window or door glass with protective film or use safety glass.
Hallway/ stairs	Falls	Child unattended No stair-gate	Supervise children when using the stairs. Ensure there is a stair-gate at the top and bottom of the stairs and that it is in place at all times.
Bathroom	Drowning	Children allowed to bath themselves	Supervise children at all times.
	Scalds	Bath water too hot	Always put cold water into the bath first and test the temperature before putting a baby into the bath.
	Poisoning	Medicines and toiletries left in the child's reach and eaten or drunk	Store medicines and toiletries in a high, wall-mounted cabinet.

Area	Risk	Hazard	Prevention
Bedrooms	Falls	Children unattended may fall from a window or furniture	Fit and use window locks on upstairs windows. Keep furniture away from windows to avoid climbing. Do not use bunk beds for children under 7.
	Burns	Flammable night-wear/ bedding	All bedding and night-clothes must be fire retardant.
Garden	Falls	Falls from climbing equipment, unattended ladders, trees	Supervise the children in the garden. Use soft surfaces under climbing equipment, ensure that all other gardening equipment is locked away.
	Drowning	Children falling into ponds or swimming pools	Supervise children, fence off or cover ponds. Teach children to swim.
	Road traffic accident, getting lost	Children wander off or go out of the garden with other friends	Ensure that the outside gates are locked and that the children cannot undo them.
	Poisoning	Children eat plants, berries, seeds and nuts that they find	Check the garden for poisonous plants and if possible remove them. Teach them not to eat things they find without permission.
Garages/ sheds	Poisoning electrocution	Drinking or eating garden chemicals. Playing with lawnmowers and other garden equipment	Ensure that sheds and garages are always kept locked. Always supervise and know where the children are.

What to check before using the outdoor play space

- Are the gates securely locked and the boundary fences secure?
- Can strangers come into contact with the children?
- Are there any litterbins and are they properly covered?
- Is the area clear of rubbish, poisonous plants, broken glass, dog or cat faeces?
- Is there any risk from water?
- Are there any items or equipment left about that could cause accidents?
- Is the play equipment properly assembled and checked for defects?
- Are the surfaces suitable for the play equipment?
- Are any mats required in place?
- Is the number of staff supervising the children adequate?

Safety equipment

Using safety equipment can avoid some common hazards. Accidents often happen because simple safety precautions were ignored or the safety equipment was not used properly. Any safety equipment used should be fit for its purpose. It is possible to find this out by checking that safety equipment has a safety mark on the label. The labels will show that toys and other equipment, such as prams and cots, are safe and that they are suitable for the age group shown. It is very important to check for the safety mark before buying equipment or toys.

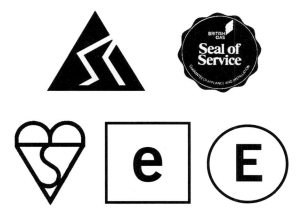

Safety marks

Safety equipment	Use
Harnesses, reins	To prevent falls from prams, pushchairs and high chairs. To stop children running into the road. Harnesses and reins should be purchased with the pram etc.
Safety gates	To prevent access to kitchens, stairways, outside. Always guard the top and bottom of stairways.
Locks for cupboards and windows	To prevent children getting hold of dangerous substances or falling from windows.
Safety glass/safety film	Prevents glass from breaking into pieces that would cause injuries.
Socket covers	Prevent children poking their fingers or other objects into electric sockets.
Play pens	Create a safe area for babies.
Smoke alarm	Detects smoke and sounds the alarm.
Cooker guard	Prevents children pulling pans from the cooker.
Corner covers	Protects children from sharp edges on furniture.
Fire-fighting equipment, such as a fire extinguisher, fire blanket	May be used to tackle *minor* fires.

Supervision

Safety equipment can be a useful and practical aid to ensuring children's safety. However, this is no substitute for close supervision. It is always important to know where children are and what they are doing. The level of supervision needed will vary according to the age of the child and what they are doing. In general, the younger the child the more careful the supervision will need to be. As children get older they understand more. It is very important that they are taught about safety and why rules that keep them safe have to be followed.

Always check the apparatus and supervise the children

Providing a good role model

Children are great imitators but they will learn and copy both good and poor behaviour. It is very important that adults always follow the safety rules and never compromise their own safety. This is especially important where road safety is involved. Always set a good example. Talk to children about road safety and use the Green Cross Code yourself. If there is a controlled crossing, use it and don't be tempted to cross at a red light even if the road appears clear.

Preventing infection

Infections like coughs, colds and tummy upsets can be passed from one person to another. This is very likely to happen in places where children are cared for in groups where they have close contact with each other. Teach children the basic rules of hygiene like washing their hands after visiting the toilet and before eating. This will help to prevent germs being spread. There is more information about this in unit C1.

Checking and maintaining toys and equipment

All places where children are cared for will have a routine for cleaning and inspecting equipment.

Any equipment should be used correctly. It is important to follow any instructions provided by the manufacturer for its safe use. In addition there will be directions for proper care and maintenance. Cleaning toys and equipment provides a good opportunity to check for defects and signs of wear. This can then be reported and the item removed.

Cleaning toys and equipment is important to ensure good standards of hygiene and to prevent infections spreading. Feeding equipment and toys used by babies should be cleaned each time they are used (see unit C13). Any toys that are regularly handled should be cleaned each day using soapy water or a disinfectant solution. Surfaces also need to be cleaned, at least daily, using a suitable anti-bacterial cleaner.

Most settings will have a routine for cleaning. This will include washing floors, bathrooms and toilets, kitchens, vacuuming and cleaning carpets. Cleaning staff may well do major cleaning jobs, such as the daily washing of floors, emptying the waste bins and cleaning the windows.

Disposing of waste materials

All child care settings should have a health and safety policy that tells staff how to dispose of hazardous waste. Care must be taken with all bodily waste (blood, faeces, urine and saliva) to prevent infections.

The following guidelines should be followed when handling and disposing of waste materials:

- cover any skin cuts or grazes with a waterproof dressing
- wear disposable latex gloves when dealing with bodily waste
- cover blood with a 1% hypoclorite solution, such as bleach before wiping up spills
- wash hands with an antiseptic soap
- dispose of nappies, dressings and used gloves in a sealed bag and place this in a sealed bin for burning
- provide covered bins for different types of waste.

Security in establishments

Child care establishments have strict security measures:

- Doors and gates that lead to the outside or to areas where children are not allowed must have a suitable lock. The lock must be well out of the reach of the children. All the adults in the setting must make sure that the locks are used at all times.

- Fire exits must be checked to see that they are not locked or blocked with equipment.
- Window locks must be fitted and used.
- Name badges must be worn by all staff and students.
- Door entry phones and bells must be installed. These will give the staff the opportunity to enquire about the nature of the business of any visitors before letting them enter the building.
- Outdoor playtimes are supervised.

Element E2.1 Are you ready for assessment?

Maintain a safe environment for children

How to present evidence that you can competently maintain a safe environment for children.

Direct observation by your assessor

Your assessor will need to see you carry out these performance criteria (PCs)

E2.1 1, 3, 4, 7, 8, 9, 10

During these observations your assessor must see you cover at least ONE aspect in each range category listed in this element.

Remember the range category for this element is:

1. Doors, gates and windows

Preparing to be observed

You will need to show your assessor that you can maintain and clean equipment. This is often done as the equipment is put out and put away. Make sure that, as you use any equipment, you follow any instructions and guidance provided. Your assessor will need to see that you can safely dispose of waste materials, so make sure that you know how to wrap waste and which bins are used for different types of waste. Be sure that you wear the gloves and any protective clothing provided. Your assessor will need to see that you work in a safe way so make sure that you pay attention to the locks on doors and windows. Be ready to act if you can see a hazard to the children's safety.

Read the performance criteria and range carefully before your assessment. Make sure that you cover as much as you can. ▶▶

Other types of evidence

You may need to present different types of evidence in order to:

- cover criteria not observed by your assessor
- show that you have the required knowledge, understanding and skills
- cover other parts of the range.

The amount and type of evidence you need to present will vary. You should plan this with your assessor.

Element E2.2 *Maintain the supervision of children*

KUS
1, 12, 13

Supervision

The number of adults required to care for children in day care is regulated by National Standards and Regulations for each of the four countries in the United Kingdom (see appendix). For example, the National Standards for Under Eight's Day Care and Child Minding (2001) regulates the number of adults required to care for the children in England. This is also related to the age of the child. These figures are described as ratios. See the table below.

The number of children who can be cared for by one adult in these age groups in full day care is:

Children under 2 years	*1 adult to 3 children*
Children aged 2 years	*1 adult to 4 children*
Children aged 3–7 years	*1 adult to 8 children*

These numbers are the minimum requirements. You would expect to have fewer children per adult if some of the children had special needs. Children also need to get out and about to enjoy local outings to the shops or park. You would need more adults in these circumstances. Different ratios apply to childminders and these are also described in the National Standards.

The adult–child ratios relate to staff available to work directly with the children. Suitable arrangements must be made to cover unexpected emergencies and staff absences. There should be enough staff to cover breaks, holidays and time spent with parents. All this will need careful planning by the management to make sure that the ratios are kept up and the children's safety ensured.

The adult role

Having the adults there is only the beginning of good supervision. Adults must be alert and aware of what the children are doing. Supervising the children well makes sure that they remain safe but also lets them try out new and more challenging activities. Child care workers must always be aware of potential hazards (see element E2.1 above). Then they can see any possible dangers for the children, before there is an accident, and take action to stop this happening. However, children do need to learn to do new things and to become more independent, so it is important not to limit the children to activities that are too easy. For example, you may need to supervise a child more closely if they are trying out their climbing skills on more difficult climbing apparatus or using the woodwork tools.

All settings will have safety rules and the adults must make sure that children follow the rules. However, it is also very important to explain to the children why there are rules and how the rules will help to keep them safe as they play and learn. For example, child care workers can explain the safety rules to the children before they use the apparatus. They must also explain the rules again during the activities if the children are not playing safely. Always explain why the child is in danger or putting others in danger.

Children will be able to play safely as they begin to understand about the dangers that are around them. However this awareness takes time to develop and all children will always need supervising as they play. Younger children and babies, because of their stage of development, will be less aware of dangers and will require greater supervision.

Children and adults can make a list of the safety rules together. This can give the children a chance to talk about what is safe behaviour and what is not. Make sure the list is not too long and that it includes the most important points. Examples that the children might suggest could be:

- no running indoors
- no pushing, shouting or fighting
- no walking around with scissors.

Include some positive rules such as:

- let everyone take turns
- always fetch an adult if someone is hurt or crying
- sit down when having a drink.

Home times

Child care workers must ensure children's safety at home times. Most settings have a policy that only allows children to be collected by a named adult. Parents should inform staff about who will be collecting the child if they cannot do so themselves. Every setting should have a procedure for collecting children.

Playground rules

Collecting Laurie

**KUS
13**

Laurie's mum, Wendy, came to the nursery today to collect him. She asked to speak to Janice who is in charge. She explained that she would not be able to collect Laurie herself the next week, as she would be delayed at work. She said that Laurie's granny would come and fetch him. Janice explained that there would be several things that Wendy needed to do to make sure that the staff at the nursery could be certain that it was his Granny collecting Laurie.

➤ *What arrangements do you think Janice could make with Wendy to ensure that Laurie was safely collected?* **KUS 13**

Element E2.2

Are you ready for assessment?

Maintain the supervision of children

How to present evidence that you can competently maintain the supervision of children.

Direct observation by your assessor

Your assessor will need to see you carry out these performance criteria (PCs)

E2.2 1, 2, 3, 4, 5, 6, 7, 8

During these observations your assessor must see you cover at least ONE aspect in each range category listed in this element.

Remember the range category for this element is:

1. Children

Preparing to be observed

Your assessor will need to see you supervising the children during their usual activities. Make sure that you can tell your assessor how many adults there should be for the number and age of the children. As you supervise the children you will need to make sure that the children are safe. You should explain any safety rules to them. Help them as they attempt more difficult things, perhaps in their physical play, while still making sure that they are safe. When the children are collected check carefully that you know about and follow the policy of your setting.

Other types of evidence

You may need to present different types of evidence in order to:

- cover criteria not observed by your assessor
- show that you have the required knowledge, understanding and skills
- cover other parts of the range.

The amount and type of evidence you need to present will vary. You should plan this with your assessor.

E2.3 *Carry out emergency procedures*

KUS
14, 15, 16

Emergency procedures

All establishments should have:

- written emergency procedures
- staff who have been trained in first aid
- first aid equipment
- an accident book for accurate recording of all incidents requiring first aid
- regular review of incidents of accidents to highlight areas of concern.

Evacuation and fire procedures

Evacuation and fire procedures must be clearly displayed and pointed out to anyone who comes into the building. Law requires regular practices. All staff must be familiar with evacuation procedures. A fire officer will make regular checks.

Part of the introduction to your setting will include an explanation of the emergency procedures. Any visitors to the setting, such as parents staying with their children, will be shown the procedure for evacuating the setting if there is a fire or other emergency. Emergencies other than fire could involve a gas escape, electricity failure or leaking water. These procedures should be displayed in every room where everyone can see and read them. They should be simple, easy to follow and if necessary have a plan to show more clearly where the fire exits are positioned. *Fire exits must never be locked or blocked by furniture or any other equipment.*

Important things that must be included in emergency procedures:

- A reminder that the alarm should be sounded.
- A clear statement or plan to show where the assembly points and fire exits are located.
- The route to follow to get out of the building.
- The way to call for help, e.g. where the nearest telephone outside the building is located.
- A reminder *not* to go back into the building.
- The name of the person responsible for the procedure and collecting the registers and parents' contact numbers.

Children should leave the building by the quickest route. This will be shown on the evacuation procedure. It is important that someone is responsible for taking a register outside. An accurate count can then be done as soon as the children and staff get to the assembly point. The first thing the emergency services will want to know when they arrive is if anyone is still in the building. As well as the register it is important to have a record of the parents' contact numbers. These need to be kept close to the register or actually written in the register.

Regular practices, to make sure that all staff and children know how to leave the building quickly and safely, should be done. It is then the responsibility of the staff to look carefully at how well the practice was done. They can then decide if any changes need to be made to make the procedure safer and quicker in the future.

If you work in a home setting you will be required to work out an evacuation procedure for each room in your home. You will need to practise leaving the building and to keep records of these practices.

Fire-fighting equipment

Settings will have fire-fighting equipment; it is important to know where any fire blankets, fire extinguishers and other equipment are kept and how to use them safely. There are different kinds of fire extinguishers that are used for different kinds of fires. It is important that you have been fully informed about the fire-fighting equipment before you attempt to use it. Never put yourself at risk by attempting to put out a fire. It is much better to sound the fire alarm and evacuate the building safely.

**Fire-fighting
equipment**

Fire extinguishers

To burn, a fire needs:

- fuel, anything that will burn
- oxygen
- heat.

Fire extinguishers work in the following ways:

- A fire blanket is good for smothering a fire so that no oxygen can get to it.
- Water or special foam is used to cool a fire.

There are different types of fire extinguishers. It is important that you know what kind of fire they can be used for. For example, fire extinguishers containing water must not be used on fires involving electrical equipment. There are special extinguishers that can be used for these fires. Suitable fire-fighting equipment should be placed near any potential fire hazard. For example, a fire blanket would be most useful in a kitchen.

Practising the evacuation procedure

Discussing the evacuation procedure and explaining what will happen will help to make the practice go more smoothly. The children will also need time to talk about the practice afterwards. Parents need to be aware of any fire practices. They can also talk this over with their children at home. Stories about fire fighters and fire engines will help the children to talk about any worries they may have. Successful practices that have gone smoothly will mean that there is a good chance that all will be well in a real emergency.

A record must be kept of each practice and the staff should discuss how well the practice went. Changes should be made to the procedure if there are any difficulties, or if staff can see how to make the procedure work better to ensure the children's safety. It is also very important to have practices that take place without any prior warning so that staff and children can respond as they would in a real emergency.

Responding in a calm and reassuring way

A real emergency that leads to an evacuation of the setting will be a worrying and frightening experience for the adults and children. However, it is important to stay calm and to reassure the children by talking to them, while carrying out the evacuation procedure as quickly and safely as possible. Give clear and positive instructions in a clear, calm voice. It will help if you and the children have practised what you need to do.

Element E2.3 — Are you ready for assessment?

Carry out emergency procedures/ Maintain the supervision of children

You need to show that you can competently carry out emergency procedures and maintain the supervision of children. You will need to be directly observed by your assessor and present other types of evidence.

Direct observation by your assessor

Your assessor will need to see you carry out these performance criteria (PCs)

E2.3 PCs 2, 3, 4, 7

During these observations your assessor must see you cover at least ONE aspect of each range category listed in this element.

Remember the range categories for this element are:

1. Emergencies
2. Equipment

Preparing to be observed

You will need to make sure that you know all about the emergency procedures for your setting. Be ready to show your assessor where the information about how to evacuate the building is displayed and be familiar with what you would be expected to do. Find out where all the fire-fighting equipment is located and be sure that you know how it can be used and for what kind of fire. You will need to show your assessor where the registers and the information needed to contact the parents are kept. Show your assessor the records of previous practices at your setting, including the discussions and comments about the practices and any action taken.

Read the performance criteria and range carefully before your assessment to be sure that you cover as much as you can.

Other types of evidence

You may need to present different types of evidence in order to:
- cover criteria not observed by your assessor
- show that you have the required knowledge, understanding and skills
- cover other parts of the range.

The amount and type of evidence you need to present will vary. You should plan this with your assessor.

Cope with accidents and injuries to children

KUS
2, 18, 19

What follows is an outline of basic first aid for children; it is not intended to replace a recognised training in first aid. It is important that all child care workers undertake recognised training in first aid so that they can act confidently and safely in the event of an accident. The British Red Cross and St John Ambulance run recognised first aid courses in most areas. A recognised first aid certificate will provide evidence for this element.

First aid box

All establishments and homes should have a first aid box. The first aid box should be clearly labelled and put in a dry place, where the children cannot reach it. All the staff should know where the first aid box is kept and it should be in a place where it can be easily and quickly reached in an emergency. The first aid box may contain all the items shown in the illustration below. There should be a list of the contents kept in the box.

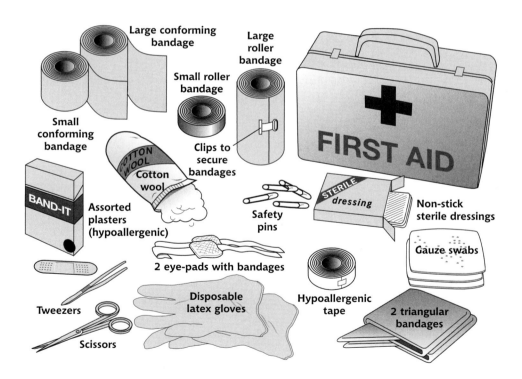

The contents of a first aid box

It is very important that the contents of the first aid box are checked. Things that have been used must be replaced at once as people using the first aid box will be relying on everything being there. Most settings will have a designated member of staff responsible for first aid. There should be a foolproof system for checking and replacing first aid items as they are used.

First aid in emergencies

First aid aims to:

- **p**reserve life
- **p**revent the worsening of the condition
- **p**romote recovery.

It is important to remain calm in any emergency situation. If you are the first person on the scene you should do the following:

- *Assess the situation.* Find out how many children are injured and whether there is any continuing danger. Are there any other adults who can help? Is an ambulance required?
- *Put safety first.* Include the safety of all children and adults, including yourself. Remove any dangerous hazards; move the injured child only if it is absolutely essential.
- *Prioritise.* Treat the most serious injuries first. Conditions that are immediately life threatening in children are:
  - *not* breathing
  - severe bleeding.
- *Get help.* Shout for help or ask others to get help and call an ambulance. If you are not trained to give emergency aid you should concentrate on getting help as quickly as possible. When the trained first aider arrives she will take charge, so follow instructions carefully.

If you are told to telephone for an ambulance:

- dial 999
- ask for the ambulance service
- answer the questions that you will be asked accurately and clearly
- know the telephone number from which you are calling
- know the exact place of the accident
- give the details of the accident and what you know about any injuries
- do not put the phone down until you have given all the information requested.

Examining a casualty

Find out if the child is *conscious* or *unconscious*:

- Check for response – call the child's name, pinch the skin.
- Open the airway and check for breathing.
- Check the pulse.

How to manage an unconscious child who is breathing

An unconscious child who is breathing and has a pulse should be put into the recovery position (shown below). This will keep the airway clear. Keep checking the airway and pulse until medical help arrives.

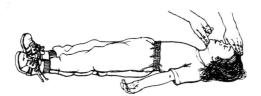

1 Lay the child on their back
Tilt the head back
Lift the chin forward
Ensure the airway is clear

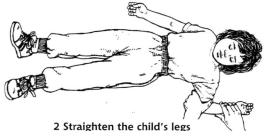

2 Straighten the child's legs
Bend the arm nearest to you at a right angle

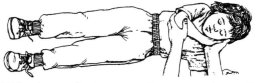

3 Take the arm furthest away from you and move it across the child's chest; bend it and place it on the cheek

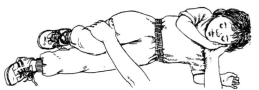

4 Keep the inside leg straight
Place the foot flat on the ground
Clasp under the thigh of the outside leg and bend it at the knee

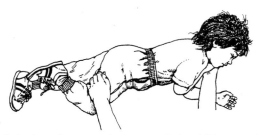

5 Pull the bent leg towards you to roll the child on to their side
Use the knees to stop the child rolling on to their front
Keep hand against the cheek

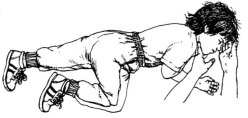

6 Bend top leg into a right angle to prevent the child rolling forward
Tilt the head back to keep the airway open
Adjust hand under the child's cheek

The recovery position

How to manage an unconscious child who is *not* breathing

If a child is *unconscious* and *not breathing* the heartbeat will slow down and eventually stop.

Follow the *ABC of resuscitation*.

The ABC of resuscitation

A: Unblock the **a**irway.

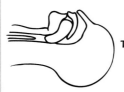

BLOCKED AIRWAY
Head is not tilted
Tongue has fallen back
Airway is blocked

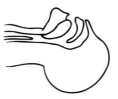

UNBLOCKED AIRWAY
Head is tilted
Tongue is forward
Airway is unblocked

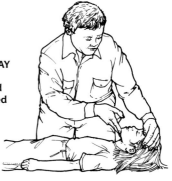

B: **B**reathe for the casualty.

Breathe into the baby's
mouth and nose

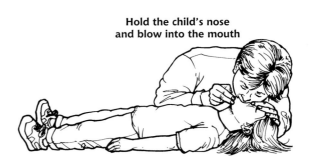

Hold the child's nose
and blow into the mouth

C: Maintain the **c**irculation.

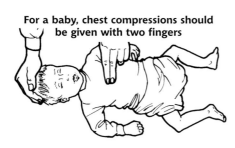

For a baby, chest compressions should
be given with two fingers

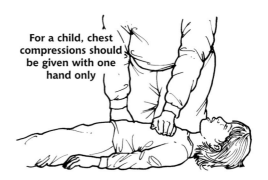

For a child, chest
compressions should
be given with one
hand only

(NB: You will need to have undertaken a recognised first aid course to be able to do this.)

First aid for minor injuries

It is essential to remain calm when dealing with an injured child. They need to be reassured that they are in safe hands and everything will be all right.

Burns and scalds

Immerse the burnt area in cold water for at least 10 minutes. Avoid touching the burn or any blisters. Cover with a clean cloth such as a tea towel and seek medical aid.

Bleeding

Minor bleeding wounds should be cleaned and covered with a dressing.
Major bleeds must be stopped:

- send for help immediately
- apply direct pressure to the wound and raise the injured part.

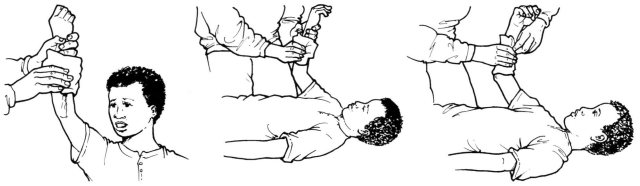

1 Apply pressure to the wound and raise the injured part

2 Lay the child down, while continuing to apply pressure and keep the injured part raised

3 Keeping the injured part raised cover the wound with a firm, sterile dressing and a bandage

Dealing with bleeding

Nose bleeds

Sit the child leaning forwards and pinch the soft part of the nose above the nostrils for 10 minutes.

Managing a nose bleed

Remember that you should always wear gloves when dealing with blood or any other body fluids. This will protect you from infection.

Splinters

Children may get splinters of wood from rough wooden objects so check equipment carefully.

If the splinter is sticking out from the shin, for example, it may be possible to remove it using a pair of tweezers. The wound should be cleaned carefully.

If the splinter is deeply embedded medical aid will be needed.

Check to make sure the child's tetanus immunisation is up to date.

Sprains

Raise and support the injured limb to minimise swelling. Remove shoe and sock if it is a sprained ankle. Apply a cold compress – a polythene bag of ice or a pack of frozen peas would do. Keep the limb raised.

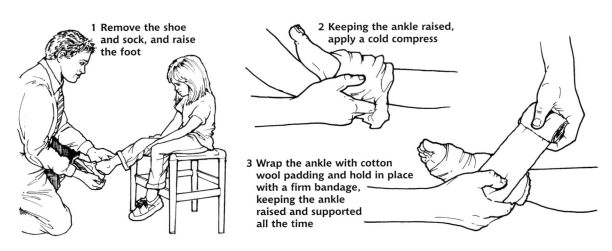

1 Remove the shoe and sock, and raise the foot

2 Keeping the ankle raised, apply a cold compress

3 Wrap the ankle with cotton wool padding and hold in place with a firm bandage, keeping the ankle raised and supported all the time

A sprained ankle

Things in noses or ears

Children who have poked anything into their nose or ears should be taken to the nearest Accident and Emergency Department. The object will be safely removed.

Choking

If you are dealing with a young child, put the child over your knee, head down, then:

- send for help immediately
- slap sharply between the shoulder blades up to five times
- check to see if the object has become dislodged and is in the mouth
- if the object cannot be removed, call for medical aid – take the child to the phone with you if you are alone

- check ABC (see page 228)
- try the back slaps again until help arrives or the object can be removed.

Poisoning

Eating poisonous plants or medicines, swallowing bleach or cleaning fluids are all serious situations. In such a case:

- send for help immediately
- check to see if the child is breathing and conscious
- put into the recovery position if unconscious
- take any samples of what has been eaten or drunk to the hospital with the child.

Asthma

Asthma attacks are very frightening for children. The airways go into spasm, making breathing difficult.

Management of an asthma attack

- Reassure the child.
- Sit the child upright and leaning forward against a support, such as a table, supporting themselves with their hands in any comfortable position.
- Stay with the child.
- Give the child their inhaler if they are known asthmatics.
- Continue to comfort and reassure.
- If the condition persists, call for an ambulance and contact parents.

When to call an ambulance

Call an ambulance immediately or get someone else to do so if:

- this is the child's first asthma attack
- the above steps have been taken and there is no improvement in 5–10 minutes.

Cuts and grazes

Any cut or graze that breaks the skin will mean that there is a risk of infection:

- Sit the child down and comfort them.
- Explain what you are going to do.
- Wash your hands.
- Put on gloves.
- Gently clean the graze or cut using clean water and a gauze pad (do not use cotton wool or any fluffy material that could stick to the wound).
- Cover the cut or graze with a pad and a light bandage.

- Put all the soiled material and gloves into a sealed bag for disposal.
- Wash your hands thoroughly.
- Some settings may use plasters but this is risky as many children are allergic to them. It is best to use special plasters (hypo-allergenic) that are specially made to avoid allergic reactions.

Maintaining standards of hygiene when dealing with accidents and emergencies

When dealing with accidents and injuries it is important to make sure that you protect yourself and the injured child from infection.

Always:

- wear protective clothing, such as gloves and aprons
- wash your hands before and after attending to an injury, even if you wear gloves
- make sure that anyone helping you also wears protective clothing and washes their hands
- avoid touching the cut or graze or the dressing that will touch the cut (don't let the child or anyone else touch either)
- avoid coughing or sneezing over the injury by you or others
- clean up carefully and get rid of any dirty dressings or other material by sealing in a marked plastic bag for disposal, preferably by burning
- clean up spills, of blood, urine or other bodily waste, carefully – wear gloves and use a solution of bleach (one teaspoon to a $\frac{1}{2}$ litre of water) to clean surfaces
- dispose of the waste from cleaning up by sealing in a marked plastic bag, as above.

Recording accidents, injuries and other incidents

All settings will have a way of recording any accidents, injuries and other incidents, often in a special book (the accident book). All accidents, injuries and incidents, however small or minor, must be recorded as soon as possible. This information should be shared with parents so that they are fully aware of what has happened. It may be that a child who has had a minor accident at nursery and seems fine, will become ill later in the day, or during the night.

The records should include:

- the full name of the child
- the date and time of the accident
- the exact details of the accident and any injury
- who was involved

- what treatment was given
- who was informed
- what action was taken
- the signature of the member of staff dealing with the accident.

Accident books should be kept for at least 3 years.

Settings will usually ask the parents to sign the book to show that they have read the details.

Informing parents

If an accident is serious the parents should be contacted immediately. This is usually the responsibility of the senior member of staff or person in charge. If the child has to go to hospital then the parent will need to go with them, or meet the ambulance there if this is a quicker option. Parents will need to be involved in any decision about their child's treatment so it is very important to be able to contact parents as quickly as possible. Parents' contact telephone numbers must be kept up to date. When speaking to a parent about an accident involving their child staff must be able to give clear, accurate information about what has happened and about what is to happen next.

More minor accidents are usually reported to parents when they collect their children at the end of the session. Parents may well be upset about accidents, however minor. It is very important to keep accurate records so that you can give parents clear information about what has happened and what was done. Parents will need time to talk about this, perhaps more than once. They may need to talk over their worries about what has happened with the person in charge.

Children's reactions to accidents and emergencies

After any accident children may be upset and crying. This is often because they have been frightened by what has happened. They may have injuries that need treatment and it is important to get help and to treat any injuries. However, it is also very important to comfort and reassure children after an accident. Take care not to blame children for accidents. It may well be that they were acting in a dangerous way but save the discussions about this for later. The important thing to do immediately is to sit with the child and talk to them while they recover. Children may want a particular comfort object, such as a toy. Try to fetch this or ask someone else to get it for the child as soon as you can. Children may also ask for a parent. The decision to send for a parent will depend on what has happened and how the child recovers.

Other children, who were not directly involved in the accident, may also be upset. They may be worried about a friend who has been hurt. Try to give simple explanations about what has happened and help the children to settle back into their normal activities. There should be a time later for the children and adults to talk about what has happened.

Element E2.4

Are you ready for assessment?

Cope with accidents and injuries to children

You will need to show that you can competently cope with accidents and injuries to children. You will need to be directly observed by your assessor and present other types of evidence.

Direct observation by your assessor

Your assessor will need to see you carry out these performance criteria (PCs)

E2.4 PCs 1, 2, 7

During these observations your assessor will need to see you cover at least ONE aspect of each range category listed in this element.

Remember the range categories for this element are:

1. Accidents
2. Type of attention

Preparing to be observed

You will need to show your assessor where the first aid box is, how you check that the contents are all in place and how this is recorded. Be ready to show your assessor how you would make sure that any missing items are replaced and how this is done following the policy of the setting.

Show your assessor the accident book and an actual entry completed by you.

Read the performance criteria and range carefully before your assessment. Make sure that you cover as much as you can.

Other types of evidence

You may need to present different types of evidence in order to:
- cover criteria not observed by your assessor
- show that you have the required knowledge, understanding and skills
- cover other parts of the range.

The amount and type of evidence you need to present will vary. You should plan this with your assessor.

E2.5 *Help protect children from abuse*

KUS
3, 4, 5, 18,
19, 24, 25,
26, 27, 28

Child protection

Children of all ages, male and female, from all cultures and all social and economic groups, can be the victims of abuse. Abuse includes:

- the deliberate harming of children, physically, sexually or emotionally
- the neglect of children's basic needs.

There are laws that aim to protect children from harm in any setting. In England this is the Children Act 1989. Wales, Scotland and Northern Ireland have their own laws (see appendix).

All those who work with children must put the interests and welfare of children first and protect them from harm. To be able to do this, a child care worker must know:

- the signs and symptoms of the different forms of abuse
- how these signs might show themselves in everyday situations
- what to do if they suspect abuse, including following the policies of their setting, the observation and recording of possible signs of abuse, and reporting these signs accurately and appropriately.

Types of abuse

The four main types of abuse are:

- physical abuse and injury
- neglect
- emotional abuse
- sexual abuse.

Physical abuse and injury

Physical abuse involves someone deliberately harming or hurting a child physically. It includes hitting, shaking, throwing, biting, squeezing, burning, scalding, attempted suffocation, drowning and giving children poisonous substances. This includes giving a child inappropriate drugs or alcohol. It includes the use of excessive force when punishing children or when carrying out tasks like feeding or nappy changing.

Signs of physical abuse

Bruises are a common sign of physical abuse. Where the bruises are on the body is important. Bruises on the cheeks, eyes, chest, back and shoulders are more likely to have been caused deliberately. Frequent bruising or bruises that are in a pattern may also be an indicator of abuse. Bruises resulting from deliberate injuries may be in the shape of fingertips, hands or other implements.

Bruising on the legs, below the knees, and arms, below the elbows, often occurs accidentally as a result of physical play.

Other possible physical signs of abuse include the following:

- Unexplained marks such as bites, outlines of weapons, nail marks, scratches and cuts, burns (particularly from cigarettes), scalds, certain fractures, internal damage and poisoning.

- Signs of head injury. These signs may include irritability, drowsiness, headache, vomiting or head enlargement. Medical attention is needed urgently. Head injury can result in brain damage, blindness, coma and death. Shaking a child or injuring the head can result in a subdural haematoma (bleeding into the brain).

- A torn frenulum in a young child (the frenulum is the web of skin joining the top gum and the lip). This usually results from something being forcibly pushed into the mouth, such as a spoon, bottle or dummy. It hardly ever occurs in ordinary accidents.

Blue spots

Blue spots (sometimes called Mongolian spots) are smooth, bluish grey to purple skin patches, often quite large. They are sometimes seen across the bottom of the spine or buttocks of infants of young children of Asian, Southern European and African descent. It is very important that Mongolian spots are *not* confused with bruises or seen as a sign of abuse. Children are born with them; they may disappear as the child gets older.

Behavioural indicators of physical abuse

Significant changes in a child's behaviour might show that a child is being abused. These may include:

- clinging, being withdrawn, aggressive behaviour, 'acting out' behaviour in role play
- developing learning difficulties including a lack of concentration
- having an inability to enjoy life
- showing symptoms of stress, for example, regression including wetting, tantrums, strange behaviour, eating problems. Abused children often appear sad, preoccupied and listless.

Effects of physical abuse

Children's development is likely to be affected if they live in a family where violence, aggression and conflict take place. Children's reactions to abuse vary. Their reactions may often be observed in their behaviour. Physical abuse can affect all aspects of children's development. It may:

- lead to physical injuries, brain damage, disability and death
- be linked to aggressive behaviour, emotional and behavioural problems and educational difficulties
- cause long-term damage to a child's self-esteem and this may last into adult life.

Neglect

Neglect involves failing to meet the basic needs of a child over a period of time and not protecting their health, safety and well-being. It involves failing to meet children's need for adequate food, clothing, warmth, medical care, hygiene, sleep, rest, fresh air and exercise. It also includes failing to protect children, for example, leaving young children alone and unsupervised.

Signs of physical neglect

- Constant hunger, a large appetite, large abdomen, too fat or too thin, failure to thrive. Inadequate, dirty clothing, inappropriate for the weather.
- Constant ill-health, untreated medical conditions, long-term nappy rash, repeated stomach upsets and diarrhoea.
- Uncared-for appearance, poor personal hygiene, dull matted hair, wrinkled skin, dirt in skin folds.
- Learning difficulties or poor social relationships, aggression or withdrawal.
- Constant tiredness or sleepiness.
- Frequent lateness or non-attendance at nursery or school.
- Repeated accidental injuries.

Effects of physical neglect

- Severe neglect affects health, physical growth and development. The term 'failure to thrive' is used to describe children who fail to grow normally. Growth charts (percentile charts) are used to record and assess such children. It can result in death.
- Children may find social relationships difficult and their educational progress can be limited. Children who are neglected are more likely to be victims of other forms of abuse.

Bruises are a common sign of physical abuse and may be in the shape of fingertips

Emotional abuse

Emotional abuse can be extremely damaging. It can create an environment in which children's needs are not recognised or nurtured. Neglecting children's emotional needs damages their development. Some adults may be emotionally abusive to children. They harm children by using constant threats, verbal attacks, taunting or shouting at them and rejecting the child. Domestic violence, adult mental health problems and parental drug/substance misuse may exist in some families where children are exposed to this form of abuse.

Signs of emotional abuse

As with physical abuse emotionally abused children will usually show signs in their behaviour. They may turn their reactions outwards and become aggressive, destructive and uncooperative with others, or they may withdraw and become quiet and unhappy. They may show similar behavioural signs to the physically abused child.

The effects of emotional abuse

There is increasing evidence of long-term negative effects on children's development where they have been subjected to continual emotional abuse. Emotional abuse affects children's developing mental health, behaviour and self-esteem and can be especially damaging to very young children.

Sexual abuse

Sexual abuse is the inappropriate involvement of dependent, developmentally immature children in sexual activities. Sexual abuse covers a range of abusive behaviour not necessarily involving direct physical contact. It can include allowing children to witness sexual activity or watch pornographic videos. It includes exposure and self-masturbation by the abuser, through to actual body contact such as touching or penetration.

Child sexual abuse is found in all cultures and socio-economic groups. It happens to children in all kinds of families and communities. Boys and girls, including babies, are victims of sexual abuse. Both men and women sexually abuse children. It is becoming clear that the majority of children who are sexually abused know the abuser. This may be a member of the child's family, a family friend or a person the child knows in a position of trust.

Signs of sexual abuse

Early recognition of the signs (indicators) of sexual abuse is essential. Otherwise it can continue undiscovered for many years and cause great harm. There may be no obvious physical indicators of sexual abuse, so particular attention should be paid to behavioural indicators.

The effects of sexual abuse

Sexual abuse can lead to disturbed behaviour, inappropriate sexualised behaviour, sadness, depression and loss of self-esteem. The effects are likely to be more severe if the child is older and the experience of abuse is prolonged. The effects can last into adult life. However, only a minority of children who are sexually abused go on to become abusers themselves.

A child's ability to cope with this experience can be helped by the support of a worker who believes the child, helps the child to understand, and offers help and protection.

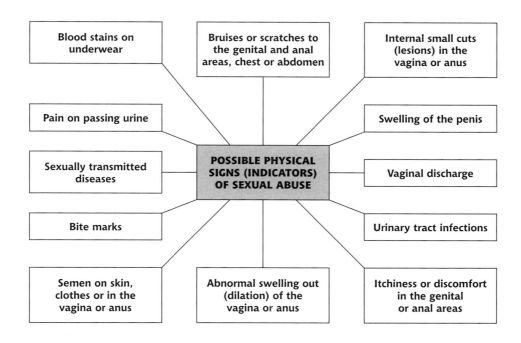

Blood stains on underwear

Bruises or scratches to the genital and anal areas, chest or abdomen

Internal small cuts (lesions) in the vagina or anus

Pain on passing urine

Swelling of the penis

POSSIBLE PHYSICAL SIGNS (INDICATORS) OF SEXUAL ABUSE

Sexually transmitted diseases

Vaginal discharge

Bite marks

Urinary tract infections

Semen on skin, clothes or in the vagina or anus

Abnormal swelling out (dilation) of the vagina or anus

Itchiness or discomfort in the genital or anal areas

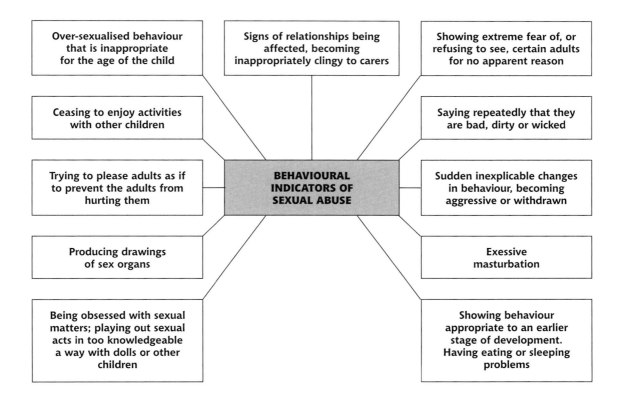

Over-sexualised behaviour that is inappropriate for the age of the child

Signs of relationships being affected, becoming inappropriately clingy to carers

Showing extreme fear of, or refusing to see, certain adults for no apparent reason

Ceasing to enjoy activities with other children

Saying repeatedly that they are bad, dirty or wicked

Trying to please adults as if to prevent the adults from hurting them

BEHAVIOURAL INDICATORS OF SEXUAL ABUSE

Sudden inexplicable changes in behaviour, becoming aggressive or withdrawn

Producing drawings of sex organs

Exessive masturbation

Being obsessed with sexual matters; playing out sexual acts in too knowledgeable a way with dolls or other children

Showing behaviour appropriate to an earlier stage of development. Having eating or sleeping problems

Observing the signs of abuse in everyday situations

Child care workers are in a good position to observe the signs and symptoms of injuries to children. These may also include changes in their behaviour.

Babies and infants

Careful observation of babies can take place during routines such as nappy changing, when changing or removing clothing, during washing and hygiene routines, and while feeding and playing with babies.

Toddlers and young children

Any hygiene, feeding or changing routines can be used to observe young children carefully. Play provides a good opportunity to observe and assess behaviour. Any play that requires children to push up sleeves or remove clothing also enables carers to observe signs of injury unobtrusively. Good opportunities to observe the condition of older children occur when they are changing for physical exercise and swimming.

Child care workers are in a good position to observe the signs and symptoms of injuries to children, including significant changes in their behaviour

Protecting children from abuse

The Children Act 1989 is the law that aims to protect children from harm in any setting. This Act is based on the principle that all children have a right to protection. There are written procedures to protect children in all settings. Parents have a right to be consulted in most circumstances. Any disclosure by a child must be dealt with sensitively and professionally. There are ways to help children to protect themselves from abuse.

The Children Act came into force in England and Wales in 1991 and in Scotland and Northern Ireland in 1995 (see appendix).

The policies and procedures of work settings

Every setting, where children are cared for, has policies and procedures that aim to protect children from abuse. In England these are based on the procedures written locally by each Area Child Protection Committee (ACPC). Procedures are also in place in Wales, Scotland and Northern Ireland. It is very important that all workers know about their local procedures and follow them. Policies and procedures ensure that all workers know what their duties are, provide clear instructions about what to do, and the steps that must be taken to protect children are made clear.

The policies child care and education workers should follow *may* include these:

- Routine and specific observation and assessment of children's behaviour and development. Settings will have ways of doing this and of recording observations. Policies may include keeping accurate, relevant records and signing and dating them.

- Using the Framework for the Assessment of Children in Need and their Families. This framework was published by the Department of Health in England in April 2000. It provides a way of collecting and analysing information.

- Discussing possible signs of abuse with a senior colleague, who may be the specifically named person in the organisation, or with a health visitor. If someone is working alone they may have access to a specially trained worker from the National Childminding Association (NCMA) (Northern Ireland Childminding Association (NICMA) and Scottish Childminding Association (SCMA)).

The procedures child care workers should follow will include these:

- Reporting concerns to a specific person in the setting. The specific person will decide whether there are grounds to refer suspicions to the statutory body. This is the Social Services Department (in England the police and the NSPCC can also receive referrals).

- Reporting the concerns themselves directly to the Social Services Department if working alone.

- Recording specific observations of what has been observed, signing and dating them.

After an investigation social workers will decide whether there are grounds to call a case conference with a view to placing the child on the Child Protection Register, or even going to court to have a child removed from home. A child care worker may be asked to go to a case conference and present a report based on their observations.

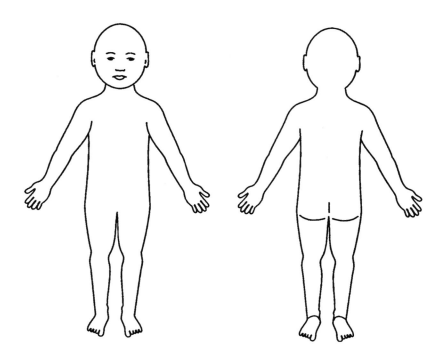

Physical indicators may be recorded on a chart like this

Joseph

A 2–year-old child Joseph often comes to the day nursery with fresh bruises on his arms and upper body. His mother explains that these are the result of minor accidents while playing.

➤ *What might lead you to suspect that the child was being injured non-accidentally?*

➤ *Describe the procedures you would follow in your setting. Describe what would you record.*

KUS
3, 5, 25, 26, 27

Involving parents

One of the principles of the Children Act 1989 is that people who work with children must also work in partnership with their parents. It is important to involve parents in the early stages of any inquiry into possible child abuse (with the exception of suspected sexual abuse). This is because:

● parents may be able to provide a clear and satisfactory explanation

● alternatively, the way parents respond may give a clear sign that all is not well, particularly so if parents give an unsatisfactory explanation, are vague or inconsistent, delay seeking medical attention, or if they lack concern or blame others, or the child, for an injury

● positive partnership with parents is the best way to create good, constructive relationships with families

● if abuse is occurring, the best outcome is to work positively with a family to prevent further abuse and where possible to keep the child within the family

● enquiries that are not carried out sensitively and respectfully, involving parents, can bring unnecessary distress both to children and their parents.

The role of the child care worker in responding to disclosure

In any day care setting, it is possible that children will tell or demonstrate to a worker that they are being abused. In other words they will disclose. This could happen in an open way, or through hinted words or behaviour. Adults need to respond sensitively and appropriately. You should:

● listen and be prepared to spend time and not hurry the child

● not ask leading questions, putting words into children's mouths

● reassure them truthfully, telling them they are not odd or unique, you believe them; you are glad they told you; it is not their fault; they were brave to tell; you are sorry it happened

● find out what they are afraid of, so you know how best to help, for example, they may have been threatened about telling

● be prepared to record what the child tells you as soon as possible (within 24 hours), in detail, accurately and legibly, including the date of the disclosure

● let the child know why you are going to tell someone else

● consult a senior person or an appropriate professional who will be able to help

● seek out support for your personal emotional reactions and needs from an appropriate colleague or professional

● not attempt to deal with the issue alone.

Helping children to protect themselves

Child care workers can help children to protect themselves by ensuring that children:

● understand they have a right to be safe and learn how to do this

● develop an awareness of their own bodies, understanding that their bodies are their own and that no one should touch them inappropriately

● learn to recognise, trust and accept their own feelings

● gain self-confidence, and assertive skills to help them, for example, to say 'no'

● recognise that they should talk and share their worries, and that they have a right to be listened to and believed

● learn that kisses, hugs and touches should never be kept secret, even if they feel good.

These principles and the skills that children need to put them into practice can be taught through the existing curriculum in schools. They can also be incorporated into themes and topics in pre-school settings. If taught well, they will promote children's confidence, assertiveness and communication skills, as well as contributing to their protection. They are relevant to all children, including disabled children and children with learning difficulties who may be especially vulnerable.

Listen and be prepared to spend time and not hurry the child

Element E2.5

Are you ready for assessment?

Help protect children from abuse

Direct observation by your assessor is not required for this element.

To show that you can competently help protect children from abuse you will need to present other types of evidence. The amount and type of evidence you present will vary. You should discuss this with your assessor.

Element E2.6

Maintain the safety of children on outings

KUS
6, 7, 20, 21, 22, 29

Outings with children

Children enjoy going on outings. These can be short trips to the shops or to post a letter, or longer outings to farms or parks. All will provide valuable learning opportunities. The amount of preparation needed depends on the scale of the outing. Whenever you are taking children outside the setting always make sure that you know about the regulations and follow them carefully.

These are things to consider when planning to take children on an outing:

- safety
- permissions
- the place
- supervision
- transport
- food
- clothing
- cost.

Choosing where to go

It may be easy to decide where to take the children. There may be a place that has been visited successfully before.

Outings are also a very good way of helping children to understand about their world. An outing can be linked to the setting's plans for the children's learning.

There may be a place nearby

When planning any trip remember to consider the following:

The age and stage of development of the children

There are differences in the physical capabilities of children. Very young children will be restricted to areas where you can push a buggy. Children will vary in their ability to concentrate and sit still. Choosing a destination that meets the needs of all the age groups you are taking is important. It may be necessary to group children. Each group can then do different things. For example, during a visit to a park the younger children will enjoy feeding the ducks. The older ones will also wish to play ball games, or follow the nature trails.

Outings with young children should be educational and fun

The distance of the destination will decide whether the trip will last for a morning, afternoon or whole day. Younger children do not like spending a long time travelling. This should be thought about when choosing where to go.

Permission

Permission to take children outside the setting will always have to be obtained from the person in charge of the setting.

Parents will want to have their wishes taken into account when an outing is being planned. They may have useful ideas or previous experience of visiting a place. Parents may also be able to give practical help and perhaps come on the outing themselves.

It is important to inform parents about the outing and get their written permission for children to take part. Parents will need to know:

- the destination
- timings and programme for the visit
- transport arrangements
- who will be responsible for their child
- the arrangements (food, clothes, footwear)
- any ways that they could help prepare their child for the outing
- emergency procedures
- cost.

The best way to do this is to send a letter including all the information. Provide a tear-off consent slip for parents to sign.

It is worth following up a letter by talking to parents to make sure everything is clear. Discuss any concerns before the outing. It may be possible to have a meeting to do this.

Adult help/supervision

It is essential to arrange to have a higher adult–child ratio on any outing away from the setting.

A general guide for ratios on trips away from the setting is:

1 adult to 1 child   0–2 years

1 adult to 2 children   2–5 years

1 adult to 5 children   5–8 years

It is always good to have extra adults to help cover any emergencies, for example, if a child becomes separated from the group and is lost. Extra adults will be free to search, while the remaining children are still adequately supervised.

Cost

If there is an entry fee or travelling costs, some families may not be able to afford to pay. Check whether there is enough funding to cater for all the children.

Transport

Is the place within walking distance or will transport be required? If arranging transport with an outside organisation, make sure that:

- they are insured
- the vehicle is large enough to seat everyone – adults and children
- there are sufficient child restraints, booster seats and seat belts
- the vehicles are safe.

Records must be kept about vehicles in which children are to be transported. This includes:

- insurance details
- a list of named drivers.

Drivers using their own vehicle to carry any children must have insurance cover. Avoid travelling during rush hours. When on foot plan to use the safest route.

Stages in the planning process

1   **Check** the national and local authority regulations that apply to your setting that cover outings. Any arrangements must comply with these regulations.

2   **Find out** about the destination, for example, travel routes, opening times and accessibility for children, toilet facilities, picnic areas, refreshments, first aid provision. It may be possible to visit to find out before you go.

3 **Prepare** a timetable for the day. Everyone will need to know times of departure and arrival. Ensure that your programme is practical and there is enough time to do everything that you have planned for.

4 **Plan** to take all the necessary equipment with you, for example:
- the first aid kit
- emergency contact phone numbers and a mobile phone
- registers
- any medicines and inhalers
- camera
- money
- audio tapes for the journey
- worksheets and bags for collecting items of interest
- packed lunches
- wet weather wear
- sun cream, sun hats
- spare clothes
- younger children may need pushchairs, nappies, harnesses.

5 **Consult** parents. It is necessary to get written consent from parents for any trip away from the establishment. They will need to know about the cost, the day's programme, transport, special requirements – lunch, clothing etc. A letter home with a consent slip is the best way to achieve this, perhaps combined with posters or notices displayed in the establishment.

6 **Prepare** the children for the outing. Discuss the outing and explain what will be happening, talk about safety issues, such as staying with adults, not speaking to strangers. Discuss any activities related to the outing. Make sure the children know what to do if they become separated from the group (e.g. not to wander about but to stay in the same place. Older children may be shown a central meeting point or the ticket office. Show children the staff uniform or name badges so they know whom to ask for help).

7 **Brief** all the adults who are helping on the outing. They will need to have all the information about the outing, who is in charge and has the registers and the contact numbers. They must also have a list of all the children and know which children they are responsible for. Make sure adults know what to do in an emergency.

8 **Plan** to have regular head counts and register checks.

9 **Consider the 'what ifs'.** Planning includes taking proper safety precautions, supervising the children carefully and preparing for the unexpected. However, unexpected events may still happen during an outing. It is important to think about what these might be beforehand. You can then think about how to cope.

Follow-up work

Children should be encouraged to record their experiences. They could do a drawing or painting, write a story or poem, and display items collected on the outing. Photographs will also provide a record of the day. All these things can be put into a book to provide a record of the outing.

Are you ready for assessment?

Maintain the safety of children on outings

Direct observation by your assessor is not required for this element. However, it may be possible for your assessor to observe you and this evidence can be used.

To show that you can competently maintain the safety of children on outings you will need to present other types of evidence. The amount and type of evidence you present will vary. You should discuss this with your assessor.

Check your knowledge

- What are the physical and emotional signs of:
  (a) physical abuse?
  (b) emotional abuse?
  (c) sexual abuse?
  (d) neglect? **KUS 3**
- How can outings promote children's learning? **KUS 6**
- What is the policy in your setting for dealing with bodily fluids and waste? **KUS 17**
- What should be included in a first aid box? Why do the contents need to be checked regularly? **KUS 19**
- What are the procedures for identifying and reporting any safety hazards in your setting? **KUS 9**

Contribute to the achievement of organisational requirements

This unit focuses on the responsibilities of child care workers to know what their role is within a setting and to be aware of the purpose and organisation of the setting in which they work. It covers the importance of identifying existing knowledge and skills, and continuing to develop professional knowledge and skills. Individual workers' contribution towards developing good practice within a setting is outlined.

This unit contains two elements:

⌣ **M3.1** *Carry out instructions and provide feedback*

⌣ **M3.2** *Contribute to the development of good practice*

⌣ Introduction

In order to function effectively within an organisation you need to be clear about your own role and responsibilities. You also need to be aware of other team members' roles and responsibilities. You need to be able to form good working relationships. This unit outlines how to be a good team member and a reliable and responsible member of staff. You will learn about the skills that you need to carry out instructions effectively and to feedback all the necessary information. You will also learn how to make a positive contribution towards improving practice. The importance of developing your own knowledge through attending training is outlined.

Element M3.1 *Carry out instructions and provide feedback*

KUS
2, 3, 4, 7, 8, 10, 15

⌣ Carrying out instructions

Showing responsibility and accountability involves willingly doing what you are asked to do within your area of responsibility. You may need to jot down instructions to make sure that you are able to follow them accurately. You must then carry out the tasks to the standard required, and in the time allocated, making sure that you are aware of the policies and procedures of your workplace.

You may need to ask your line manager or someone in a supervisory role if you do not understand what to do, or if you think the task is not your responsibility. You may need to refuse to do some tasks until you have been shown how to do them by someone in a supervisory role, or until you have received appropriate training.

Recording information

Your role is likely to involve recording information. That means writing information down. You may need to record instructions that have been given to you to help you remember them. You may also need to record any information to feedback to other staff members. Writing information down means that instructions and feedback are accurate. It also means that you can carry out tasks correctly and independently, because you are sure of what you need to do.

Recording instructions will help you to remember them

Confidentiality

All child care workers have a responsibility to maintain confidentiality at all times. Sensitive information concerning children and their families will only be available to you if you need it to meet the needs of the child and family concerned. Maintaining confidentiality means that any information given to you should not be given to others, or received from others, for any other reason than to meet a child's needs.

Although the idea of confidentiality may be easy to understand, the practice can be complex and will require self-control and commitment to the welfare of the child and their family. However, information about children and families will need to be exchanged within the work setting and you should ask your line manager about how and with whom it can be shared. You should not discuss identifiable children and families with anyone outside the work setting. Breaking confidentiality is a serious matter and can lead to you losing your job.

Personal time management

You will need to manage your time effectively in the work setting if you are to achieve all the tasks within your role and responsibilities. You will need to arrive promptly at your work setting and not leave before your finishing time unless instructed to. You may also find it helpful to:

- make lists and add dates/times by which the task needs to be accomplished
- prioritise the tasks on the list, i.e. put them in order, which is most important, which must be achieved first etc.
- observe and learn from experienced staff how they manage to achieve their tasks within the allocated time
- ask your line manager for feedback about how you manage your time.

Practical Example

Carrying out instructions and feeding back information

KUS
2, 3, 4

Kate was asked by the nursery manager to set up a box modelling activity for the following day. They looked together at the box modelling activity plan and discussed what was needed and how it would be set up. The manager asked her to report back on any equipment or materials that were missing or in short supply so that she could get them out of the stock cupboard before tomorrow. Kate noticed that a number of things were needed. She decided to make a list of them so that she didn't forget any when talking to the manager. Having set up the activity she found the manager and gave her the list of things that were needed. The following day all the necessary equipment and materials were there for the children to do the activity.

➤ *Why was it necessary to feedback this information to the manager?*
  KUS 4
➤ *Why did Kate decide to make a list of the equipment needed?* **KUS 3**
➤ *How did Kate's feedback contribute to making the activity successful?*
  KUS 2

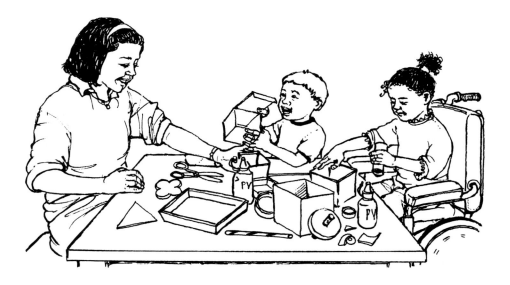

Element M3.1

Are you ready for assessment?

Carry out instructions and provide feedback

You need to show that you can competently carry out instructions and provide feedback. To do this you need to be directly observed by your assessor and present other types of evidence.

Direct observation by your assessor

Your assessor will need to see you carry out these performance criteria (PCs)

M3.1 PCs 1, 3, 4, 5, 6, 7, 9, 10

During these observations your assessor must see you cover at least ONE aspect in each range category listed in the element.

Remember the range categories for this element are:

1. Instructions
2. Tasks

Preparing to be observed

Your assessor will need to see you being given instructions. You will then need to follow the instructions and provide feedback on the task given to you. You will need to fully understand the instructions. If you are in doubt ask a relevant person to explain the instructions further. Record the instructions so that you can refer to them later on. Make sure that you know what information needs feeding back. When you have completed the task your assessor will need to see you feedback the necessary information to the relevant person. Make sure that the information is accurate. You may want to record the information as you do the task. Remember that you must maintain confidentiality at all times, during the task, in any notes that you make and in your feedback.

Read the performance criteria and range carefully before your assessment. Try to cover as much as you can.

Other types of evidence

You may need to present different types of evidence in order to:

- cover criteria not observed by your assessor
- show that you have the required knowledge, understanding and skills
- cover other parts of the range.

The amount and type of evidence you need to present will vary. You should plan this with your assessor.

Contribute to the development of good practice

KUS
1, 5, 6, 9,
10, 11, 12,
13, 14, 15

Working as part of the team

In the work setting, child care workers usually work with other people as part of a team. (Those who work as nannies or childminders may find it helpful to see themselves as part of a team with the child's family.) You will need to know who leads/manages the team and what they expect of you as part of the team.

Within the work setting there will be many different groups of people who you work alongside individually and in teams: other staff, parents/carers, children and other professionals.

Teams can be very effective in many ways, for example:

- thinking of new ideas
- organising and managing projects
- making decisions
- looking at progress
- supporting other team members.

Teams operate effectively when all members consider their own behaviour and how it contributes to the aims of the team.

Personal responsibility within a team

Effective child care workers need to think carefully about what they do. It is important to remember that all members of a team are responsible for creating a reassuring, stimulating and effective environment for the children. Good practice in providing an effective environment for children involves the following.

Planning and preparation

Planning and preparation is important before an activity/experience or routine. This doesn't necessarily have to be written down but thinking things through before doing them is good practice. The activities or experiences that you plan need to be part of team planning. Routines need to be agreed within the team so that everyone follows similar procedures.

Observation

Observation is necessary throughout the session so that you can decide what worked well and what hasn't worked well. You can also observe what the children have learned by being involved in an activity or experience. This information may need to be reported back to other team members.

Evaluation

Evaluating the activity/experience or routine is important for a number of reasons:

- recognising good practice when things have gone well
- to try and work out why things haven't worked well – this may involve discussing the activity or routine with a more experienced child care worker
- to feedback information to other members of the team so that further planning is accurate.

Sharing ideas with others can lead to positive changes in practice

Teams are most effective when staff share knowledge, understanding and ideas. These skills are developed through training, experience and observation. Discussion about how the activities and routines are working provides the opportunity for staff to offer their thoughts and ideas. These discussions may take place informally or in group or team meetings. It is important to be aware of how information is shared in a setting.

Observing existing practice and offering ideas for change needs to be done in a positive way. Evaluations of existing practice must be done in a professional manner, without direct criticism of other staff members. The benefits of any changes need to be explained. It is important that any suggestions made are consistent with the setting's policies and procedures.

Occasionally you may observe staff acting in ways that are unprofessional and/or do not follow the setting's policies and procedures. It is important that you do not ignore what you have seen. You need to discuss your observations with someone in a position of responsibility. It is important that this is done in private and in a professional manner. Your observations need to be accurate and you need to explain your concerns. Any appropriate action should then be taken by the person in a position of responsibility.

All child care workers must maintain confidentiality at all times. This means that sensitive information about children and their families should be used only if it is needed to meet the needs of the child and the family. Although confidentiality may be easy to understand, the practice can be complex and will require careful thought and a commitment to the child and the family's welfare. However, information about children and families will need to be exchanged within the work setting, and you should ask your line manager about how and with whom it can be shared. You should not discuss identifiable children and families with anyone outside the work setting. Breaking confidentiality is a serious matter.

Personal and professional development

As a professional child care worker, you will need to do further training to keep your skills and knowledge up to date. You will also need to be open to suggestions for changing your methods of working. This could be achieved in a number of ways:

- supervision by experienced workers
- observation of experienced workers both at your setting and if possible in other settings
- in-service staff development
- attending courses.

Good training will give you ideas on how to improve your practice. If you are working as part of a team it is important that the whole team makes a training plan together to ensure that all areas are covered by at least one person in the team.

It is also important that those working alone find ways of getting feedback and support on their practice. Discussion with others in a similar role can be supportive. There are a number of nannying networks and childminder networks developing in various parts of the United Kingdom.

KUS
7, 10, 11, 12, 13

Sharing ideas with other people in the setting

Drink and biscuit time in the playgroup was always hectic. The staff were constantly busy trying to get round the tables to give children drinks and biscuits, to refill the cups and to mop up spills. The children spent time just sitting waiting. Observing this each day Samina thought that it would be easier if the drinks and the biscuits were put on each table and a member of staff sat with the children to help them serve themselves. At the end of playgroup Samina suggested this to the playgroup leader. She was very interested in the ideas as she also felt that this part of the session was hectic. She asked Samina to tell the other staff about this idea at the next meeting. Samina did this and together they agreed that a member of staff would sit at a table and help serve the drinks and biscuits, while one member of staff was responsible for mopping up spills. They agreed to try this system the following week and see how it worked. Samina volunteered to buy the plastic jugs to put out on the tables.

The following week the staff implemented the idea. By the end of the week they were all in agreement that it was a much better system than they had had. The session was less hectic and the children spent very little time waiting for their drink and biscuits. Also the children had an opportunity to develop their social skills and it gave the staff time to sit and talk with the children.

➤ *How did Samina identify the need for change in how drink and biscuit time was managed?* **KUS 11, 12, 13**

➤ *How did she share her ideas with the other staff?* **KUS 7, 10**

➤ *How did Samina's ideas improve the practice?* **KUS 11, 12, 13**

Working as a team

Element M3.2 — Are you ready for assessment?

Contribute to the development of good practice

You will need to show that you can contribute to the development of good practice. To do this you will need to be directly observed by your assessor and present other types of evidence.

Direct observation by your assessor

Your assessor will need to see you carry out these performance criteria (PCs)

M3.2 PCs 2, 3, 4, 5, 6, 7

During these observations your assessor must see you cover at least ONE aspect in each range category listed in the element.

Remember the range for this element is:

1. Contributions

Preparing to be observed

Your assessor will need to see you making suggestions about changes in practice or procedures, for example, a different way of organising the drinks at snack time or a different way to set up an activity. These suggestions will need to be made to the relevant person and in a professional manner. This means explaining why you think that doing things differently will improve practice or procedures. Make sure that any suggestions that you make are consistent with the setting's policies. Your assessor will also need to see you put some agreed changes into practice. Changes may have been made on your suggestion and/or because of new ideas from training. You may suggest bringing in resources from outside the setting, for example, people to talk about their experiences or jobs.

You will also need to show that you have responded to opportunities for training by using ideas from training to improve practice within the setting. Remember that you must maintain confidentiality at all times.

Read the performance criteria and range carefully before your assessment. Try to cover as much as you can.

Other types of evidence

You may need to present different types of evidence in order to:

- cover criteria not observed by your assessor
- show that you have the required knowledge, understanding and skills
- cover other parts of the range.

The amount and type of evidence you need to present will vary. You should plan this with your assessor.

Check your knowledge

- Why is it important to attend training courses and use the ideas from them in your work? **KUS 1**
- Why is it important to listen to instructions carefully and implement them correctly? **KUS 4**
- What should you do if you don't understand the instructions given to you? **KUS 3**
- What should you do if you observe practice that is unsatisfactory? **KUS 14**
- How do you identify good practice and possible changes to improve practice? **KUS 11, 13**
- How can suggestions for changes in practice be made in a professional manner? **KUS 10**
- What is your role in maintaining confidentiality in the workplace? **KUS 15**

Relate to parents

*T*his unit covers the important area of interaction between child care workers and parents. It recognises that such interaction is essential for the effective care and education of children.

This unit has close links with unit P9.

This unit contains two elements:

- *P1.1 Interact and share information with parents about their children*
- *P1.2 Share the care of children with their parents*

Introduction

It is important that child care workers recognise the important part that parents play in the care and education of their children. By the time they arrive at the child care setting, children will have acquired many skills and know a great deal about who they are and the world that they live in. They will have learned all this from within the family. The skills, attitudes and beliefs gained from parents provide the foundation for children's learning and development throughout the early years and beyond. An effective partnership between parents and the child care setting will ensure that as children learn new skills, these will be recognised and supported by both parents and professionals.

Why relate to parents?

- Parents have the most knowledge and understanding of their children. If they are encouraged to share this with staff, all will benefit.
- Children need consistent handling to feel secure. This is most likely to occur if there are good relationships between parents and staff.
- Legislation contained within the Education Reform Act 1988, the Children Act 1989 and the Special Educational Needs Code of Practice 2001 places a legal responsibility on professionals to work in partnership with parents. Services provided for children in the public, private and voluntary sector must take this into account.

- It is a condition of receiving public funding for educational provision for 3 and 4 year olds (known as nursery grant) that settings work in partnership with parents.

- Research has demonstrated conclusively the positive effect that parental involvement in the education process has on the progress of children. If parents become involved early on in the child's care and education, they are likely to maintain this involvement throughout the child's educational career.

- Children's learning and development is not confined either to the child care setting or the home. An exchange of information from centre to home and from home to centre will reinforce learning, wherever it takes place.

- Where parents are experiencing difficulties with their children, they may be able to share these problems and work towards resolving them alongside sympathetic and supportive professionals.

To ensure good relationships with parents, child care workers should:

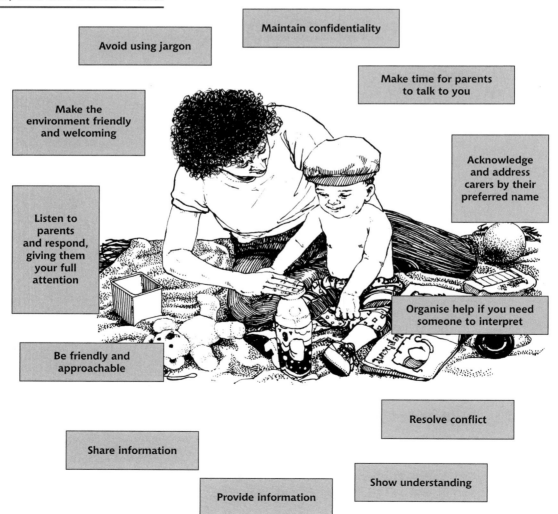

Maintain confidentiality

Avoid using jargon

Make time for parents to talk to you

Make the environment friendly and welcoming

Acknowledge and address carers by their preferred name

Listen to parents and respond, giving them your full attention

Organise help if you need someone to interpret

Be friendly and approachable

Resolve conflict

Share information

Show understanding

Provide information

Relating to all parents

It is the responsibility of those who work with children to do everything that they can to make parents feel welcome and valued. The needs and feelings of all parents should be considered. This may include some parents who have had previous negative experiences of child care or education settings and who may need encouragement to feel comfortable. Parents who are unfamiliar with the methods and approaches used in the setting may require explanation and reassurance. Parents may be concerned that their child's cultural and religious background is understood. Provision should be made to ensure that parents who do not use the language of the setting are provided with the full range of opportunities to be involved in their children's care and education.

Element P1.1 *Interact and share information with parents about their children*

KUS
2, 3, 5,
6, 7

Making effective relationships

Parents will begin to have an impression of a child care setting and its staff from the moment they first make contact, either by phone or face to face. Many establishments operate an 'open door' policy, where parents are made welcome whenever they choose to call and so it is important that the centre is always welcoming.

The physical environment

First impressions count for a great deal, and most establishments will recognise this and take particular care to make the way into the building clear, with signs directing visitors to an appropriate person. Notice boards and displays in entrance halls and foyers give an immediate impression of the philosophy and approach of the centre. Carefully mounted and imaginatively displayed children's work demonstrates professional standards and shows what the children do and that you value their work. Named photographs of staff and their roles give parents an indication of how the centre operates. A well-maintained notice board giving information about current activities and topics may attract a parent's attention and encourage them to become involved. The physical condition and upkeep of the building also creates an impression; no parent would choose a gloomy, unsafe or unhygienic environment for their child.

Staff attitudes

But perhaps even more important than the welcome communicated by the physical environment is the response of the staff. In many establishments there will be a particular person with responsibility for dealing with enquiries and settling in new children and families, but this does not mean that other members of staff should not be involved. Everyone should have time for a greeting and a smile

A welcoming entrance creates a positive impression

while the required person is found. Remember that parents may feel ill at ease in an unfamiliar setting. Leaving a child for the first time is almost certainly going to be stressful and they will need your support. Remembering the following may help you to put parents at their ease:

- Smile or nod when you see a parent, even if they are making their way to another member of staff.
- Make time to talk with parents. If they have a concern that requires time and privacy, try to arrange a mutually convenient appointment.
- Try to call people by name. 'Ellie's mum' may do in an emergency but might not be the most appropriate way to address someone.
- Remember that there are many different types of families and that it is not at all unusual for parents to have a different surname from that of their child or of their partner. In our culturally diverse society, be aware that communities have their own naming customs and may not follow the western naming custom of personal names followed by family names. Ask colleagues or consult records to find out parents' preferred forms of address. If you are unsure of the correct pronunciation, ask the parent.

Exchanging information

Working with young children is likely to mean that you are in daily contact with their parents when they bring and collect them. This means that information about children, whether achievements or concerns, can be exchanged informally between parents and workers. This helps to build the relationship between parents and the staff, and shows children that home and the child care setting are working together.

It is particularly important that parents have confidence in staff and feel that they are able to pass on information about events at home that might affect the child. Illness in the family, a new baby or a parent leaving home will all have an effect on the child. The more that the exchange of this type of information is encouraged, the smoother the process of sharing care is likely to be. Some centres use a key worker system, where one member of staff has a responsibility for a particular group of children. This can be helpful to parents as they can build a relationship with their child's key worker.

Remember that some parents may have difficulty with filling in forms and with written information. If this is the case, then it is particularly important that they have regular opportunities to exchange information face to face.

Sometimes information received in conversations with parents will need to be recorded. You should make sure that any information received in this way is recorded promptly and accurately, either by yourself or the person who is responsible for keeping records up to date.

KUS
1, 7

Expressing concerns

Shamila had been coming to nursery for over a year. She was a bright and outgoing child who had plenty of friends and joined in with all the activities. One morning she came in looking very pale and tired. She spent the whole of the session curled up in the book corner, often with a rug over her, pretending to be asleep. At home time, the nursery nurse made a point of having a word with Shamila's mother and described her behaviour. Her mother seemed very upset. She explained that Shamila's grandmother, who lived with them, was seriously ill and had been admitted to hospital the previous day, and the whole of the family had been affected.

➤ *What do you think was wrong with Shamila?*
➤ *Why was it helpful for the staff to know what was upsetting her?*
➤ *What opportunities do parents in your setting have to share this kind of individual information?*

Parents and records

All establishments are required to keep records of the children and families that they work with. The content of these records will vary depending on the type of care that is being provided. They will always include personal data about the child supplied by parents. There will also be records that track the child's progress and achievements during their time at the centre. These should be made available for parents to refer and contribute to.

Initial information

Usually parents are asked to complete a form that includes the following:

- Personal details about the child: full name, date of birth, etc.
- Names, addresses and phone numbers of parents and other emergency contacts.
- Medical details that will include the address and telephone number of the child's doctor and any information about allergies and regular medications.
- Details about any particular dietary needs.
- Details about religious or cultural customs, which might have a bearing on the care provided for the child.

Additionally, there may be sensitive information that is necessary for the centre to have; for example, are there any restrictions on who may collect the child from the centre? Are social services involved with the family?

Parents will need to be assured that such information will be confidential and stored securely. Centres need to make sure that this essential information is correct and up to date.

Other types of information will also be very helpful, particularly around settling in. These might include the following:

- any comfort object the child might have
- food likes and dislikes
- any particular fears
- special words the child might use, for example, for the lavatory.

Progress and achievements

Where children spend a great deal of their time at the child care setting, it is important that parents are kept informed about their children's day-to-day achievements as well as the more significant milestones. Praise is important to children's self-esteem and sharing what children have been doing at the setting on a regular basis gives parents an opportunity to recognise and respond to their children's achievements. This emphasises the importance of the partnership between parents and professionals in the shared care of children. Much is to be gained from sharing records with parents. This does not mean merely making children's records available to parents, but encouraging parents to contribute by offering their own observations of their children, thus putting the child into the wider context of home and community. Parents can be involved in the process of recording their children's progress and achievements in a number of ways.

- Parents will often help staff to compile a profile of their child at admission. This is usually organised around areas of development and shows what the child can do. It may also include space to refer to the child's preferences, for example, 'likes painting', and any other related information, including concerns. These initial profiles will serve as a starting point and will be added to as the child progresses and achieves new skills.

- An informal chat with parents at the beginning and/or end of sessions can be very useful, providing an opportunity to talk about what children have been doing in the session, handing on paintings, models etc. and sharing any concerns.

- Most settings and parents would agree that there is a place for a regular, more structured exchange of information where records can be updated by parents and by staff and progress discussed. This will give parents the opportunity to add to the records compiled by staff and supplement these with additional information from their own observations. Plans for the next steps for their children should also be discussed with parents, emphasising the partnership between parents and staff, and recognising the parents' key role in promoting their children's development.

- Many settings maintain folders of children's work, showing their developing skills and achievements. Children will enjoy adding to these and sharing them with parents.

Children will enjoy choosing items to add to their profiles

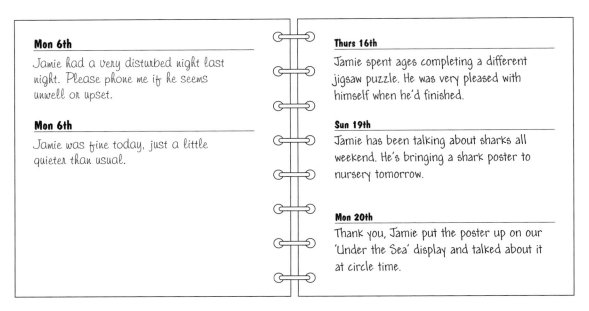

Mon 6th

Jamie had a very disturbed night last night. Please phone me if he seems unwell or upset.

Mon 6th

Jamie was fine today, just a little quieter than usual.

Thurs 16th

Jamie spent ages completing a different jigsaw puzzle. He was very pleased with himself when he'd finished.

Sun 19th

Jamie has been talking about sharks all weekend. He's bringing a shark poster to nursery tomorrow.

Mon 20th

Thank you, Jamie put the poster up on our 'Under the Sea' display and talked about it at circle time.

Diaries provide a useful way of exchanging information

- Diary-type booklets that are regularly written up and sent home with children for parents to read and comment on provide another useful channel for exchanging information, particularly for those parents who are unable to get to the centre on a regular basis.

Confidentiality

The nature of your work with children means that you will learn a great deal about individual children and their families. Parents will expect you to treat the information about their child and their family life that they have shared with you as confidential, and only to be discussed with others where this is in the best interest of their child.

Respecting confidentiality means the following:

- You should not gossip about details of children or their families with others, either in your workplace or outside. Imagine how you would feel if you were sitting on a bus and heard someone a couple of seats in front discussing your private life!
- You should discuss relevant information in a professional way with your supervisor and others who work with the child.
- Understanding that sometimes you will have to pass on information, even when a parent has asked you not to. You cannot guarantee to keep something to yourself if there could be a risk, however small, to the child.
- You should refer to and become familiar with any workplace policy on confidentiality. Ask your supervisor to go through this with you.

Element P1.1 — Are you ready for assessment?

Interact and share information with parents about their children

You need to show that you can competently interact and share information with parents about their children. To do this you may be directly observed by your assessor and you will need to present other types of evidence.

Direct observation by your assessor

There is no requirement for your assessor to observe any of the performance criteria for unit P1.1. However, evidence from observation may be presented.

Remember the range categories for this element are:

1. Confidence
2. Contact

Preparing to be observed

Arrange for your assessor to observe at a time when parents are present in your setting, perhaps either at the beginning or the end of a session. Make sure that you make parents feel comfortable in the setting and that you provide an opportunity for them to talk about their children, as well as for you to talk about what has been going on in the setting.

Read the performance criteria and range carefully before your assessment. Try to cover as much as you can.

Other types of evidence

You may need to present different types of evidence in order to:

- cover criteria not observed by your assessor
- show that you have the required knowledge, understanding and skills
- cover other parts of the range.

The amount and type of evidence you need to present will vary. You should plan this with your assessor.

Element
P1.2 *Share the care of children with their parents*

KUS
4, 10

Admission/settling-in procedures

Everyone recognises the importance of the settling-in period for both the child and the parent, and will encourage parents to play a full part. Centres will generally make sure that the following takes place to help make transition a positive experience:

- Parents will often stay with their child until, with the encouragement of staff, they feel comfortable about leaving. At this stage the exchange of information is vital: staff will want to know all about the child and parents will want to know all about how their child is doing during these early days. Parents who have full-time jobs may find it difficult to stay during these sessions, but will be just as concerned; giving them plenty of notice of arrangements for starting may mean that they can organise other commitments and be there.

- Day nurseries that cater primarily for working parents will often have a programme for introducing parents and children to the setting, providing evening sessions where children and parents can meet staff and visit the building. When the child starts, there is usually someone at the end of a telephone to report back and reassure parents.

- Some centres will have their own pre-school (or pre-nursery) group where children come with their parents for a number of sessions before they start officially.

- Some centres will make home visits to families prior to their children starting nursery or school. Parents often feel more comfortable in their own homes rather than in a strange, perhaps intimidating environment.

Parents will often stay to help children settle in

For some children, starting at nursery or playgroup will be the first time they have been separated from their parent. Unit C4 on children's social and emotional development will help you understand and anticipate how children are likely to react and how you can support them through what is often a difficult time for them. But it is important to remember that the settling-in period can sometimes be more stressful for parents than for the child. Parents may take some time to adjust to a new role. Child care workers can help during this time by being sensitive to this and making sure that they take time to let parents know how the child is getting on and filling them in on the routine of the day. If parents seem over-anxious or fussy during this period, you can help by being approachable and reassuring.

Different ways of parenting

The ways that parents choose to bring up their children will vary from family to family. Being a parent is a very demanding role and parents develop their own ways of managing these responsibilities. They will be influenced by their own experience of being parented and, if they have close family ties, they will receive advice and support from their own parents, brothers and sisters. For some parents there will be cultural and community influences to balance alongside other advice. However, all families are individual and you should not make assumptions that all families from a particular cultural, religious or ethnic group will parent their children in an identical way. There may be similarities, but there are likely to be as many differences. You need to be able to show that you can relate to parents and families as individuals.

Parents must have confidence that the setting and its workers will take a professional and non-judgemental view that, providing the child is happy and healthy, respects the rights of parents to bring up their children in the way that is most comfortable for them.

Element P1.2 **Are you ready for assessment?**

Share the care of children with their parents

You need to show that you can competently share the care of children with their parents. To do this you may be directly observed by your assessor and you will need to present other types of evidence

Direct observation by your assessor

There is no requirement for your assessor to observe any of the performance criteria for unit P1.2. However, evidence from observation may be presented.

Remember the range category for this element is:

1. Care

▶▶

Preparing to be observed

Arrange for your assessor to observe you when parents are likely to be present in the setting. If you have new children starting, this will be a good opportunity for you to demonstrate how you share the care of children with their parents. Make sure that you talk to parents about what their children have been doing or are about to do. You should also be able to show that you listen to parents and that you respond sensitively and, where appropriate, act on their wishes and concerns.

Read the performance criteria and range carefully before your assessment. Try and cover as much as you can.

Other types of evidence

You may need to present different types of evidence in order to:

- cover criteria not observed by your assessor
- show that you have the required knowledge, understanding and skills
- cover other parts of the range.

The amount and type of evidence you need to present will vary. You should plan this with your assessor.

Check your knowledge

- Why it is important for child care settings to develop good relationships with parents? **KUS 1, 8**
- Why might some parents feel ill at ease or lack confidence in the child care setting? **KUS 5**
- How can you ensure that parents can be involved in settling in their children? **KUS 4**
- Why is confidentiality such an important aspect of working with parents? **KUS 3**
- Why is it important for child care workers to have open minds, and not make assumptions about children and families from particular cultural and religious groups? **KUS 10**

Optional units

Feed babies

This unit covers all aspects of preparing feeds and feeding babies: sterilising equipment, making up formula feeds and weaning. It includes taking account of parents' wishes.

This unit contains three elements:

- **C12.1** *Prepare equipment and formula feed*
- **C12.2** *Feed babies by bottle*
- **C12.3** *Prepare food and feed babies*

Introduction

The nutritional needs of babies

All babies should be fed on milk only for at least the first 4 months of life. The decision to breast-feed or bottle-feed is a very personal one. Most women have an idea of how they will feed their babies before they become pregnant. This may be influenced by how their mother fed them or how their friends feed their babies. There are advantages and disadvantages to both methods, but breast milk is the natural milk for babies. It is the ideal source of food for the few first months of life.

Breast-feeding
Advantages of breast-feeding

- Breast milk is the ideal food: it is made especially for babies. It contains all the right nutrients in the right proportions to meet the changing needs of the baby.
- The first milk produced by the breast is called colostrum. Colostrum has a high concentration of maternal antibodies. Antibodies are produced by the mother and can protect the baby from some infections.
- It contains no germs and reduces risk of infection.
- There are fewer incidences of allergies, such as asthma, in breast-fed babies.
- It is always available at the correct temperature.
- It is more convenient; there are no bottles to prepare.
- It is less expensive than buying formula milk.

Managing breast-feeding

Demand feeding (the baby is fed when hungry) is usually the best way to approach breast-feeding. Babies have different requirements and some will feed more often than others. Babies will often have established their own 3–5 hourly feeding routines by the time they are 3–4 weeks old. It is important that the mother has a good diet and plenty of rest. Extra help at home will benefit the mother and the baby.

Bottle-feeding (formula feeding)

Most modern infant formulas (modified baby milks) are based on cow's milk. However, some are derived from soya beans, for babies who cannot tolerate cow's milk. Manufacturers try to make these milks as close to human breast milk as possible. All modified milks must meet the standards issued by the Department of Health. There are basic differences between breast and modified milks. Cow's milk can be difficult to digest as it has more protein and fat than breast milk. Cow's milk also has a higher salt content; salt is dangerous for babies as their kidneys are not mature enough to excrete it. Making feeds that are too strong or giving unmodified cow's milk can be very dangerous, and may cause damage to the baby's kidneys and brain.

Advantages of bottle-feeding

- It is possible to see exactly how much milk the baby is taking.
- Other people can help with the feeding.
- The baby can be fed anywhere without embarrassment.

C12.1 *Prepare equipment and formula feed*

KUS
2, 6, 8,
12, 16,
17, 18, 22

Cleaning and sterilising equipment for feeding

All equipment for bottle-feeding must be thoroughly cleaned and sterilised. The normal washing and drying methods are satisfactory for adults and older children. Equipment that is used to feed small babies, under 1 year of age, needs to be sterilised to kill germs that are not removed using normal washing and drying methods. This includes feeding bottles, teats, teat caps, plastic spoons, bowls and feeding cups. Equipment can be sterilised using cold water sterilising solutions. These come in tablet or liquid form. A more common method now is to use a steam steriliser.

Equipment must be washed and rinsed before it is sterilised. Do not use salt to clean teats, as this will increase the salt intake of the baby if the salt is not rinsed off properly. Use a proper teat cleaner, which is like a small bottle brush. When it has been thoroughly washed the equipment is ready to be sterilised. Follow the manufacturer's instructions on the sterilising solution bottle, packet or steam steriliser.

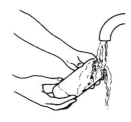

(1) Rinse the bottles, teats and other equipment with cold water, then wash in hot water and detergent. Use a bottle brush for the inside of the bottle and a teat cleaner for the teats. Do not use salt.

(2) Rinse everything thoroughly in clean water. Check that the holes in the teats are clear by squeezing water through as you rinse them

Cleaning and sterilising feeding equipment

(3) Fill the steriliser with clean, cold water and add the sterilising tablets or solution. Follow the manufacturer's instructions.

(4) Place the bottles, teats and other equipment into the solution and ensure that everything is completely covered and that there are no air bubbles. Do not put any metal equipment into the solution. Cover and leave for the stated time. Follow the manufacturer's instructions.

Making a formula (bottle) feed

Feeds should be made up according to the guidelines on the modified milk container. The following equipment will be needed:

- bottles (some have disposable plastic liners)
- teats
- bottle covers
- bottle brush
- teat cleaner
- plastic knife
- plastic jug
- sterilising tank, sterilising fluid or tablets, or steam steriliser.

These are the important points to remember:

- Always wash your hands before and after making up feeds or weaning foods.
- Wipe down the work surface before preparing feeds using hot soapy water or anti-bacterial spray.
- Rinse the feeding equipment with boiled water after it comes out of the sterilising fluid.

When making up a feed, **always**:

- use the same brand of baby milk; do not change without the advice or recommendation of the health visitor or doctor
- put the water into the bottle or jug before the milk powder
- use cooled boiled water to make up feeds.

When making up a feed, **never**:

- add an extra scoop of powder for any reason
- pack the powder too tightly into the scoop
- use heaped scoops.

These actions would result in the feed being too strong. This is dangerous for the baby.

If the feed is not being used immediately, cool and store in the fridge. Throw away any feed that has been stored in the fridge for 24 hours. If a feed has been taken from the fridge and warmed to feed a baby it should be used within 45 minutes and the teat should always be covered when not in use.

If feeds have been stored in a fridge they will need to be warmed before they are given to a baby. Put the bottle into a jug of hot water for a few minutes to heat through. You will need to shake the bottle to distribute the heat through the milk. Test the temperature of the milk before feeding. An easy way to do this is to drop some milk on to the inside of your wrist. It should feel just warm. Beware of using a microwave to heat up feeds as they can heat unevenly, producing hot spots in the feed.

How much milk?

Bottle-fed babies should be fed on demand (when they are hungry) and they usually settle into their own individual routine. New babies will require about eight feeds a day – approximately every 4 hours – but there will be some variations. A general guide to how much to offer babies is 150 ml per kg of body weight per day (24 hours). For example:

a 3–kg baby will require 450 ml over 24 hours
a 4–kg baby will require 600 ml over 24 hours
A 5–kg baby will require 750 ml over 24 hours

Divide the daily amount by the number of feeds a day to work out how much milk to offer the infant at each feed. When a baby finishes each bottle offer more milk.

Choice of milks

There are many different kinds of formula milk available. Parents choose the type of formula for their baby and this should be continued when the baby is being cared for at nursery or in other situations. A decision to change the type of milk

1 Check that the formula has not passed its sell-by date. Read the instructions on the tin. Ensure the tin has been kept in a cool, dry cupboard.

2 Boil some fresh water and allow to cool.

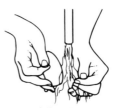

3 Wash hands and nails thoroughly.

4 Take required equipment from sterilising tank and rinse with cool, boiled water.

5 Fill bottle, or a jug if making a large quantity, to the required level with water.

6 Measure the <u>exact</u> amount of powder using <u>the</u> scoop provided. Level with a knife. Do not pack down.

7 Add the powder to the measured water in the bottle or jug.

8 Screw cap on bottle and shake, or mix well in the jug and pour into sterilised bottles.

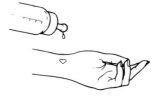

9 If not using immediately, cool quickly and store in the fridge. If using immediately, test temperature on the inside of your wrist.

10 Babies will take cold milk but they prefer warm food (as from the breast). If you wish to warm the milk, place bottle in a jug of hot water. <u>Never keep feeds warm for longer than 45 minutes</u>, to reduce the chance of bacteria breeding.

Note: whenever the bottle is left for short periods, or stored in the fridge, cover with the cap provided.

Preparing a feed

used may be made for medical or other reasons. Some babies have difficulty in digesting cow's milk products and so soya-based milk may be advised by the baby's doctor. There are some medical conditions such as phenylketonuria (PKU) that require the baby to be fed with very special formula milk.

Element C12.1

Are you ready for assessment?

Prepare equipment and formula feed

You need to show that you can competently prepare equipment and formula feeds. You will need to be directly observed by your assessor and present other types of evidence.

Direct observation by your assessor

Your assessor will need to see you carry out these performance criteria (PCs)

C12.1 PCs 1, 2, 4, 5, 6, 7, 8

During these observations your assessor must see you cover at least ONE aspect of each range category listed in this element.

Remember the range categories for this element are:

1. Equipment
2. Sterilisation

Preparing to be observed

You will need to arrange to clean bottles and other equipment and to prepare a formula feed for your assessment. Try to ensure that you cover all of range 1 by including bottles, teats, plastic cups, dishes and spoons in the articles you clean and sterilise. For range 2 use either liquid or tablet methods of sterilisation.

Read the performance criteria carefully before your assessment. Try to cover as much as you can.

Other types of evidence

You may need to present different types of evidence in order to:

- cover criteria not observed by your assessor
- show that you have the required knowledge, understanding and skills
- cover other parts of the range.

The amount and type of evidence you need to present will vary. You should plan this with your assessor.

C12.2 *Feed babies by bottle*

KUS
3, 4, 7,
13, 20

Feeding babies

When feeding babies remember the following:

- Check the feed chart to make sure that you prepare the correct amount of feed and that you are aware of any special requirements for the baby's feed.
- **Some babies are allergic to milk protein and other ingredients in baby milks and weaning foods. It is very important to be sure that you have checked that the feed you are preparing to give the baby is the correct one. Never give milk or food to a baby without checking first.**
- Ensure that you have everything ready before beginning to feed the baby.
- Wash your hands.
- Make sure that you are comfortably seated and that you are holding the baby securely.
- Fasten the baby's bib to protect her clothes.
- Use this time throughout the feed to make eye contact with the baby and to talk to her. Make this an enjoyable time.
- Test the temperature of the milk. An easy way to do this is to drop some milk on to the inside of your wrist. It should feel just warm.
- Check the size of the hole in the teat: Tilt the bottle to allow the milk to flow. It should come out of the teat in steady drops. If the hole is too small the baby will take in air as she sucks hard to get the milk, causing wind; if the teat is too large the feed will be taken too quickly and the baby may choke.
- Make sure that the bottle is held at an angle, so that the baby cannot take in air as she is fed.
- Wind the baby once or twice during a feed and at the end of the feed. To do this sit the baby upright on your lap, or you may like to gently stroke or rub her back. This should help the air in the baby's stomach to be brought up. The baby may also bring up a very small amount of the feed during winding so have a tissue or bib ready.
- Settle the baby, clean and wash her face, change the nappy if necessary.
- Clear away. Wash and re-sterilise feeding equipment.
- Record information about the amount taken and any other relevant points on the baby's feed chart so that you can give information to the parents at the end of the day.
- Ensure that any other information about any feeding difficulties is passed on to the relevant member of staff.

Feeding a baby should be a one-to-one experience

Special equipment for feeding babies

Some babies may need adaptations to the feeding equipment or specialised equipment for feeding. For example, some babies may require a larger or smaller hole in the teat or a softer or harder teat. In more specialised cases such as babies with a cleft lip and palate a special teat or spoon may be used and the baby may need to be fed in an upright position. These requirements should be clearly recorded on the baby's feed chart so that child care workers can follow parental and medical advice consistently.

Colic

Whether breast-fed or bottle-fed, some babies may experience colic, which is caused by air taken in during feeding or crying. This wind passes through the stomach and becomes trapped in the small intestines resulting in painful contractions of the intestines.

Signs of colic

The signs of colic are the baby crying, a reddened face, drawing knees up and appearing to be in pain. It is common in the evenings in breast-fed babies. However, some babies are affected by colic in the day and night. Any concerns should be discussed with the parent who may consult the health visitor or doctor.

Care of a baby with colic

- Comfort the baby.
- Lying the baby on the tummy on the carer's lap and rubbing the back will help.

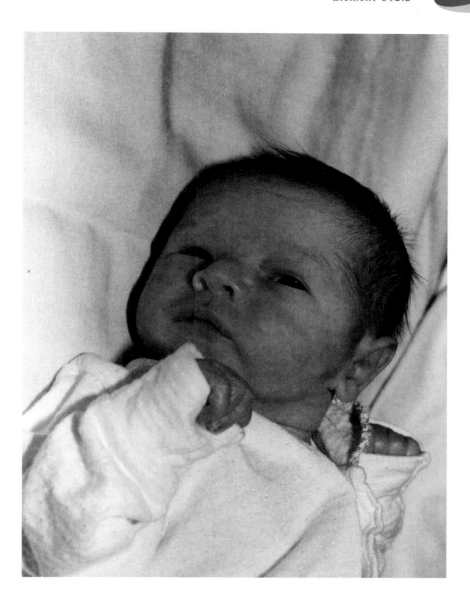

Colic usually occurs between 2 weeks and 3 months of age

- Rocking movements such as those created by car journeys, baby slings and walks in the pram may also help to relieve the pain.
- Some doctors advise breast-feeding mothers to monitor their diet to avoid foods that may exacerbate colic.
- Bottle-fed babies should be winded regularly; check the teats for hole size and flow of milk.
- The GP may prescribe medicinal drops to be taken before a feed.

Element C12.2 — Are you ready for assessment?

Feed babies by bottle

You need to show that you can competently prepare equipment and formula feeds. To do this you will need to be directly observed by your assessor and present other types of evidence.

Direct observation by your assessor

Your assessor will need to observe you carry out these performance criteria (PCs) and range in your workplace

C12.2 PCs 1, 2, 3, 4, 5, 6, 7, 8, 9, 12, 13

During these observations your assessor must see you cover at least ONE aspect in each range category listed in this element. Remember the range categories for this element are:

1. Babies' needs
2. Feeding process

Preparing to be observed

Arrange to feed a baby. Check the feed charts and make all the necessary preparations. Ensure that you and the baby are comfortable during the feed and that you talk to the baby. Smile as you talk to the baby and make eye contact. Make sure that you keep the teat covered when the bottle is put down. Clean and settle the baby after the feed and fill in the relevant records.

Read the performance criteria and range carefully before assessment. Try to cover as much as you can.

Other types of evidence

You may need to present different types of evidence in order to:

- cover criteria not observed by your assessor
- show that you have the required knowledge, understanding and skills
- cover other parts of the range.

The amount and type of evidence you need to present will vary. You should plan this with your assessor.

Prepare food and feed babies

KUS
1, 3, 10,
11, 14,
15, 21

Weaning

Weaning describes the stage when babies begin to take solid foods. This process should not be started before 4 months, and not later than 6 months.

Why is weaning necessary?

Milk alone is not enough for a baby over the age of 6 months. The baby has used the iron stored during pregnancy and must begin to take iron in their diet. Starch and fibre are also necessary for healthy growth and development. Weaning also introduces the baby to new tastes and textures of food.

Weaning and development

Babies at around 6 months are ready to learn how to chew food. The muscular movement of chewing helps the development of the mouth and jaw, and also the development of speech.

Mealtimes are sociable occasions and babies need to join in with this. As weaning progresses, they learn how to use a spoon, fork, feeding beaker and cup. They also begin to learn the social rules in their cultural background associated with eating. To do this they need good role models. Rules may include using a knife and fork, chopsticks, chewing with the mouth closed or sitting at the table until everyone has finished eating.

When to start weaning

Between 4 and 6 months, babies will begin to show signs that milk feeds alone are not satisfying their hunger. They may still be hungry after a good milk feed, wake early for feeds or not settle to sleep after feeding. It is important to work closely with the parents when a baby is weaned as babies will differ in when they need to be weaned. Some parents will be more anxious to wean a baby than others.

How to wean

As young babies cannot chew, first weaning foods are runny so that the baby can easily suck it from a spoon. Start weaning at the feed at which the baby seems hungriest: this is often the lunchtime feed. Give the baby half their milk feed to take the edge off their immediate hunger, then offer a small amount of baby rice, puréed fruit or vegetables mixed with breast or formula milk to a semi-liquid consistency from a spoon.

Remember that the baby is still open to infections. All the weaning utensils must be sterilised and careful preparation of the food and food preparation area will be needed, as described in element C12.1.

There should
be a relaxed
atmosphere with
no distractions

It will be easier if the baby is in a baby chair. There should be a relaxed atmosphere and no distractions. The carer should sit with the baby throughout the feed. It may take a few days of trying for the baby to take food from the spoon successfully.

Guidelines for weaning

- Try different tastes and textures gradually – one at a time. This gives the baby the chance to become accustomed to one new food before another is offered. If a baby dislikes a food, do not force them to eat it. Simply try it again in a few days' time. Babies have a natural tendency to prefer sweet foods. This preference will be lessened if they are offered a full range of tastes.

- Gradually increase the amount of solids to a little at breakfast, lunch and tea. Try to use family foods so that the baby experiences their own culture and becomes familiar with the flavour of family dishes.

- As the amount of food increases, reduce the milk feeds. Baby juice or water may be offered in a feeding cup at some feeds.

- Milk will still form the largest part of a baby's diet during the first year of life.

Weaning Tom

Tasleem has been Tom's nanny since he was 6 weeks old. Tom is now 4 months old and his mother has returned to work. Tom is showing signs that milk feeds are not enough and Tom's mother is going to discuss giving Tom some other foods with Tasleem. Tasleem is going to prepare a plan for Tom's weaning.

KUS
5, 10

➤ What signs have Tasleem and Tom's mother noticed that lead them to believe that Tom needs some weaning food? **KUS 5, 10**

➤ What should Tasleem include in her weaning plan for the next week? **KUS 5, 10**

Cow's milk

After 6 months, babies may be given cow's milk in family dishes. They should not be offered it as a drink until they are over 1 year old. Milk drinks should continue to be of modified milk or breast milk.

Iron

By 6 months, the baby's iron stores are low, so foods containing iron must be given. These include:

- liver
- lamb
- beans
- dahl
- green vegetables
- wholemeal bread
- cereals containing iron.

Weaning stages

Stage 1

Early weaning foods are puréed fruit, puréed vegetables, plain baby rice or baby cereal and dahl. Milk continues to be the most important food.

Stage 2

The baby will progress from puréed to minced to finely chopped food.

Stage 3

Offer lumpy foods to encourage chewing. The baby may be offered food to hold and chew, such as a piece of toast or apple. A cup may be introduced. Three regular meals should be taken as well as drinks.

Remember:

- Weaning is a messy business. Babies love to touch their food and to try to feed themselves. Just make sure that the baby's hands are washed before feeding and that the floor is washable or covered to allow for spills.
- Encourage independence by allowing the baby to use their fingers and offering a spoon as soon as the baby can hold one.
- Offer suitable finger foods.

Weaning plan

Feeds	Stage 1 (4–5 months)	Stage 2 (6–7 months)	Stage 3 (9–12 months)
On waking	Breast or bottle feed	Breast or bottle feed	Drink of milk, bottle or breast
Breakfast	Breast or bottle feed	Baby cereal mixed with breast milk or bottle milk. Breast or bottle feed	Cereal, yoghurt, fruits. Milk to drink (bottle or breast)
Lunch	1–2 teaspoons of baby rice or puréed fruit or vegetables mixed with breast or bottle milk	Finely chopped or mashed vegetables, meat or fish, mashed or stewed fruit. Water to drink from a feeding cup	Well-chopped meat, fish or cheese with vegetables. Fruit, yoghurt or fromage frais. Water or well-diluted fruit juice to drink in a cup
Tea	Breast or bottle feed	Puréed fruit or baby dessert. Breast or bottle feed	Pasta, rice or sandwiches. Fruit. Breast or bottle milk
Evening	Breast or bottle feed	Breast or bottle feed	Breast or bottle milk in a cup

- Allow the baby to find eating a pleasurable experience.
- Babies are not conventional and may prefer to eat things in a different order. Never start a battle by insisting that one thing is finished before the next is offered. When the baby has had enough of one dish, calmly remove it and offer the next.
- Babies will normally want to eat so refusing food could be a sign that a baby is ill.

Food allergies

Food allergies can be detected most easily if a baby is offered new foods separately. Symptoms may include:

- vomiting
- diarrhoea
- skin rashes
- wheezing after eating the offending food
- severe reactions such as convulsions, difficulty in breathing.

Always check before you give a baby any food to make sure that it is safe to do so.

Element C12.3

Are you ready for assessment?

Prepare food and feed babies

You will need to show that you can competently prepare equipment and formula feeds. To do this you will need to be directly observed by your assessor and present other types of evidence.

Direct observation by your assessor

Your assessor will need to see you carry out these performance criteria (PCs)

C12.3 PCs 2, 4, 5, 6, 7, 8, 9, 10

During these observations your assessor must see you cover at least ONE aspect of each range category listed in this element.

Remember the range categories for this element are:

1. Babies' needs
2. Food
3. Methods

Preparing to be observed

You will need to arrange to prepare and give a baby weaning food from a spoon and if possible provide some finger food. Try to make sure that this is relaxed and that you communicate and interact with the baby. Protect the baby's clothing and wash their hands before and after feeding. Consult the baby's feed chart before feeding and make your own entry afterwards.

Read the performance criteria and range carefully before your assessment. Try to cover as much as you can.

Other types of evidence

You may need to present different types of evidence in order to:

- cover criteria not observed by your assessor
- show that you have the required knowledge, understanding and skills
- cover other parts of the range.

The amount and type of evidence you need to present will vary. You should plan this with your assessor.

Check your knowledge

- What medical conditions might affect the weaning process? **KUS 5**
- When might vitamin and mineral supplements be necessary? **KUS 21**
- What are the stages of weaning? **KUS 3**
- What is the difference between sterilisation and social cleanliness? **KUS 12**
- Why should you always check before giving any feeds or weaning food to a baby? **KUS 14**

Provide for babies' physical development needs

UNIT C13

*T*his unit is about caring for babies aged from 0–12 months. Babies are cared for in domestic and day care situations. It includes caring for babies' physical needs and also encouraging babies' development. Information about the development of babies aged 0–12 months is in the introductory development section.

This unit has close links with C12.

This unit contains four elements:

- **C13.1** *Wash babies*
- **C13.2** *Change nappies and dress babies*
- **C13.3** *Encourage development through stimulation*
- **C13.4** *Clean and maintain clothing and nursery equipment*

Introduction

Working with babies under 1 year requires special skills. Babies are completely dependent on an adult to meet all their needs.

Emotional needs are:

- continuity and consistency of care
- physical contact
- security
- socialisation
- stimulation.

Physical needs are:

- food
- warmth, shelter, clothing
- cleanliness
- rest, sleep, exercise
- fresh air, sunlight
- safety and protection from injury and infection
- medical intervention if necessary.

To help with this many nurseries have a key worker system, where a worker is responsible for a particular baby. Babies need constant care and attention if they are to grow and develop successfully. Babies are cared for in different ways and in different settings. This could include a registered childminder working in the childminder's home, a nanny working in the child's home or a day nursery registered to care for babies. Some registered childminders are now allowed to care for babies in their own homes.

The National Standards for Under Eights' Day Care and Child Minding has additional criteria related to the care of babies.

Element C13.1 *Wash babies*

KUS
2, 4, 6, 8, 12, 13, 15, 16, 25

Caring for a baby's skin and hair will ensure the child stays comfortable and free from infection. Caring adults need to be flexible and patient. Be aware that child care practice varies. Know about and respond to the needs of the baby's parents.

Bathing and washing babies

Most babies and small children will have a daily bath. However, this may not always be necessary and parents may not wish the baby to be bathed each day. An all over wash may be enough. In most day nurseries you will only need to 'top and tail' babies (see page 291).

When preparing to wash or bath a baby ensure the following:

- The room is warm – at least 20°C (68°F) – and the windows are closed and there are no draughts.
- The room and equipment are clean and safe.
- You use protective clothing. This may include aprons and gloves. It is standard procedure in day care settings to use latex disposable gloves while washing and changing babies. In private homes high standards of personal hygiene should be followed. This includes covering any cuts and thorough hand washing.
- The water is at body temperature, 37°C (98.6°F).
- Cold water is put into the bath first.
- You have collected all the equipment together before starting the bath.
- You never leave a baby or young child alone in the bath or on the changing mat while washing.
- The baby is completely dry, after washing or bathing, especially in the skin creases. This will prevent soreness.

Equipment needed

- Baby bath and stand. At home the baby bath is often put into the big bath or used on the floor.
- Chair (if you are sitting to bath the baby).
- Changing mat. This can be placed on the floor or on a safe, raised surface.
- Protective clothing (apron, gloves).
- Bath thermometer.
- Bins with lids or plastic bags for nappies, used cotton wool, dirty clothes.
- Clean clothes.
- Clean nappy.
- Towels.
- Cotton wool swabs/balls. Sponge or flannel for older baby.
- A bowl of cooled, boiled water for washing the baby's face and eyes.
- Hair brush and comb.
- Nail scissors.

Method (for a baby under 3 months old)

- Gather all the equipment needed.
- Put on your apron and wash your hands.
- Put the water into the bath. A liquid baby bath preparation can be used according to the instructions on the label. Remember to start with cold water, then add hot. Test the temperature (it should be 37°C/98.6°F).
- Carefully lift the baby, supporting the head well. Undress her but leave the nappy on. Wrap the baby in a warm towel. Doing this on a changing mat is safest.
- Put the used clothes into a bucket or bag.
- Gently wipe each eye with a cotton wool ball, moistened with cooled, boiled water. Wipe from the inner corner to the outer (nose to ear). Use a separate cotton wool ball for each eye. This will avoid causing or spreading any infection.
- Wipe the face, neck and ears with moistened cotton wool balls.
- Dry with clean cotton wool balls. Pay good attention to skin creases, especially the neck creases.
- Clean the baby's hands, using a sponge or flannel. Check that nails are short and that there are no jagged edges that may scratch. Cut them straight across.
- Pick the baby up, still wrapped in the towel. Support the baby's head with one hand and tuck her legs under your arm.
- Hold the baby's head over the bath and with your free hand gently wet the baby's head. Apply a small amount of the preferred shampoo. Wash and rinse thoroughly.
- Move the baby back to the changing mat and dry her head with the towel.

- Unwrap the baby from the towel. Put on gloves if you are using them and take off the nappy. Clean the bottom area, using cotton wool or a separate flannel. *Always* wipe in a front to back direction. If the baby has soiled the nappy, soap is advisable to clean the area. Wet wipes may be used, but these may sometimes cause soreness.
- Place wipes and nappy into a plastic bag for disposal.
- Pick the baby up, supporting the baby's head and neck with one arm and hand. Use your other hand to support the bottom and legs. Gently lower her into the water. You can now let go of the baby's bottom and legs and use this hand to wash the baby. Pay attention to the creases around the arms and tops of the legs and the bottom. For baby boys leave the foreskin alone; do not attempt to pull it back as this will cause damage.
- Allow a short time for play and kicking but don't let the baby get cold.
- Lift the baby out of the water, supporting the bottom and legs again.
- Wrap in a towel and put her on the changing mat while you dry her thoroughly.
- Apply any creams or oils that you know are required.
- Put on a clean nappy and clothes.
- Brush or comb the hair.
- Settle the baby.
- Wash your hands and give any feeds.
- Clear away the equipment and dispose of the waste safely in the designated bins.
- Check that you clean the bath, changing mat and any other equipment and leave it clean and ready for use.

Safety while washing and bathing

Babies must be supervised at all times while in the bath or while being washed. Always hold a small baby securely while bathing and washing. As the baby gets older, she may feel more comfortable in a sitting position in the bath. Constant physical support must be given to prevent the baby from sliding under the water, or feeling insecure. A non-slip bath mat is essential for safety. Discourage older babies from standing up in the bath, as serious injuries could result from a fall.

Bathtime is fun

If the baby is safe in the bath, they will feel secure and begin to enjoy the experience of kicking and splashing. Once babies can sit up in the bath there are many toys available or you can use household objects. For example, empty washing-up liquid bottles will squirt water; plastic jugs will enable filling and pouring. In the first year a baby is more interested in physical contact and play. Blowing bubbles or singing songs with actions will all amuse and give pleasure. Hair washing can be fun too. If the baby is accustomed to getting her face wet from an early age, hair washing should be easy. If it proves difficult, leave it for a couple of days. Wipe over the head with a damp flannel and gradually reintroduce the hair

Bathtime is fun

washing gently, using a face shield if necessary. Above all, never let this area become a battle. It is not that important and may create a real fear of water that could hinder future swimming ability.

Bathtime with Iona

KUS
4

Laura is a nanny for Iona who is 8 months old. Iona has never been very happy at bathtime and washing her hair has always meant tears and upset for both Iona and Laura. Now Iona is older and is beginning to play outside she really does need her bath to get properly clean.

➤ *What would you advise Laura to do to make bathtime a better experience for them both?* **KUS 4**

➤ *How should Laura manage hair washing?* **KUS 4**

Topping and tailing

Topping and tailing involves cleaning the baby's face, hands and bottom.

Preparation

Put on protective clothing such as an apron and gloves. Collect all the necessary equipment:

● a bowl of warm water

- a separate bowl of cooled, boiled water for the eyes in the first month or so
- cotton wool balls
- baby sponge or flannel
- towel
- change of clothes
- nappies
- creams, if used
- blunt-ended nail scissors.

Method

- Lie the baby on a towel or changing mat. While lifting a small baby it is important to support the baby's head. To do this put one hand under the head and one under the body as you lift the baby.
- Remove outer clothing, if the baby is to be changed. Leave the nappy in place.
- Gently wipe each eye with a cotton wool ball, moistened with cooled, boiled water. Wipe from the inner corner to the outer (nose to ear). Use a separate cotton wool ball for each eye.
- Wipe the face, neck and ears with moistened cotton wool balls.
- Dry with clean cotton wool balls. Pay good attention to skin creases especially the neck creases.
- Clean the baby's hands, using a sponge or flannel. Check that nails are short and that there are no jagged edges that may scratch.
- Remove the nappy and clean the bottom area, using cotton wool or a separate flannel. *Always* wipe in a front to back direction. If the baby has

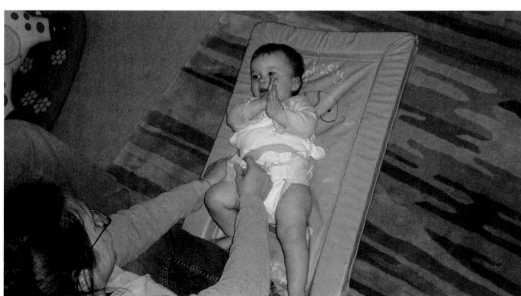

Topping and tailing

soiled her nappy, soap is advisable to clean the area. Wet wipes may be used, but these may sometimes cause soreness.

- Place wipes and nappy into a plastic bag for disposal.
- Put on a clean nappy, after the bottom has been thoroughly dried.
- Replace clothing.
- Remember, like bathing this is a time when you can talk to the baby. Communicate and have fun!
- Dispose of waste materials and nappies. Put clothes ready for collection or laundering.
- When washing, bathing and changing babies it is important to know about any preferences the parents may have. For example, they may prefer certain skin creams, shampoos, oils or lotions. The baby may have a reaction to some skin products. Always check first.

Care of black skin

All babies may have dry skin, but it is especially common in black children and they should be given special care. Always consult the parents about any special care that needs to be given to a baby's skin and hair. The following are *general* guidelines:

- Oil may be added to the bath water but do not use detergent-based products, as these are drying.
- Oil or cream may be massaged into the skin after bathing. Oil may also be massaged into the hair to help prevent dryness and damage.
- Observe the baby frequently for signs of dryness and irritation – scaly patches need treating with a moisturising cream.
- Beware of sunshine. Always use sun block on a baby's skin in the sun, and a sun hat.
- Comb very curly hair with a wide-toothed comb.
- Avoid doing tight plaits in the hair as this can pull the hair root out and cause bald patches.

Common skin problems

Cradle cap

Cradle cap affects the scalp. It is seen as a scaly, greasy or dry crust usually around the soft spot (fontanelle) on the baby's head. Prevent cradle cap by washing the hair once or twice a week, and rinsing it very thoroughly. If it becomes unsightly or sore, the crust can be removed by special shampoo.

Heat rash

Heat rash is caused by over-heating and appears as a red, pinpoint rash, which may come and go. Remove surplus clothing, bath the baby to remove sweat and to reduce the itching and make the baby feel comfortable.

Eczema

Eczema is fairly common in babies, especially if there is a family history of allergies. It begins with areas of dry skin, which may itch and become red. Scratching will cause the skin to weep and bleed. Cotton scratch mittens should prevent this. Avoid perfumed toiletries; use oil such as Oilatum in the bath and an aqueous cream instead of soap. Biological washing powders and some fabric conditioners may irritate the condition, so use an alternative. Cotton clothing is best, as it is absorbent and not irritating to the skin. The GP should be consulted if the condition is severe or causing distress.

Are you ready for assessment?

Wash babies

You need to show that you can competently wash babies. To do this you will need to be directly observed by your assessor and present other types of evidence.

Direct observation by your assessor

Your assessor will need to see you carry out these performance criteria (PCs**)**

C13.1 PCs 1, 2, 3, 5, 6, 7, 8, 9, 10, 12, 13, 14

During these observations your assessor will need to see you cover at least ONE aspect in each range category listed in this element.

Remember the range category for this element is:

1. Babies

Preparing to be observed

You will need to arrange for your assessor to see you wash or bath a baby. This is a complex procedure so you need to make sure that you have done this before and feel confident handling a baby. Read through the information given above and check that you know the sequence of the procedure. Make sure that you prepare well. Ensure that the room is clean and warm, and that all the equipment is at hand before you begin. Try to make sure that the baby is not hungry nor tired so that you can both enjoy the experience. Talk to the baby and try to make this as enjoyable as you can.

Read the performance criteria and range carefully before your assessment. Try to cover as much as you can.

Other types of evidence

You may need to present different types of evidence in order to:
- cover criteria not observed by your assessor
- show that you have the required knowledge, understanding and skills
- cover other parts of the range.

The amount and type of evidence you need to present will vary. You should plan this with your assessor.

Change nappies and dress babies

KUS
5, 11, 17, 18, 19

When to change nappies

Small babies wet and soil their nappies frequently, so it is important to change them as often as necessary. Most settings will have a routine for doing this. The usual times will be at feed times and before settling the baby down for a sleep. Extra changes will often be needed to keep the baby comfortable, dry and clean. Nappy changing should suit the needs of the baby and the wishes of the parents.

Protective clothing and personal hygiene

Aprons and gloves will be provided in settings outside the home. A plastic apron will protect your clothes. Gloves will lessen the risk of transferring germs from one baby to another. It is also essential to wash your hands before and after changing a baby. This will protect you from infection. Gloves and disposable plastic aprons must always be disposed of, well wrapped, in the correct bin.

The environment

Most settings will have an area set aside for changing babies. There may be a separate bathroom for the babies. It is important that this area is warm and free from draughts. All the equipment needed should be stored in this area so that it can easily be reached. This will include clean nappies, toiletries, clothes and bags and bins for disposing of wet and dirty nappies. In some settings parents will provide nappies and toiletries for their baby. Other settings may provide them. Strict hygiene procedures must be followed. Changing mats and surfaces must be thoroughly cleaned after each baby has been changed.

Nappies and toiletries

There are two types of nappy available, reusable (terry) nappies and disposable nappies. The choice of nappy is based on personal preference. This is something that will need to be discussed with the parents so that their preferences are followed.

These are the things to consider when choosing nappies:

- Cost – reusable (usually terry nappies) involve a larger initial cost (24 will be needed), but they are thought to be cheaper in the long term.
- Time – disposable nappies certainly take less time generally.
- Hygiene – disposable nappies need to be disposed of in a hygienic way. In the nursery a special bin is usually provided. Terry nappies need to be disinfected before washing.

Both types of nappy are quite adequate if they are used with care. Whichever type is used, babies should be changed 3–4 hourly, at each feeding time, and between if they are awake and uncomfortable. Talk to the baby, while you are changing the nappy, and let them enjoy some freedom without the restriction of a nappy.

Disposable nappies are available in a wide range of sizes. They are made to suit all ages and may be shaped for boys and girls. Terry nappies are either shaped or the standard rectangle. Rectangular nappies will need to be folded to fit each baby. Terry nappies are fastened with one or two nappy pins. These are large safety-type pins and have a safety cap that prevents the pin opening accidentally. Plastic pants are used with terry nappies. These are available in different sizes to suit each baby.

If one-way nappy liners and a disposable nappy liner are being used with a terry nappy arrange the layers like this:

One-way nappy liners help to keep the baby dry. They let the wetness through to the terry nappy but stay dry themselves. Disposable liners make dealing with dirty nappies easier as they can be flushed down the lavatory. Terry nappies are rinsed,

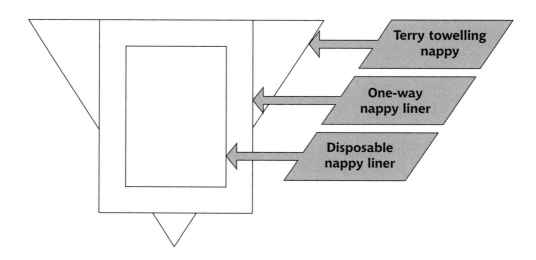

Terry towelling nappy

One-way nappy liner

Disposable nappy liner

Using a nappy liner

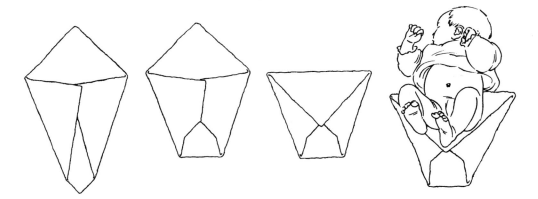

Folding terry nappies

then put to soak in nappy sterilising solution. Use a bucket with a well-fitting lid for this. Disposable nappies are well wrapped in a plastic bag and put into the correct bin. Some settings may have a special nappy unit that seals nappies into plastic bags.

In some cultures nappies are not used and babies may simply have a piece of cloth placed under them. When babies are bigger clothing is designed to make using a potty quicker and easier.

Toiletries

Many toiletries are specifically made for use with babies. These include:

- soap
- baby wipes
- lotions
- creams
- bath products
- barrier creams
- shampoo
- body powder
- sun protection creams and lotions.

There are some creams, oils and lotions that are specially made to use when changing a nappy. They help to protect the baby's bottom and prevent rashes and soreness developing. It is important to find out which toiletries are used for each baby. Parents will have particular preferences and will wish certain products to be used. Some toiletries may cause skin reactions. Babies with very sensitive skins may have special creams prescribed by their doctor.

Nappy rash

Nappy rash usually begins gradually with a reddening of the skin in the nappy area; if this is not treated it will blister and become raw and sore. It is extremely uncomfortable for the baby, who will cry in pain when the nappy is changed. Causes of nappy rash are:

- a soiled or wet nappy left on too long – this allows ammonia present in urine to irritate the skin
- an allergy to, for example, washing powder, wet wipes or baby cream
- an infection, such as thrush
- inadequate rinsing of terry nappies, and using plastic pants.

Treatment is as follows:

- Remove the nappy.
- Wash the bottom, rinse and allow to dry thoroughly.
- Let the baby lie with the nappy off as much as possible, to expose the bottom to the air.
- Change the nappy as soon as the baby has wet or soiled it, at least every 2 hours.
- Apply cream sparingly and make sure the baby's bottom is completely dry before putting on any cream.
- Do not use plastic pants.
- If there is no improvement, consult the health visitor or GP.

Changing a nappy

Prepare the changing area before you start. Make sure that the area is clean and that there are no draughts. Keep other children away from this area.

Gather all the things you will need including:

- a changing mat
- wipes or bowl of water for washing the baby's bottom
- towel or cotton wool to dry the baby
- clean clothes
- clean nappy
- a bucket with a lid for the soiled nappy
- a container for any dirty clothes.

The procedure is as follows:

- Put on an apron, wash your hands and put on gloves.
- Collect the baby from the cot or pram and lay her on the changing mat. The mat should be placed on a safe surface or on the floor. Very careful supervision is needed to ensure the baby's safety. **Never leave a baby for any reason; do not look away or get distracted.** It is best to keep one hand on the baby at all times.

- Undress the baby so that you can get at the nappy. Remove the nappy and any soiled clothes and put them into the containers.

- Clean the baby's bottom thoroughly using water, baby wipes or other chosen toiletries. Make sure her bottom is dry before applying any creams, oils or lotions chosen by the parents.

- If the baby is happy then give her time to kick free from the nappy. This is a good time to observe the baby's skin and note any marks or soreness.

- Put on a clean nappy and dress the baby.

- Place the baby back in her cot, pram or other safe place.

- Dispose of the dirty nappy and clothes.

- Wash your hands (with your gloves on), clean the changing mat and area and leave it ready for the next user.

- Remove and dispose of your apron and gloves.

- Wash your hands.

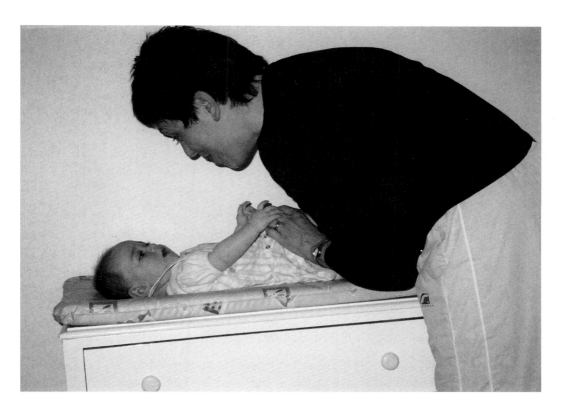

Always make time to play with the baby and talk to her while changing her nappy. Take your time and don't rush this and the baby will enjoy being free from her nappy for a while and having the full attention of her carer

Reporting any concerns

Nappy changing is a good time to observe a baby's skin. Any concerns should be recorded and reported to a senior member of staff for advice and guidance. For example, you may see:

- soreness
- a rash
- bruising.

When a baby dirties its nappy the contents are often referred to as stools. A normal stool is usually of a soft consistency and yellow in colour. Variations may mean that the baby has a problem. For example:

- streaks of blood may indicate an injury
- small, hard green stools could mean that the baby is constipated
- very frequent stools (diarrhoea) may indicate an infection.

A baby's nappy is normally wet at each nappy change. If the nappy stays dry, there is a decrease in the amount of urine passed and this may be a sign of illness. A chart to record information about feeds and urine and stools is a helpful way of identifying any cause for concern.

Dressing babies

When choosing baby clothes there are some important points to remember:

- Choose clothes that are easy to wash and dry.
- Natural fibres such as cotton are the most comfortable as they are more absorbent than synthetic fabrics.
- Clothing should be comfortable, and not too tight. This will allow for easy movement. Tight clothing, especially around the feet, can cause bones to become deformed.
- Clothes made of stretch fabric and with wide sleeves make dressing and undressing much easier.
- Avoid suits with feet, as it is tempting to continue using them after they have been outgrown. A footless suit with a pair of correctly sized socks is a better alternative.
- Clothes should have a flame-retardant finish.
- Avoid ribbons and ties. They may cause strangulation.

Baby clothes are usually made of material that can be easily washed. It is important to check before you buy that the clothes can be washed in a machine. Hand washing sounds fine, but if you are busy it takes time so restrict this to one or two special items. A baby's clothes will need washing often; always read the care label and follow the instructions. You may wish to avoid biological washing powders and conditioners for some babies whose skins are sensitive.

Clothing for the first year

Babies grow very quickly, so it is a good idea to avoid buying too many first size clothes. Shoes are not needed until a child needs to walk outside. Bare feet are preferable if it is warm enough and the flooring is safe. Choose clothes that will allow freedom of movement, as the child becomes more mobile throughout the first year.

Choose clothes that are comfortable and allow for free movement

Clothing for the first year

Element C13.2

Are you ready for assessment?

Change nappies and dress babies

You need to show that you can competently change nappies and dress babies. To do this you need to be directly observed by your assessor and present other types of evidence.

Direct observation by your assessor

Your assessor will need to see you carry out these performance criteria (PCs)

C13.2 PCs 1, 2, 3, 6, 7, 9, 10, 11, 12, 13

During these observations your assessor will need to see you cover at least ONE aspect in each range category listed in this element.

Remember the range category for this element is:

1. Babies

Preparing to be observed

You will need to arrange for your assessor to see you dress a baby and change a baby's nappy. Like washing and bathing a baby, this is a tricky procedure so make sure you have done it a few times and feel confident. Make sure that you have everything ready before you fetch the baby you are going to change. Carry out the changing and dressing in a careful and unhurried manner, and follow the guidelines above. Pay particular attention to hygiene and safety. Don't forget to talk to the baby and make sure that time is taken to let the baby be free from the nappy. When you have finished changing the baby make sure that the changing area is thoroughly cleaned and left ready for the next user. Make any records needed.

Read the performance criteria and range carefully before your assessment. Try to cover as much as you can.

Other types of evidence

You may need to present different types of evidence in order to:

- cover criteria not observed by your assessor
- show that you have the required knowledge, understanding and skills
- cover other parts of the range.

The amount and type of evidence you need to present will vary. You should plan this with your assessor.

Element C13.3 *Encourage development through stimulation*

KUS
1, 7, 9,
10, 20, 26

Promoting early development

Babies are completely dependent on their main carers to meet all their needs. Babies need constant care and attention. They also need appropriate simulation if they are to grow and develop successfully.

Babies will progress at their own rate but child care workers need to be aware of the stages of development so that they can provide what is needed to interest and encourage a baby's development. Babies learn using all their senses: touch, taste, smell, sight and hearing.

For more information about early development see the introductory section on development.

Babies enjoy repeating activities; it helps to perfect their skills, so it is important to allow babies the time to do this and not to rush them when they are concentrating on their play. Daily routines like feeding and changing provide very good opportunities to play and talk with babies.

Encouraging physical development

Babies make great progress in their physical skills in their first year. At birth they have little control of their bodies but by the time they are one year old they will be well on the way to walking. To encourage the development of walking it is important to know about the stages of physical development:

- At 6 weeks to 3 months babies will enjoy kicking vigorously. Time should be allowed in the baby's routine for her to kick with the nappy off and to lie on her back and her tummy.

- At around 5 to 6 months the baby will begin to sit and take her weight on her legs. Provide safe opportunities for sitting. Hold in a standing position so that she can bounce and practise taking her weight.

- At 9 to 12 months she may be pulling herself up to stand or walking with help. Provide safe walking opportunities by having stable furniture for the baby to use to pull herself up. Getting from one piece of furniture to another is a favourite game. Make sure that the pieces of furniture are steady and not too far apart. Hold the baby up in a standing position and support walking. Babies love this and will progress from having two hands to one hand held. Encourage babies to walk from one person to another. Make the distances short to begin with and hold your arms out to her to give confidence. Baby walkers and push along toys can also be helpful. However they need very careful supervision while they are being used as they can tip over or move too quickly for the baby.

Stimulating development

Age	Development	Role of the adult	Equipment/toys
0–6 weeks	Smiles; watches faces and near objects intently	Talking to the baby, especially when feeding or changing	Mobiles; musical cot toys; pram toys
6 weeks–6 months	Watches and plays with fingers; holds a rattle briefly; vocalises, especially when spoken to; beginning to control the head	Talk to the baby and allow the baby to 'reply'; provide opportunities to kick with the nappy off and lie on their tummy; play finger and hand games like 'Round and Round the Garden'	Bouncing cradle (ensure that this is used safely); activity blankets; baby gym and pram toys to encourage reaching and investigation; different rattles to hold
6–9 months	Sits with support; grasps objects using the whole hand; bounces if held in a standing position; laughs, vocalises; puts everything in the mouth	Provide safe opportunities for babies to sit; put cushions around them in case they topple over; provide safe object of a suitable size for the baby to grasp and put in their mouth; hold in a standing position so they can practise taking their weight and bouncing; talk and copy the sounds they make; allow time for the baby to be on the floor on the back and on the front; encourage rolling over; make time for the baby to experience the outside environment	Soft, hand-sized, washable toys; small plastic bricks; small soft balls especially those with a rattle inside; pop-up toys; books with thick pages and bright pictures; outings in the pram or buggy to look at the outside world, point out the birds, ducks, cars etc.
9–12 months	Sits well; crawls or bottom shuffles; may pull to standing and walk holding on; points at object; uses a pincer grasp to hold smaller object; claps hands; understands some words, e.g. 'bye bye'; likes to repeat sounds, e.g. 'da da'	Provide safe opportunities to develop walking skills; play Peep-bo' games and clapping games; point and name objects; allow the baby to feed herself; read books and encourage the baby to repeat words and name pictures; sing songs, repeat the names of people and objects; take the baby outside in a pram or buggy; sitting outside on a rug to view the environment	Safe, everyday objects, e.g. wooden spoons, saucepans, boxes, plastic jugs; stacking beakers; shape sorters; bath toys, jugs, sponges; bricks; soft play and climbing toys; pull along toys; books; supervised water play; may enjoy baby bouncer; outings in the pram or buggy

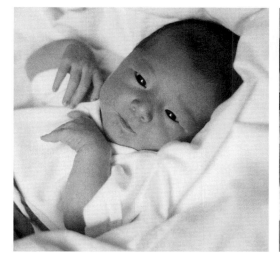
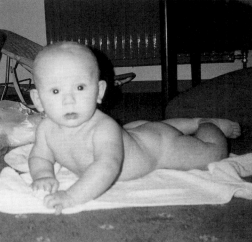

Stages in the development of walking

Safety

Babies walk at different ages, usually between 12 and 18 months. Once they can walk they are very keen to use their new skill to explore the environment. This means that ensuring their safety is very important. Fire guards and plug socket covers should be in place. Stair gates should be used to keep babies away from dangerous areas. Reins can be used to keep the baby close to you when starting walking outside. Harnesses should always be used to keep babies secure when they are in a high chair, pram or pushchair. Constant careful supervision of babies is crucial to ensuring their safety. Don't take your eye off them for a minute!

There is more information about providing a safe environment in units E1 and E2.

How babies learn through everyday interactions with their primary carers

The first year of life is an important time for the development of the infant brain. The quality of the environment and the interactions babies have with their carers are very important in ensuring babies' progress.

Interactions with babies

Babies are naturally social and seek out contact with those around them. They are likely to receive this contact from adults and older children, not from other babies. They need carers who recognise and are responsive to these early attempts at communication. If there is no response, babies will give up and opportunities to learn will be lost.

The following points are suggestions for ways to support early learning and communication:

- Provide a calm atmosphere that allows the baby to pick out familiar sounds and voices. This does not mean silence but acknowledges that baby cannot make sense of a very noisy environment.

- Use care routines as opportunities for communication with babies. Physical care may take up much of the baby's wakeful time. Changing and washing are good opportunities for close contact and chatting with a baby. Babies respond to the splash of the water and the feel of the cream on their skin. Time should be taken over these activities, and a conveyor belt approach, where babies are whisked through the procedure as quickly as possible, should *never* be used.

- Ensure that feeding is relaxed and pleasurable. Bottle-feeding should be a one-to-one experience and there should always be time for a cuddle. When babies are being weaned, the spoon should be offered at a pace that suits the baby, not the child care worker. It will not be a pleasurable experience for anyone concerned if the child care worker is spoon-feeding more than one baby at a time.

- Carers need to give babies their full attention. Babies thrive on this and will lose interest if the carer's attention is elsewhere.

- Take advantage of any opportunity to stimulate babies' curiosity about the world. Talk to them about the birds perching on the fence, the rain gushing out of the drainpipe. Point out and show them these things.
- When planning activities for babies, have realistic expectations about how they will respond and what they will get out of them. For example, hand printing on paper will be a meaningless task to an 8-month-old baby. She will be far more interested in touching and tasting the paint.

Tips for talking with babies

Babies love to communicate. But for those who have had no previous experience of working with babies, talking with babies can be daunting. You don't have to be the parent to be 'tuned in' to the baby!

Think about the following:

- Get close to the baby. Babies love faces and respond to smiles.
- Use short phrases and ordinary words, not baby talk.
- Consider the tone and modulation of your voice. Babies respond to a slightly higher pitch than usual and to expressive speech.
- Remember that you are talking with, not at the baby.
- Pause and listen so the baby can reply. This rhythm should reflect the pattern of normal conversation.
- Repetition of the same or similar phrases is helpful but don't overdo this.
- Follow the baby's lead and allow her to initiate the conversation. See what she's looking at or pointing to and respond.

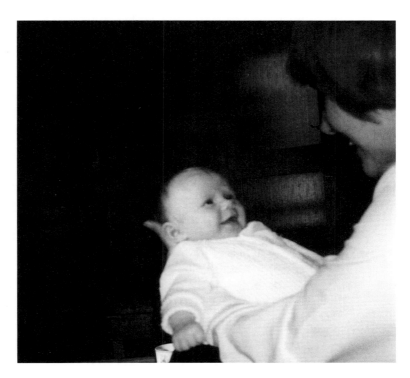

Talking with babies

Sharing information with parents

Babies make very rapid progress in their development during their first year. Most parents will be very anxious to know about their baby's progress. They will also wish to know about their baby's day, for example, what they have done, how well they have fed and what they have eaten.

Many nurseries and childminders keep a daily written record for the parents to see at the end of each day. Feed charts will also provide information, for the nursery and the parents, and can be used to record any changes.

Written records should also be used to give parents an opportunity to provide information for the nursery. Sharing information is a two-way process. This is very important when caring for babies as changes in the care needed are frequently made. A good example of this is feeding requirements. This will also help to ensure that parents' wishes and suggestions are put into practice.

Element C13.3 — Are you ready for assessment?

Encourage development through stimulation

You need to show that you can competently encourage the development of babies through stimulation. To do this you need to be directly observed by your assessor and present other types of evidence.

Direct observation by your assessor

Your assessor will need to see you carry out these performance criteria (PCs)

C13.3 PCs 1, 2, 3, 4, 5, 6, 8

During these observations your assessor will need to see you cover at least ONE aspect in each range category listed in this element.

Remember the range category for this element is:

1. Environment

Preparing to be observed

Your assessor will need to see you interacting and playing with babies in different situations. Try to include caring routines like feeding and changing as well as planned activities to stimulate development. Choose the play equipment carefully to suit the developmental stage of the baby. Don't forget the importance of eye contact and talking with the baby. Look back at the information above to help you with this. Show your assessor how your setting shares information with parents including records of activities and

▶▶

development. If possible include indoor and outdoor activities so that you can cover the range.

Read the performance criteria and range carefully before your assessment. Try to cover as much as you can.

Other types of evidence

You may need to present different types of evidence in order to:

- cover criteria not observed by your assessor
- show that you have the required knowledge, understanding and skills
- cover other parts of the range.

The amount and type of evidence you need to present will vary. You should plan this with your assessor.

Clean and maintain clothing and nursery equipment

Element C13.4

KUS
21, 22, 23, 24

Providing a safe, clean environment for babies

Keeping the environment hygienic

It is very important that strict hygiene procedures are followed in child care settings, especially where babies are being cared for. Cross-contamination and cross-infection can be avoided.

There is more information about the spread of infection in unit C1.

Checklist for a hygienic environment

The environment

- Keep kitchen work surfaces and implements clean.
- Use disinfectant to clean work surfaces regularly.
- Wash surfaces and implements with hot soapy water after they have come into contact with raw food, particularly meat, fish and poultry.
- Wash tea towels, dish cloths and other cleaning cloths regularly on the hottest cycle of the washing machine, or use very hot water if washing by hand.
- Clean babies' toys at least each day or after each session with hot soapy water or disinfectant.

- Keep toilet areas clean. Disinfect the seats, handles, door handles and sink taps at least after each session. Keep rubbish bins securely closed and out of the reach of the children.
- Nappies and other waste involving bodily fluids must be securely wrapped and disposed of in the designated bins following the policy of the setting. Child care workers must ensure that they wear latex gloves when handling any waste contaminated with bodily fluids. Wash your hands after doing this even if gloves have been worn.
- Any spills or accidents involving bodily waste must be mopped up using a 1% bleach solution, and gloves and aprons must be worn.
- Any spills should be mopped up immediately; separate mops should be assigned to the different areas of the setting, e.g. kitchen and bathroom.
- The bathroom area where babies are changed must be checked and cleaned regularly.
- Changing mats should be disinfected after each nappy change.
- Babies should have their own potty.
- Babies should have their own cot. If this is not possible then the cot should be cleaned and the bedding changed before another baby uses it.
- Babies should not share dummies or teething rings/rattles and these items should be sterilised regularly.

Personal hygiene (this refers to workers and to the older children)

Hands must be washed before:

- preparing food
- preparing babies' bottles or weaning food
- eating or drinking
- attending to skin or nappy rash
- giving a baby's medicine.

Hands must be washed after:

- going to the toilet
- handling raw food
- changing nappies
- wiping noses
- coughing or sneezing
- touching pets or their equipment.

Animals

- Keep pets free from infection.
- Keep pets out of food preparation areas.

- Wash and store pets' equipment separately.
- Keep pet food and litter trays out of children's reach.

Food preparation

- Ensure that food is handled and stored correctly.
- Prepare food following the instructions on packaging and in recipes.

Refer to unit C12 for more information on preparing baby feeds and baby foods.

Nursery equipment

All equipment must comply with safety regulations and must be used following the manufacturer's instructions. Look for the British Standards Institute and other marks of safety.

Cleaning equipment

All equipment should be cared for correctly. This will include cleaning and checking equipment regularly. Cleaning should be carried out following the manufacturer's instructions. Washable items can be cleaned using hot, soapy water then rinsed and allowed to dry. Anti-bacterial sprays are useful but be careful that they don't replace thorough washing. Soft toys can often be washed in the washing machine, but some soft toys can only have a surface wash. Follow the manufacturer's instructions. Cleaning should be regular, how often will depend on the number of children using toys and equipment, but at least at the end of each play session or more often if there is a lot of use by a large number of children. It is useful to check on the cleaning methods when buying toys. Choose those that can be washed and cared for easily. Anything that needs dry cleaning will not be a practical buy.

Checking the equipment

Assessing the safety of the equipment used should include checking:

- for any signs of wear
- for signs of actual breakage, e.g. missing parts, holes or cracks
- brakes work correctly
- harnesses are correctly fitted and show no signs of wear
- moving parts are guarded
- equipment is stable and correctly assembled
- equipment is used correctly following the instructions supplied.

Any equipment that is damaged or broken should be removed and reported to your supervisor. It may be possible to do minor repairs, like repairing a book. Repairs to equipment will need professional attention to ensure safety. Check with your supervisor.

Cleaning clothes and bedding

Baby clothes are usually made of material that can be easily washed. It is important to check before you buy that the clothes can be washed in a machine. Hand washing sounds fine but if you are busy it takes time, so restrict this to one or two special items. A baby's clothes will need washing often; always read the care label and follow the instructions. You may wish to avoid biological washing powders and conditioners for some babies whose skins are sensitive.

If bedding and clothing is very dirty it will need to be thoroughly rinsed (sluiced) to remove vomit or faeces before it is washed. Terry nappies should be put into a sterilising solution before they are washed. This procedure is described in element C13.2.

Clothes and bedding should be dried thoroughly and aired. It is good to dry clothes outside on a line as this helps to kill any germs. However, you will often find that day nurseries use a tumble dryer. Consult the manufacturer's instructions to make sure you use the right time and temperature setting. Check that the clothes are properly dry before you take them out.

Some clothes may need ironing, but things like terry nappies and sleep suits will only need to be folded. All the clothing should be stored in a warm, dry place until needed. It is much more convenient if clothes can be stored near to the changing area ready for use. This is a good time to check for any missing buttons or other things that will need a minor repair.

Care symbols for laundry

> **Only wash laundry that is labelled with the following care symbols:**
>
> 〚95〛 〚90〛
> **90°C Cottons + Linens**
>
> 〚60〛 〚40〛 〚30〛
> **60°C, 40°C, 30°C Cottons + Linens**
>
> 〚60〛 〚40〛 〚30〛
> **60°C, 40°C, 30°C Easy-care**
>
> 〚40〛 〚40〛 〚30〛 〚30〛
> **40°C, 30°C Delicates**
>
> 〚✋〛 〚40〛 〚40〛 〚30〛 〚30〛
> **40°C, 30°C Woollens (hand and machine-washable)**
>
> **Laundry that is labelled with the following care symbol must not be washed in the washing machine:**
>
> ⊠ = **do not wash**

Nursery equipment

All babies need:

- a place to sleep
- provision for bathing and changing
- to be safely transported.

To prevent cot deaths current research recommends that all babies should sleep:

- on their backs
- without a pillow
- feet against the bottom of the cot
- using sheets and blankets NOT a duvet
- in a room temperature of 18°C (64.4°F).

Checking on sleeping babies regularly or using a baby monitor can also be helpful in ensuring safety.

Practical Example

Sleeping safely

KUS 13

Jasmine is a young mother who has a new baby, India, who is just a few weeks old. Jasmine and her partner have had lots of advice about how to look after India from relatives and friends. Some say she should sleep on her tummy, others say the side or back is best. They are most anxious about the baby when they put her down to sleep and they are not in the room.

➤ *What advice would you give Jasmine about caring for India when she is sleeping?* **KUS 13**

➤ *How could they reassure themselves that India is safe when they are not in the room?* **KUS 13**

➤ *What is the policy of your setting when babies are put in their cots to sleep?* **KUS 13**

Items for sleeping, bathing, transport (what to look for)

Item	Features	Illustration
Cradle	Wooden crib or wicker basket. Ideal secure space for the baby to sleep in for the first few weeks. Ensure that the baby is moved into a larger cot as the baby grows and becomes heavier	
Carry cot	Rigid structure, carrying handles, waterproof coverings and hood. May be available with transporter (wheels), easily moved and can be used outdoors	
Pram	Look for a strong, rigid frame-built structure, waterproof with a hood and cover. Efficient, easily applied brakes. Needs to be able to accommodate the baby for at least the first year. May convert into a pushchair for an older baby	
Cot	Should be strong and stable. Bars should be no more than 7 cm (2½ in) apart to prevent the baby getting stuck. Waterproof safety mattress that fits tightly within the frame leaving no gaps. Cots with sides that lower should have childproof catches. Babies should be put to sleep on their backs (see page 313)	
Car seats	There are many types of car seat. They are all designed to be used in different ways, e.g. some are used facing forwards, some facing backwards. Some use the car's safety belts, while others are designed to be anchored to the car and have their own safety harness. Whichever car seat is selected it is *very important* that it is fixed and used according to the particular manufacturer's instructions. Always ensure that that you have had a demonstration of how to use the car seat before you attempt to use it yourself	

Items for sleeping, bathing, transport (what to look for) (cont.)

Item	Features	Illustration
Bouncing cradle	Soft fabric seat, suitable from about 6 months. Can only be used for a short time as they can move about if a baby bounces vigorously. *Needs constant supervision*	
Baby sling	Enables the baby to be carried leaving two hands free. Watch for signs of strain as the baby gets bigger	
Baby bath	Should be big enough to use until the baby can use the adult bath. A stand could be useful, but is best used inside the big bath	
Changing mat	A well-padded mat will provide a comfortable changing area. Should be washable and waterproof. There are more portable versions that can be carried in a changing bag. Changing mats should not be used on high surfaces because of the danger of the baby falling off. Much better to put the changing mat in a cot or on the floor	

Element C13.4 Are you ready for assessment?

Clean and maintain clothing and nursery equipment

You need to show that you can competently clean and maintain clothing and nursery equipment. To do this you need to be directly observed by your assessor and present other types of evidence.

Direct observation by your assessor

Your assessor will need to see you carry out these performance criteria (PCs)

C13.4 PCs 1, 2

During these observations your assessor will need to see you cover at least ONE aspect in each range category listed in this element.

Remember the range categories for this element are:

1. Articles and items
2. Hygiene procedures

Preparing to be observed

Your assessor will need to see you deal with articles that are soiled. These could include terry nappies, clothing or bedding. Make sure that you follow the hygiene procedures of the setting for cleaning and for disposing of any waste. Your assessor could also observe you as you clean and check equipment.

Read the performance criteria and range carefully before your assessment. Try to cover as much as you can.

Other types of evidence

You may need to present different types of evidence in order to:
- cover criteria not observed by your assessor
- show that you have the required knowledge, understanding and skills
- cover other parts of the range.

The amount and type of evidence you need to present will vary. You should plan this with your assessor.

Check your knowledge

- How can babies' development be stimulated during caring routines? Why is this important? **KUS 3, 10**
- What common skin conditions might you observe and report? **KUS 5, 6**
- What health and safety procedure will you observe to protect you from infection? **KUS 14**
- List the safety equipment needed when caring for babies. **KUS 20**
- Why is it important to listen to parents' wishes and advice when caring for babies? Give some examples. **KUS 25**
- Why is it important for parents to know about the daily activities of their babies? **KUS 26**

Monitor, store and prepare materials and equipment

This is a basic unit that covers giving administrative and technical support when you are asked to. It includes setting up a variety of technical equipment such as audio (listening), visual (watching) and scientific (like a computer) equipment for use by others. It also includes preparing copies of papers, sets of art and craft materials, and other play and learning resources. You must also show you can monitor (check and record) stock levels; this includes levels of stationery, play and learning materials.

This unit contains three elements:

⌣ **M1.1** *Prepare equipment*

⌣ **M1.2** *Prepare materials*

⌣ **M1.3** *Monitor and store materials*

⌣ Introduction

Resources

Child care and education settings have varying amounts of audio, visual and other electronic equipment, such as computers, available for use. Some settings have very little equipment; others have a wide variety. Similarly, the quality and amount of other materials varies between settings.

Settings use the equipment and materials they have differently. Some have fewer resources, but may use them more effectively than those that have more.

Settings also vary in the way they monitor and store their materials and equipment, and in the way they make them available for use by children.

Resources, storage and access

The amount of resources a setting has, its storage capacity and the ease of access to resources are affected by a number of things. These include:

Some settings use the equipment and materials they have more effectively than others

The setting has more money to spend on resources	The setting has a relatively low income
The premises are for the sole use of the setting (e.g. a private day nursery, a nursery class)	The premises are used by different people at different times of the week for a variety of purposes (e.g. a pre-school in a community hall)
Equipment is stored where it is available for use. It does not have to be put away in another place	All equipment has to be cleared away at the end of a session into a storage area
There is ample purpose-built storage	There is little space for storage
Storage areas are secure	There is low security for storage

We should never judge the quality of the child care and education provision of a setting by the amount or value of the equipment and materials it has. The sensitivity of the staff to the children and the richness of interaction between staff and children is of far greater importance.

However, all registered child care settings are required to have some materials for children to play with and use. The quality of these materials will affect the children's experiences. It is important to make the best use of equipment and materials.

Part of your role is to help support staff in preparing, monitoring and storing equipment and materials, and to make the best use of these resources. If resources are badly stored and monitored there will be:

- more wastage
- less for the children to use

and this will affect the quality of their experiences.

Element M1.1 *Prepare equipment*

KUS
1, 2, 3, 4

Preparing equipment

It is very important that you prepare equipment for use by following the manufacturer's instructions correctly. This is to ensure that:

- children's health and safety is protected
- your own and other adults' health and safety are protected
- best use is made of the equipment to promote learning and enjoyment.

Equipment can present possible dangers to children and adults if prepared or used incorrectly. The use of electricity, the mechanism of the equipment, how heavy it is to carry or where it is positioned all present dangers. It is your responsibility to minimise any danger by following the manufacturer's instructions correctly. This will also ensure that everyone can make best use of the equipment in safety.

It is very important that you prepare equipment for use by following the manufacturer's instructions correctly

Special requirements

There may also be some special requirements for preparing equipment in your setting and you need to be aware of these. A supervisor may tell you about the particular operating procedures and safety requirements of your setting regarding the use of equipment. These requirements may be written down as a policy. It is important that you take note of these and follow them carefully.

Special requirements may be linked to the type of premises and the age of the children.

How you prepare equipment will depend on things such as:
- the space available (or lack of it)
- the position of doors and sources of water
- rules laid down by whoever owns the premises
- how heavy the equipment is
- having suitable tables or other surfaces to put equipment on
- the age of the children (the presence of very young children who are crawling or moving around freely presents a particular hazard).

It is useful to develop a good awareness of the environment in which you work. You should also use your 'common sense' when dealing with equipment. If something looks dangerous to you, use your initiative, take action to prevent an accident and tell someone about it. Do not wait until somebody tells you to do something about it.

Equipment that you may have to prepare

The equipment listed below can have a value in promoting learning in an enjoyable and effective way. You may be required to help prepare any of this equipment for use by the children either on their own or together with a member of staff.

The types of equipment you may need to prepare may include:

Audio equipment	Radio, cassette, CD, mini disc recorders and players
Visual equipment	Television, VHS video recorders, DVD players, digital cameras, overhead and slide projectors
Computers	Small battery-powered games and computers, programmable toys, PCs, printers, scanners and photocopiers

Instructions about how to assemble (put together) and use equipment may be described in words or as a series of diagrams in a booklet supplied by the manufacturer. You should follow the instructions one step at a time. These instruction booklets should be stored in a well-ordered way in a place that all staff know about and can easily access. Similarly, any accessories and spare parts, such as headphones, remote controls, tapes and disks required for different types of equipment, should be stored where staff can find them easily.

If you can, you should spend time reading, understanding and practising carrying out the manufacturer's instructions before you need to prepare any equipment for use. It is also a good idea to practise setting up equipment when the children are not there. In this way you can learn how to do it without feeling under pressure. It also gives you time to ask for some advice and be shown by another member of staff if necessary.

Setting up equipment

Once you have read the manufacturer's instructions and have practised setting up a piece of equipment you should be ready to use it. Another member of staff may ask you to prepare some equipment for them or you may need to prepare it as part of an activity that you have planned yourself. You should always check with a supervisor that you are permitted to use a piece of equipment.

The correct time and place and position

It is your responsibility to know when and where a piece of equipment is needed. You will know this if you have planned the activity yourself. Alternatively, someone may ask you to provide it at a certain time or it may be part of the activity plan that you are following for the day. Equipment may be needed for the whole or part of the day; for example, a computer all day or a tape recorder with several sets of headphones for part of it. You should ensure that the use of equipment is supervised if this is necessary. You should never set it up and assume someone else is watching it.

You should refer to activity plans so that you know where the equipment is needed. This should be in an area that is safe and best suited to its use. For example, you should not put noisy equipment near a quiet area or electrical equip-

Equipment needs to be in a position for adults and children to make the best use of it

ment near water or in an unventilated space.

The position of equipment can be very important. It needs to be in a position for adults and children to make the best use of it. Equipment that children use on their own should be at their height, dependent on whether they will be standing or sitting to use it.

Particular care should be taken with the position of equipment that needs to be plugged into an electric socket. An appropriate officer should routinely check plugs and sockets. Sockets should be covered until in use. Wires should be treated carefully. They should be covered or taped down to prevent tripping over them.

Links with E1 and E2.

If a group of children are using audio or audio visual equipment (listening or listening and watching), it is important that they can all hear and see it. It should be positioned so that children with a hearing or visual impairment have full access to it.

Faults in equipment

You should make sure that you know the procedures of the setting for dealing with faults in equipment.

These will usually include:

- checking equipment before it is used to make sure there are no faults
- if there are faults, removing the equipment from use
- reporting the fault to the relevant person
- recording the fault according to the procedures of the setting
- if requested, making sure that the equipment is discarded safely or is mended by an appropriate person
- finding a replacement if possible.

Practical Example

KUS
1, 2, 3, 4

Playing 'Sound Lotto'

Ann worked as an assistant in a private day nursery, in a room with eight 3 and 4 year olds. The nursery officer in charge of the room asked her to prepare a game called 'Sound Lotto'. Ann put two tables together and a chair for each child and one for herself and the nursery officer. She placed the tables near to an electric socket on the wall. She fetched the game from the shelf in the room. She collected a tape player from the office and briefly re-read the instructions for its use. She removed the socket cover and plugged the tape player in. She covered the wire with a rubber mat. She inserted the tape and checked that the player was working correctly, and then rewound the tape. Ann then paced eight lotto cards in front of each place and nine counters beside each card.

She then called the nursery officer and the children to the table. Everything was ready for the sound tape to be played. She placed the tape player near her in a position so that each child in turn would be able to come and turn the player on and off in turn to play each sound. She ensured that the youngest children in the group sat closest to her.

➤ *Why did Ann arrange the tables in the way she did?* **KUS 4**
➤ *How did she meet health and safety requirements?* **KUS 2**
➤ *How did she check for possible faults?* **KUS 1**
➤ *Describe and comment on what Ann did.* **KUS 1, 2, 3, 4**
➤ *Why did she sit the youngest children nearest to her?* **KUS 3**

Element M1.1

Are you ready for assessment?

Prepare equipment

You need to show that you can competently help to prepare equipment. To do this you will need to be directly observed by your assessor and present other types of evidence.

Direct observation by your assessor

Your assessor will need to see you carry out these performance criteria (PCs)

M1.1 PCs 1, 2, 3, 4, 5, 7

During these observations your assessor must see you cover at least ONE aspect in the range category listed in this element.

Remember the range category listed for this element is:

1. Equipment

Preparing to be observed

Your assessor will need to see you preparing at least one type of equipment listed in the range. This could be audio or video equipment or a computer. When you prepare this equipment you should make sure that you follow the manufacturer's instructions for preparing it. You should also correctly follow any special requirements for preparing the equipment and any health and safety requirements. Your assessor should see you set up the equipment in the correct place and time. You should position it correctly. You should make sure that any necessary accessories and information are readily available and within easy access.

Read the performance criteria and range carefully before your assessment. Try to cover as much as you can.

▶▶

> ## Other types of evidence
>
> You may need to present different types of evidence in order to:
> - cover criteria not observed by your assessor
> - show that you have the required knowledge, understanding and skills
> - cover other parts of the range.
>
> The amount and type of evidence you need to present will vary. You should plan this with your assessor.

Element M1.2 *Prepare materials*

KUS
5, 6, 7

Preparing materials

Part of your role in an early years setting will be to prepare materials for use in the setting. This may include copies of papers. It will also include preparing paper, art and craft, play and other learning materials.

Preparing copies of papers

In order to produce copies of papers you must learn how to use a copying machine. This is most likely to be a photocopier. If your setting uses an older type of copying

Part of your role will be to prepare art and craft materials

machine you may have to learn to use this. Not all settings have their own copying machines, particularly if they do not have sole use of their premises. In this case you will have to be guided by staff about where to make copies. They may go to a local shop to do this. You will have to learn to operate copying equipment. To do this you should follow the guidelines covered in M1.1 above. You should particularly follow the manufacturer's instructions and be aware of health and safety issues.

You may need to make copies for staff, for example, copies of curriculum and activity plans, magazine articles, procedures, letters and other notices. Or copies may be for the use of children during an activity.

Quantity, layout and format

Staff should tell you the correct number of copies they want; if the copies are for your own use you should estimate the number carefully. If you produce too few you may waste time making more copies or may not even be able to do this easily; if you produce too many it is wasteful of money and resources.

You may need to change the layout and format of the papers you are copying. You may need to (see range):

- change a one-sided copy to a double-sided, or the other way round
- reduce the size of a piece of writing or illustration, or enlarge it
- group together different sheets of paper in a particular order (sorting and collating).

These tasks are more complicated than reproducing one sheet of paper. To achieve them you will need to practise and become skilled in the use of the different functions (things it can do) of the copier.

In addition to reading instructions, it can be very helpful if someone demonstrates the correct use of a machine to you. They can also help you to check that you are following the manufacturer's instructions and complying with health and safety requirements. This is very important if you need to cut copies after you have made them using a guillotine machine.

Copying is expensive. The more skilled you are in using a copier correctly the less wasteful of materials you will be. The best way to cut down on waste is to become skilled and know the number of copies you need.

Dealing with faults

Any piece of equipment can develop a fault. It is important to identify a fault rather than ignore it and trying to run the machine regardless. This could lead to further damage and could also be dangerous.

If a fault develops with electrical equipment you should turn it off, then turn the socket switch off, remove the plug and insert the socket cover. You should then follow the procedures of your setting and report the fault to your supervisor or the person with responsibility for the equipment. This may include making a written record of the fault and what led to it.

Some machines come with instructions about how to deal with faults, for example, when a photocopier becomes jammed with paper. It is not uncommon for copying machines to become jammed with paper and stop working. This sometimes happens because we ask too much of them! Machines have different capacities for producing volumes of copies in a short time. You should be aware of the capacity of a machine and avoid overloading or overheating it. Jamming is the most common fault. You should keep calm and follow the instructions or ask for help.

Preparing other materials

Other materials you may need to prepare are listed below:

Materials	Examples	Preparation and presentation
Papers	Paper and card of different colours for drawing, painting, displays	Paper should be of the required size, shape, colour and type for the activity
Art and craft materials	Brushes, glue sticks, pens, pencils, crayons, scissors, glue, paint, clay, dough, junk materials	These should be: clean, dry, in good condition and non-toxic of the right size and appropriate to the age of the children (include adaptations for children with individual needs, such as left-handed scissors) in appropriate containers and pots in a position that the children can reach and use comfortably stored in a way that preserves them for future use
Play materials	Sand, sawdust, shavings, containers, small equipment, resources for role play, jigsaws, games, small toys, models, bricks, construction toys	These should all be stored in an appropriate way to maintain their cleanliness and freshness. They should be checked for damage before use and, if so, removed. Play materials for use by the children should be presented in the right containers, such as trays on stands. Floor and table protective coverings should be put out first. Role play materials should be checked for wear and replaced if worn or dirty. Jigsaws should be complete
Learning materials	Books; science materials such as magnifying glasses, gardening tools, cooking utensils and raw ingredients; natural materials, such as leaves, flowers, shells	These should be prepared and put out at the right time and in the way requested. Care should be taken to supervise the children until the specified person is ready to supervise their use

Play materials for use by the children should be presented in the right containers

Quantity and quality

As with papers, it is important to provide the correct quantity of materials. The activity plan should include an estimate of the quantities of different materials needed. This should be estimated according to the number of children who are expected to access the activity and the length of time of the activity. In this way the children will have enough materials to enjoy the activity and promote their learning. Too few materials may lead to children becoming frustrated, bored and argumentative.

Always make sure that any materials you produce are of a suitable quality. This includes manufactured and disposable materials, natural materials such as sand, water and plants. It is essential to use good quality materials, that have the appropriate safety and kite marks, to ensure the health and safety of the children.

You need to be aware of any shortages in materials before an activity is due to begin. This will be easy if you prepare for an activity in good time. Good

Make sure that any materials you produce are of a suitable quality

monitoring should enable stocks to be kept at the right level. If stocks are running low, good preparation should enable you to replace them in time.

If there are shortfalls you should refer them to the responsible person in the nursery and follow the procedures of the setting for reordering. This may include you recording the shortfall in a particular record book. Shortfalls may be caused at certain times by:

- shortage of money at the end of a financial year
- running stocks down for a holiday period
- keeping stocks low because decorating or alterations are planned.

Are you ready for assessment?

Prepare materials

You need to show that you can competently help to prepare materials. To do this you will need to be directly observed by your assessor and present other types of evidence.

Direct observation by your assessor

Your assessor will need to see you carry out these performance criteria (PCs)

M1.2 PCs 1, 2, 3, 4, 7, 8

During these observations your assessor must see you cover at least ONE aspect in the range category listed in this element.

Remember the range categories listed for this element are:

1. Copies of papers
2. Materials

Preparing to be observed

Your assessor will need to see you produce copies of papers in the correct quantity, layout and format. You will need access to a copier to do this; this may not be in your setting. It is useful if you can prepare a number of copies and cover as much of the range as you can. If the machine allows, your assessor could observe you producing one-sided, double-sided, reduced and enlarged copies, and also collating some copies of papers.

You must show your assessor that you are using the equipment according to the manufacturer's instructions.

Your assessor will also need to see you presenting an appropriate quality and quantity of materials to a person in the setting at an agreed time. In order to cover the range these could be the papers you have already copied; however, they could be some art and craft materials such as paint and brushes and/or other play and learning materials.

Read the performance criteria and range carefully before your assessment. Try to cover as much as you can. ▶▶

Other types of evidence

You may need to present different types of evidence in order to:

- cover criteria not observed by your assessor
- show that you have the required knowledge, understanding and skills
- cover other parts of the range.

The amount and type of evidence you need to present will vary. You should plan this with your assessor.

Element M1.3 *Monitor and store materials*

KUS
7, 8,
9, 10

Storing materials

Any setting you work in will have arrangements for the storage of materials. These should include following the health and safety requirements for their storage and use.

At the beginning of this unit we discussed the fact that the amount of resources a setting has, their storage capacity and ease of access to resources are affected by a number of things.

Some settings have sole use of their premises, like most day nurseries. In day nurseries some resources and materials can be kept in the room where they are used. However, even single use buildings can have limited storage space.

Other settings are used by different people during the week, like many pre-school playgroups in community halls. In these, all materials have to be cleared away at the end of a session into a storage area. The security and accessibility of these storage areas is an issue.

Accessing materials

Whether materials are stored in the room where they are used or in separate areas it is essential that users can easily access them. The use of large, disorganised cupboards that no one can reach the back of, results in equipment and materials being under-used and deteriorating from lack of attention. Each setting will have its own policy about the amount of free access children are allowed to materials. For example, some settings may allow children to choose from a wide range of art and craft materials at any time and use them as they wish; others may only have certain materials accessible at certain times.

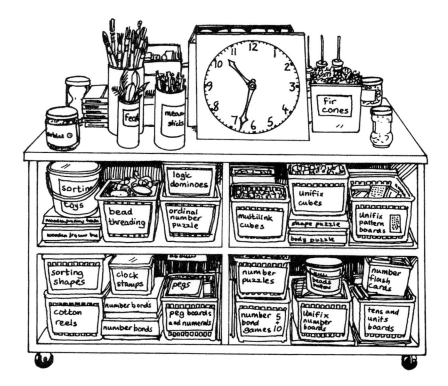

Clear labelling, that is appropriate to the user, is essential for the best use and monitoring of materials

Whatever the policy, clear labelling, that is appropriate for the user, is essential for the best use and monitoring of materials.

Involving children in storing materials

Children are involved in helping to clear away and store materials in varied ways in different settings. Their involvement may be limited by the type setting. However, many settings aim to involve children in very practical ways in the storage of the materials they use. They put materials in a place that children can both take them out of and learn to put them away again after use. This can:

- be a very effective use of time
- enhance independence and a sense of responsibility
- increase co-operation between children
- promote creativity
- help the development of good patterns of behaviour.

Adults can provide a good role model by themselves clearing away materials that they use.

Storing papers

Paper should be stored in a way that maintains it in the condition in which it was purchased. This can be difficult as it is very easy when removing a few sheets of paper to pull out others. These are then easily damaged when they are put back

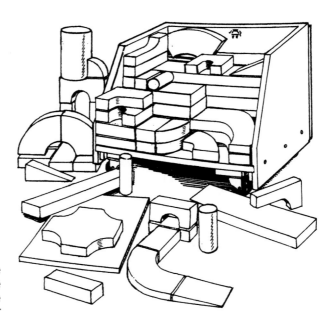

Many settings aim to involve children in very practical ways in the storage of the materials they use

on the pile. It is the responsibility of all staff, including you, to maintain the condition of paper. This is made easier if shelves are of the right size and at an accessible height. Paper is heavy and should never be stored at a height where it might injure anyone if pulled out on top of them. You may be asked to keep a storage area tidy, if so you should take this job seriously as you will be responsible for:

- maintaining the quality of materials used by children
- keeping costs down, by minimising wastage caused by damage.

Storing art and craft materials

Brushes, glue sticks, pens, pencils, crayons, scissors, glue, paint, clay, dough and junk materials should all be stored in ways that preserve them in the best condition for future use and prevent deterioration.

You should always follow the manufacturer's instructions for the storage of any of these materials, particularly where there are health and safety requirements. These instructions may also cover temperature, position and the preferred way up. Make sure that you also understand and learn the procedures of your setting for the storage of materials. There are probably agreed places to store things so that everyone knows where they are.

Any material with a moisture content will have a limited life span (paint, glue, pens, dough, clay). However, correct storage will increase the life of some of these.

Pay particular attention to materials that need to be kept in air-tight containers (such as clay) and at cool temperatures (such as dough) to prevent deterioration.

Make sure that any tops are put on jars and pens before they are stored.

Check that pens and brushes are stored with their tips upwards.

Storing play materials

Your setting will need storage space for a wide range of large play equipment such as wheeled toys, a climbing frame both for indoor and outdoor use.

It will also need to store smaller play materials, including natural materials such as:

- sand, sawdust, shavings
- containers for these and water
- small equipment and tools to use with these
- resources for role play
- games, jigsaws, small toys, models, bricks and construction toys.

Your setting will need storage space for large play equipment

When storing play materials, it is essential that:

- they are stored in a well-ordered way to prevent deterioration
- only clean and undamaged materials are stored
- appropriate shelving and containers are used
- any health and safety requirements and manufacturer's instructions about storage are followed
- the procedures of the setting for storage are followed.

Storing other learning materials

The principles outlined above for the storage of other materials should be applied to these other learning materials. They may include materials such as magnifying glasses, gardening tools, cooking utensils and raw ingredients, and natural materials such as leaves, flowers and shells. These may include some delicate items that need particular care and attention when being stored to prevent damage. It may be necessary to store some things, such as food items, in a refrigerator to prevent deterioration until they are needed.

Monitoring materials

Taking an inventory

The basis of accurate monitoring of materials is first to be aware of the materials that the setting owns or has on loan. It is a good idea to have a complete list (inventory) of all equipment and materials. These can be divided into different sections that group similar items together. The inventory should distinguish between items that need to be replaced because of wear and tear, such as books and puzzles, and those that continuously need replacing because of constant use, such as paper and paint. It should also suggest the minimum amount of disposable materials, such as paper and paint, that should be kept in store for use at any time.

Recording usage

Settings will inform you of their procedure for recording the use of materials by staff and children. It may be that every member of staff who uses materials records this use on a record sheet. You should use this to make a record of the things that you use yourself. This may be on a sheet or in a book in the stock cupboard or in a file that is kept somewhere else.

You may be given responsibility for checking the stocks of materials at regular intervals. As well as checking the amount of materials, you must also check whether items such as sand, paint and dough are safe and hygienic for use. If they have deteriorated you should report this to a relevant leader in the way that you have been told. This may include you making a written record and disposing of the materials in a safe manner.

Keeping records of stock levels

When you have checked the quantity and quality of materials you should follow the procedures of the setting to make an accurate and up-to-date record of what you have found. If there is not a system for recording stock levels you may be able to help produce one.

Dealing with shortfalls and ordering materials

If, after recording the quantity and quality of materials in stock, you think there is a need to replenish (build up the stock) or replace some items, you should tell the person who is responsible for ordering stock. You may speak to them about this but you should also show them the records you have made. This will help them to complete an order form or make a list of what they need to buy.

Element M1.3

Are you ready for assessment?

Monitor and store materials

You need to show that you can competently help to monitor and store materials. To do this you will need to be directly observed by your assessor and present other types of evidence.

Direct observation by your assessor

Your assessor will need to see you carry out these performance criteria (PCs)

M1.3 PCs 1, 2, 3, 4, 5, 6, 8

During these observations your assessor must see you cover at least ONE aspect in the range category listed in this element.

Remember the range category listed for this element is:

1. Materials

Preparing to be observed

Your assessor will need to see you carry out arrangements for the storage of some or all of the materials described in the range. You should do this according to the procedures of the setting; that is, you should put the materials in the place agreed for them. You should also show your assessor how materials are stored in accordance with manufacturer's instructions and health and safety requirements.

You should enable your assessor to inspect the setting and show your assessor how the storage allows easy access to users, and how you and others make a record of the materials you use. You should demonstrate how you monitor stock levels, when this is done and how this is recorded and kept up to date. You should also show how you monitor materials for cleanliness and deterioration, and how you report this to others.

Read the performance criteria and range carefully before your assessment. Try to cover as much as you can.

Other types of evidence

You may need to present different types of evidence in order to:

- cover criteria not observed by your assessor
- show that you have the required knowledge, understanding and skills
- cover other parts of the range.

The amount and type of evidence you need to present will vary. You should plan this with your assessor.

Check your knowledge

- What are the procedures in your setting for dealing with faults in equipment? **KUS 1**
- What happens if resources are badly stored and monitored? **KUS 8, 9**
- If equipment is prepared or used incorrectly, what might happen? **KUS 2, 3**
- Why can the position equipment is placed in be very important? **KUS 3**
- What should you do if there is a shortage of materials? **KUS 7**
- Why is it important for children and adults to be able easily to access materials and equipment? **KUS 8**
- When storing brushes, glue sticks, pens, pencils, crayons, scissors, glue, paint, clay, dough and junk materials what should your main aim be? **KUS 6, 8, 9**

Work with parents in a group

T his unit looks at how child care workers inform parents about the ways in which the setting operates. It also covers the variety of ways in which child care settings and parents can work together. It considers the different positions and perspectives of parents, and the part parents can play both in supporting events at the setting and by contributing to children's activities.

This unit has close links with unit P1 (candidates should refer to this for additional background information before starting to collect evidence for this unit).

This unit contains three elements:

- *__P9.1__ Inform parents about the operation of the group*
- *__P9.2__ Encourage parents to participate in group functions*
- *__P9.3__ Encourage parents to participate in children's activities*

Introduction

All elements of this unit require an understanding and appreciation of the role that parents play in the care and education of their children, and of the need for child care workers to value the benefits of parental involvement in the child care setting by positively encouraging this through their policy and practice.

Inform parents about the operation of the group

P9.1

KUS
1, 5, 6, 7

Settings inform parents about the operation of their group in a number of ways. When parents are thinking about which setting to choose for their child they will talk with staff about the day-to-day routine and about the facilities that are offered. Often they will visit a number of settings before deciding which is most suited to their child. Brochures, prospectuses and other written information is usually provided too, so that a full picture can be given. All of these will provide starting points for questions from parents. Parents also gain information about the way that the group operates from the physical environment and how the setting is arranged (see unit P1). Once children start attending there is a need to keep parents informed and up to date with what is happening.

A notice board will keep parents informed and encourage involvement

Skills for talking and listening

Thinking about your own communication skills and how these might have an affect on your relationships with parents can be helpful. When talking with or listening to parents, consider the following points:

- Make eye contact but be careful – a fixed stare can be very off-putting.

- Don't interrupt and make comparisons from your own experiences. Encourage further conversation with phrases such as 'I see . . .', 'Tell me . . .'.

- Make sure that you are at the same level. Try not to sit down if the parent is standing, and vice versa. Doing this will make communication seem less equal.

- If a parent seems upset or wants to discuss something in private, find some-where suitable to talk.

- Summarise the points that have been made during and at the end of a discussion. This recap will be particularly helpful if the parent has come to discuss ways of dealing with a problem.

- Keep your distance. Everyone needs a space around them. If you get too close, the person you are speaking to may feel uncomfortable. (On the other hand, people from some cultural backgrounds may have a different view of personal space and could interpret your distance as unfriendly.)

- You may feel that a parent is worrying over something quite unimportant. Try not to dismiss these concerns as insignificant as the parent may be reluctant to confide in you in future. Try to be reassuring.

- Avoid using jargon (terms that only someone with your professional background would understand). This is off-putting and limits the effectiveness of your communication.

- Recognise that all parents, not just those who speak the language of the setting, will want to share information and be consulted about their children's progress and think about any arrangements you may need to make. (See 'Communicating with everyone' below.)

- Make the limits of confidentiality clear. Assure the parent that you will deal with any information shared professionally, but be clear that you may have to pass some things on.

- Remember (particularly if you are a trainee) that you will usually need to discuss with colleagues and your line manager any requests that a parent might make. Don't make agreements or promises that you might not be able to keep!

Staff should be welcoming to parents

Written communications

Most settings provide a variety of written information for parents. This is helpful for general information that parents might want to keep and consider, and for keeping parents informed about current events and developments.

Brochures

All centres will have a brochure that they provide for parents giving them information about the service offered. Of course, these will vary, though there will be common factors. All will probably include:

- location, including address, telephone number, person to contact
- the times that the centre is open and the length of sessions
- the age range of children catered for
- criteria for admission (for example, a workplace nursery may require the parent to work in the establishment; social services establishments may require children to be referred through a social worker or health visitor)
- information about meals and snacks provided
- information about the facilities and accommodation available
- schedule of fees (if any) to be charged
- reference to any policies, especially those relating to special educational needs, equal opportunities and behaviour
- the qualifications of the staff and staff roles and responsibilities
- an indication of the daily or sessional programme for the children
- what parents are expected to provide, for example, nappies, spare clothing, sun cream

A brochure provides a great deal of information

- details of any commitments the parent must make, for example, rota days, notice of leaving, regular attendance

- details of any approach to learning followed, for example, learning through play and the curriculum followed

- information about the complaints procedure.

A brochure can provide the parent with a great deal of information, which will also be useful to refer to once the child has started at the centre.

Other types of written communications

Parents can expect to receive a whole range of written communications once their child has started at a centre. Some centres produce their own booklets, for example, about their approach to reading or other areas of the curriculum, indicating to parents the part they can play in their children's learning. Parents might also receive regular newsletters, invitations to concerts, parents' meetings, requests for assistance and support, information about the activities provided for children, advance notice of holidays and centre closures, and so on. These will often be reinforced with notices and verbal reminders. It is important that these notices and letters communicate the information in a clear and friendly manner.

Sometimes there will be a need for a more individual exchange of information, for example, if a child has an accident during the session. This might be written in a note to the parent or it might be explained at pick-up time. Parents need to know what has happened and someone needs to have responsibility for passing on this information. Many centres provide regular written reports to parents on their children's progress.

Communicating with everyone

It is the responsibility of the child care centre and its workers to ensure that they provide opportunities to communicate with all parents, remembering that, for some, they may need to make special provision.

- Some parents may not share the language of the setting. All parents, not just those who speak English, will want to share information and be consulted about their children's progress. Try to organise for someone to interpret for them – some local authorities will provide this service or have a list of interpreters. Remember that it is inappropriate to rely on an older child or another parent to interpret, particularly if the conversation is concerned with sensitive issues. Deaf parents who use sign language will require communication support too. (Sign language interpreters are usually very busy but your local deaf club or society should be able to help you to find one.)

- Don't assume that all parents are able to read and write. If you are aware of this, you can talk to parents rather than rely on written information. Parents may speak a home or community language fluently but often may not read and write in it. You should be aware of this if you are having materials translated.

- Some parents may be very pressed for time and cannot enjoy a relaxed chat with staff when they bring and pick up their children. You should not assume that they don't wish to talk about how their children are doing. Try to make alternative arrangements, perhaps for an out-of-hours appointment or a telephone conversation.

Different approaches to child rearing and play

As child care workers, it is important that you recognise that families may have different approaches to bringing up their children. Families from the same cultural, religious or ethnic background may have similarities in their approach to bringing up their children but there are likely to be many differences too. You should not make assumptions that families will respond or behave in a certain way because they belong to a particular group. Provided children are healthy and happy, you should not criticise a particular approach just because it is not what you would do.

However, there may be times when there are difficulties in the relationship between parents and the child care setting. Staff will need to take a positive approach to managing these. Below are some examples of difficult situations:

- methods of disciplining children in the setting may be quite different from those of the home
- parents who are experiencing stresses and strains in their lives may appear to react angrily and aggressively to what seems to be a minor incident, for example, paint on a child's clothes
- there may be agreements over, say, collecting children at an agreed time, paying fees in advance, that are not kept to
- parents may disagree with the methods of the centre, for example, challenging a 'learning through play' approach
- rules such as no smoking on the premises may be challenged and broken
- where there are child protection procedures in operation and a centre has a role in monitoring and reporting on contact between parents and children, the relationship between child care workers and parents may be strained.

There is no magic formula for resolving difficulties but a centre that values working in partnership will work hard to maintain the confidence of parents by trying to resolve any conflict to the satisfaction of all concerned. This is most likely to happen if:

- staff deal seriously and courteously with parents' concerns
- anger and aggression are dealt with calmly and not in a confrontational manner
- parents' feelings, opinions and skills are acknowledged and valued

- the centre has a consistent and well thought out approach to the way that it works with parents, which all staff are aware of and support
- any concerns that staff have are communicated promptly and honestly with parents.

To sum up, child care workers need to take a non-judgemental approach, that is one that recognises that parents have a great deal to contribute to the shared care of their children, and where professionals accept that parents' views and values may differ from their own.

KUS 7

Learning through play

Maria, a lively $2\frac{1}{2}$ year old, had just started at the local playgroup. She was an only child and had previously spent all her time with her mother, Sally. She settled well into the playgroup and began to join in and make friends. The staff at the playgroup chatted with Sally when she came to pick up Maria and talked to her about how well they thought she was doing. After a couple of months, Sally asked to have a private interview with the playgroup leader. She said that she was concerned that all Maria did at the group was play and asked when she was going to be taught how to write her name and the other letters of the alphabet. The leader listened to Sally, giving her a chance to put her point of view. She showed her the playgroup plans and then asked Sally to walk around the playroom with her, explaining how the play activities offered to the children contributed to developing the skills they would need later for reading and writing. She gave her a copy of a playgroup's brochure, which explained the group's commitment to a 'learning through play' approach and was able to reassure her that Maria was well on the way to becoming a writer.

➤ *Why do you think Sally was concerned?* **KUS 7**

➤ *Why was the playgroup leader's approach successful in reassuring Sally?* **KUS 7**

Element P9.1 Are you ready for assessment?

Inform parents about the operation of the group

You need to show that you are competent at informing parents about the operation of the group. To do this you will need to be directly observed by your assessor and present other types of evidence.

Direct observation by your assessor

Your assessor will need to see you carry out these performance criteria (PCs)

P9.1 PCs 1, 2, 4, 5

During these observations your assessor must see you carry out at least ONE aspect in each range category listed in this element.

Remember the range categories for this element are:

1. Parents
2. Care and education setting

Preparing to be observed

You should arrange for your assessor to observe you at a time when you are likely to be talking with parents, perhaps at the beginning or end of a session. You should think through what you want to talk to parents about and perhaps anticipate any questions they might have so that you can have information to hand or know whom to refer them to. You may have parents who need some communication support; if this is the case, make sure you have arranged for this to be in place beforehand. If you are able to include parents who are new to the setting as part of your observation, then you will cover more of the range.

(You should explain to any parents involved that your assessor is observing *you* rather than them and their responses and respect the wishes of anyone who doesn't wish to participate.)

Read the performance criteria and range carefully before your assessment. Try to cover as much as you can.

Other types of evidence

You may need to present different types of evidence in order to:

• cover criteria not observed by your assessor
• show that you have the required knowledge, understanding and skills
• cover other parts of the range.

The amount and type of evidence you need to present will vary. You should plan this with your assessor.

Element P9.2

Encourage parents to participate in group functions

Element P9.3

Encourage parents to participate in children's activities

KUS
2, 3, 4,
8, 9, 10

Why encourage parents to participate?

- Parents have a wealth of skills and experiences that they can contribute to the child care centre. Participation in this way will broaden and enrich the programme offered to all the children. Many groups rely on a parents' rota to complement their staffing.

- An extra person to work at an activity, to help out on a trip or to prepare materials can make a valuable contribution to a busy setting. Parents who are involved in this way will gain first-hand experience of the way that the centre works and an understanding of the approach.

- Provision for young children is often under-funded. Many centres have parent groups that organise social activities and raise funds.

- Parents may experience a loss of role when their child starts nursery or school. Being involved may help them to feel valued and help them to adjust to this change.

- Where parents are experiencing difficulties with their children, they may be able to be supported by playing with their children alongside sympathetic professionals in the child care setting.

Parents make a valuable contribution by supporting activities

- Many centres operate with regulations that require a parent representative on the management committee or governing body. The responsibilities here can be quite significant and will include financial management and accountability, selection and recruitment of staff, as well as day-to-day running of the centre.

- New initiatives such as Sure Start, which are aimed at improving opportunities and facilities for young children and their families, require communities to take an active part in deciding what is needed and how it should be provided. Parents of young children will play a key role in these developments.

Involving parents in the work setting

All parents will have some involvement with the centre their child attends. Just what form this involvement takes will depend on the type of centre, on the way that staff choose to work with parents and on the parents themselves. Following are some examples of how child care centres can work together with parents to the benefit of children.

Working with the children

Here parents are encouraged to stay and become involved in activities with the children, sometimes committing themselves to a regular session – as with a playgroup rota – or on an occasional basis. The children benefit from the presence of another adult, parents have a chance to see the setting at work and the child is aware of the link between home and the centre. Cooking and crafts such as sewing are often supported in this way. Outings with groups of children would neither be possible nor safe without parent volunteers to accompany them. Parents might also be able to contribute in a more specific way, for example, by talking about their job, telling a story in another language or playing an instrument. In these situations parents should be supported, rather than left to get on with activities on their

A parent might bring in a new baby to meet the children

own. Staff need to brief parents on the routine and talk about their approach and the purpose of the activities they are providing.

KUS
2, 3, 8

Giving a talk

The pre-school group had been working on a topic about 'Ourselves'. The children had examined their own features and compared them with those of their friends and taken part in many other linked activities. The group had a good relationship with its parents and they were often involved in activities. At the beginning of every topic, staff displayed their plans on the parents' notice board and asked parents for contributions, either of materials or ideas. One parent noticed that some work was planned on joints and the skeleton. As a radiographer, she had access to X-rays, which she thought might be useful for the project. After a chat with the supervisor, she was persuaded not only to donate the X-rays but to come and give a talk to the group. Although she had some reservations, she came along in her hospital uniform and talked to the children about her job. There were lots of questions after she'd finished, with many from children who'd had their own experience of X-rays after accidents. When she came in next to pick up her children, she saw the follow-up work that the group had done after her visit displayed on the boards.

➤ *What do you think the children gained from this experience?*
➤ *What do you think the parent gained from participating in this way?*
➤ *Do you think all parents would be happy taking on this role? What would it depend on?*

Working behind the scenes

Not everyone feels comfortable with or is able to work alongside the children. Making, mending and maintaining equipment is a task that can involve parents. Also in this category of involvement will be the fund raising and organisation of social events that many parent groups take responsibility for. Social events that bring together staff and parents are usually very successful in promoting good relationships and often raise funds too. Parents who are not available during the day may be able to become involved in these ways.

Special events

Most centres have occasions when parents are invited along to parties, concerts, sports, open days or stay-and-play sessions. Such events are usually very popular indeed. More parents will be able to take advantage of the invitation if other commitments are taken into account, for example, if babies and toddlers are welcome at an afternoon concert, or if there are occasional evening events so that those who are out at work during the day can attend.

Support for parents

In some centres the staff have a special brief to work with parents. This is probably because there is some difficulty in the family that affects the child and the parent needs some support. Staff work alongside parents and children in individual programmes. For this kind of work to be successful, it is crucial that the member of staff has the trust and confidence of the parent. Some centres might also offer 'drop-in' facilities and parents' groups as part of their programme.

Taking the curriculum home

When they reach that stage, most parents will expect to play a part in helping their children to read. Home–school reading diaries, in which parents and staff exchange comments on books and reading, provide a link and show children that everyone is involved in supporting their progress. But parents' involvement in the curriculum is valuable much earlier on too. Many settings keep parents informed about what their children have been doing and what they are planning to do as a group, so that parents can follow up or reinforce a skill or an interest that is developing. This approach recognises and emphasises the importance of partnership between home and setting in supporting children's development.

Official roles

Some parents will be involved with the child care centre in an official capacity. All state schools will have parents, elected by other parents, on their governing bodies and they have an important role defined in law. Playgroups are usually run by a committee of parents for the benefit of the local community. Other types of settings may have parent representatives on their management committees. Sometimes parents may be reluctant to become involved in this way and will need to be assured that they have a necessary and valuable contribution to make.

Parents who do not participate

Remember that not all parents will wish to, or be able to, be involved directly in the setting. They may have family or work commitments that leave them with little time to spare. Others may not feel confident about participating in some of the ways described above. Some parents may have a real need for some 'time out' from their children and anything associated with them. The child care worker should not make assumptions that the parent is not interested in their child if they do not participate directly but should try to understand the variety of individual family circumstances.

Are you ready for assessment?

Encourage parents to participate in group functions

You need to show that you are competent at encouraging parents to participate in group functions. To do this you will need to be observed by your assessor and present other types of evidence.

(As this element is very closely linked to P9.3, you may find that evidence can be used across both elements.)

Direct observation by your assessor

Your assessor will need to see you carry out these performance criteria (PCs)

P9.2 PCs 1, 2, 3, 4, 5, 6, 7

During these observations your assessor must see you cover at least ONE aspect in each range category listed in this element.

Remember the range categories for this element are:

1. Relationships
2. Parents
3. Functions

Preparing to be observed

Arrange for your assessor to observe you when you are with parents, perhaps talking to them as a group, otherwise as you interact with individuals. You should show that you can encourage them to join in with functions, such as helping out with a fund raising activity or coming to a social event. You should show that you are sensitive to parents' wishes and recognise that parents will participate in different ways, some becoming more involved than others.

Read the performance criteria and range carefully before your assessment. Try to cover as much as you can.

Other types of evidence

You may need to present different types of evidence in order to:

- cover criteria not observed by your assessor
- show that you have the required knowledge, understanding and skills
- cover other parts of the range.

The amount and type of evidence you need to present will vary. You should plan this with your assessor.

Element P9.3

Are you ready for assessment?

Encourage parents to participate in children's activities

You need to show that you are competent in encouraging parents to participate in children's activities. To do this you will need to be directly observed by your assessor and present other types of evidence.

(As this element is very closely linked to P9.2, you are likely to find that evidence presented for one element can be cross-referenced to the other.)

Direct observation by your assessor

Your assessor will need to see you carry out these performance criteria (PCs)

P9.3 PCs 1, 2, 3, 4, 5, 6

During these observations your assessor must see you cover at least ONE aspect in each range category listed in this element.

Remember the range categories for this element are:

1. Parents
2. Children's activities

Preparing to be observed

You should arrange for your assessor to observe you when you are working with a parent or group of parents who are participating in children's activities. You should show how you match parents' interests and skills to the kinds of activities you are asking them to support, listening and responding to any suggestions or concerns they might have. Explain to the parents what the purpose of the activity is and what you intend the children to gain from it and be clear about how they can support this. As they become involved in the activities, show how you can support and encourage them in this role.

Read the performance criteria and range carefully before your assessment. Try and cover as much as you can.

Other types of evidence

You may need to present different types of evidence in order to:
- cover criteria not observed by your assessor
- show that you have the required knowledge, understanding and skills
- cover other parts of the range.

The amount and type of evidence you need to present will vary. You should plan this with your assessor.

Check your knowledge

- Why is it important for the child care worker to recognise that all families are different and that approaches to child rearing and play will vary from family to family? **KUS 7**
- Does being involved mean that parents have to participate in children's activities? Explain your answer. **KUS 3**
- Why might some parents be reluctant to participate in children's activities? **KUS 9**
- What communication skills do you need to work effectively with parents? **KUS 5**
- What are the benefits to parents, to children and to the group of parents' involvement in the child care setting? **KUS 2**

Contribute to the effectiveness of work teams

This unit describes the role of the child care and education worker in contributing to the effectiveness of work teams. The term 'work team' refers to a group of people who work closely together. It also refers to a team of people who work together to meet the needs of children but are not in close contact throughout the day. This includes childminders. Childminders usually work on their own for long periods of time but are part of a team that includes parents and may include childminder support staff, health visitors and others.

The first element in this unit describes standards for contributing to effective team working by:

- *behaving appropriately*
- *communicating effectively*
- *passing on information*
- *receiving and acting on constructive feedback*
- *offering ideas about how to improve the team's practice*
- *seeking advice about how to deal with any problems that arise in the team; this may include clashes of personality, unclear roles and inappropriate behaviour such as bullying, discrimination or harassment.*

The second element focuses on you developing yourself through:

- *thinking about your work role and what you are capable of*
- *developing your own practice through learning from other members of the team.*

Unit wide knowledge **KUS 1, 4, 5, 20**

Introduction

Effective communication

The ability to communicate through the spoken and written word is what makes human beings different from other animals. We have many ways of communicating through papers, books and magazines, telephones, mobile phones, text messaging, emails and video connections.

However, the most important form of communication between people is direct, face-to-face communication. This type of communication is particularly important for those who work with people rather than machines. Sometimes, however, people find direct communication the most difficult. A large part of your role, if you work with children, is to communicate directly and effectively with children as

Childminders usually work alone for long periods of time but are part of a team that includes parents

well as with other adults. The adults may be parents, other professionals and your staff team. Childminders work with children and also in partnership with parents and sometimes as part of a childminding network. In order to provide the best environment for children, you need to develop good direct, face-to-face communication skills.

Face-to-face communication involves conveying a message using verbal and non-verbal methods. These include:

Method of communication	What it includes
Verbal communication:	Using spoken words appropriately Listening Writing effectively
Non-verbal communication:	Tone of voice Body language including: Facial expression Eye contact Posture, gestures, body movement and actions

To communicate effectively and to convey your message clearly and positively you must use all these methods skilfully.

Good practice when communicating with others

Verbal communication

Verbal communication involves using words in some form. For this it is important that you speak clearly, listen carefully and write clearly. You should:

- *Speak clearly* using words that you can reasonably expect the listener to understand. You should change the words you use and the way you say them to take into account:

  - the chronological and developmental age of the listener

  - whether the listener speaks English as their home language

  - any hearing or learning impairment the listener has.

- You should use an interpreter if needed.

- *Listen carefully* to what the other person is saying to you. It is important to give time to listen to the person and to show them that you understand what they are saying to you. This can be done by what is called 'reflective listening'. This includes repeating what the other person has said but in a slightly different way and also summarising what they have said. This shows them that you have understood what they have said to you. It also helps you to show warmth and concern. It is good not to interrupt a person when they are speaking.

- *Write clearly* in plain English. Use short sentences, simple words and illustrations and drawings.

Non-verbal communication

Only a small part of what we understand comes from the actual words a person says. A much bigger part comes from the way a person says it; this includes their tone of voice and their body language.

When communicating with others it important to check your tone of voice, facial expression, eye contact, posture, gestures, body movement and actions. You should check the following:

- *Your tone of voice.* You need to be aware of the tone, speed and pitch of your voice. Through these you can express a range of emotions from excitement and enthusiasm, to boredom and irritation.

- *Your facial expression.* This is very important as it shows what you are feeling and what really interests you. If you look bright and interested your communication will be much better than if you look bored and uninterested.

- *Eye contact.* Making eye contact with the child or adult you are talking with is very important. However, eye contact is interpreted differently in different cultures. For example, in British culture it is considered rude not to make eye contact but it is rude to stare. For some people from an Asian family background, making eye contact during a conversation with a stranger can be rude.

- *Your posture, gestures, body movement and actions.* Movements of different parts of the body can be very revealing. Young children quickly learn that they gain attention by moving their bodies. Movements can show how a person feels and what they are about to do, such as bring a conversation to an end. You should try to sit or stand at the same level as the person to whom you are speaking. Keep an appropriate distance. If you get too close you may 'invade' the space around a person (sometimes called their personal space). If you keep too far away you may be considered rude and distant. People also differ personally, socially and culturally in their use of physical contact with others. You need to be aware of these differences so that you do not offend other people.

Making eye contact is very important

Barriers to effective communication

The environment

You may have developed effective communication skills but there are other things that can make communication difficult. The environment can help or hinder communication.

You should avoid trying to communicate with people:

- If there is a great deal of other noise in the environment. The noise of machines, vehicles, loud music or lots of other people talking can make it difficult. You cannot give your full attention to the other person and they will not be able to hear you.
- If there is a lot of physical activity going on around you. People moving around or moving objects is very distracting.
- Try to find an appropriately quiet, calm place in which to communicate with others.

The way you speak

The way you speak includes:

- the type of language you use
- the way you use it.

When communicating with children or with adults it is important that you use language that they understand.

You should aim for the following:

- Make your vocabulary (the words you use) simple. Avoid using a complicated word if there is a simpler one.
- Avoid the use of jargon. This includes technical words, language to do with your profession and abbreviations that the other person may not understand.
- Avoid the use of slang. Slang should be reserved for communicating with friends and not be part of your professional vocabulary. It also provides a poor language role model for children who may copy you.
- Be aware of local dialects. Dialects are patterns of speech of a particular area. If part of your speech pattern includes use of local dialect words and phrases, you should be aware that not everyone you speak to is local and that it can seem to them that you are speaking another language. They may also feel left out.
- Understand your mood and attitude. We all have days when we feel low in our mood, or unhappy or cross about something. As professionals we should control the way we express our personal emotions. We should always be positive and pleasant in our communication with children and adults at work. We must not let our personal feelings affect our professional contact with others.

This unit contains two elements:

- **CU10.1** *Contribute to effective team working*
- **CU10.2** *Develop oneself in own work role*

Element CU10.1 *Contribute to effective team working*

KUS
6, 7, 8,
9, 10, 11,
12, 13,
14, 19, 21

Work relationships

Relationships at work (professional relationships) are not the same as personal relationships although you may make friends at work. We relate to people at work to achieve the aims and objectives of the work setting, such as the care and education of children. We should not develop relationships at work to satisfy our personal needs.

However, we do need some of the same skills and qualities in all our relationships. These include politeness, honesty, thoughtfulness, a sense of humour and encouraging others. Although work colleagues are not necessarily the ones we would choose as friends, work relationships can be fulfilling and also personally satisfying. We must develop good professional relationships for the benefit of children and families rather than for personal satisfaction.

Effective teams

In most work settings, child care workers work with colleagues as part of a team. You may have thoughts and feelings about the team of people that you work with. Do you feel happy and fulfilled in what you are doing? Are you all working well and providing the best possible environment for the children in your care? If the answer is yes, it probably means that you are working in an effective team.

To be effective any professional team should have the following:

- Clearly defined aims and objectives that all members can put into words and agree to put into practice.
- Flexible roles that enable individuals to work to their strengths, rather than in roles where they must conform to expectations (for example, a teacher always taking storytime, the child care worker always clearing up).
- Effective team leaders who manage the work of the team, encourage and value individual contributions and deal with conflict.
- Team members who are committed to:
  - developing self-awareness
  - building and maintaining good working relationships
  - demonstrating effective communication skills
  - expressing their views assertively rather than aggressively
  - understanding and recognising their contribution to the way the group works
  - carrying out team decisions, irrespective of their personal feelings
  - accepting responsibility for the outcome of team decisions.

Working with others in a team

You need to know who manages your team and what their expectations are of you as a team member. You may be part of a team of people who have the same professional background, for example, nursery officers working together in a day nursery. Or you may be a part of a multidisciplinary team. A multidisciplinary team has members from a number of professional groups, for example, family workers, teachers and health visitors working together in a Sure Start area.

Keeping others informed

When you are working with others in a team it is important that other members of the team know what you are doing. You can do this in the following ways:

- Verbally – face-to-face with an individual person or during a small team meeting or a whole staff meeting.
- In writing – recording what you do. This may mean using an agreed format. Records and plans should be kept in a place where others can easily refer to them.

Professional confidentiality should be maintained at all times when exchanging and recording information.

Recording information

Your role is likely to involve recording information for a variety of purposes. The following indicates what information you may need to record for and about the children in your care and for whom:

Records that must be kept	
What	**For whom?**
attendance	
health	yourself
progress	parents/carers
accidents/incidents	team members
child protection	line manager
planning	other professionals
child observations	

The way in which you need to record information will vary according to your role, the purpose of the information and for whom it is intended.

Roles within the team

Lines of management and reporting

In order to work well within any organisation you need to be clear about your own role and the role of other team members.

Be clear about roles	
Your own role, including:	**The role of other team members, including:**
what your responsibilities are	their role and responsibilities
to whom you are accountable	to whom they are accountable
what your job description includes	what their job description includes
who your line manager is (this is the person who is immediately responsible for your work)	the line management structure of the setting

A line manager is the first person that you and others should expect to report to and be guided and managed by.

Possible line management structure in a private day nursery:

Owner

↑

Officer-in-charge

↑

Deputy officer-in-charge

↑

Level 3 nursery officers (supervising others in a room)

↑

Level 2 or level 3 nursery officers working in support of others

↑

Trainee nursery officers

How teams work – what makes a team effective?

Your performance in a staff team should help to support the effective working of the team. You should be prepared to work hard, be helpful and offer ideas and information to other members of the team. If other members of your team make suggestions, you in turn should accept them positively and use them constructively to improve your practice with the children.

The advantages of team work	
Co-operation	The children see the benefits of people working together and co-operating with each other
Consistency	All workers adopt the same approach to the task of caring for children and working with their families
Encouragement	Members of the team stimulate, motivate, praise, encourage and support one another
Respect	Team membership satisfies a need to belong and to be respected, and to have ideals and aims confirmed and shared by others
Efficiency	The skills of all members are used to arrive at the best solutions
Belonging	Individual staff feel a sense of belonging and can share problems, difficulties and successes
Sharing	Responsibility and insight is shared by all
Innovation	Individuals become more willing to adopt new ways of thinking and working
Balance	The strengths and weaknesses of one person are balanced by the strengths and weaknesses of others

Participating in team meetings and groups

Within a work setting groups meet formally and informally. There are staff team meetings, groups of parents and carers, and other professionals. Groups can be effective in stimulating new ideas, managing projects, making decisions, monitoring and reviewing progress, and supporting group members.

It helps if group members consider their behaviour and think how they can establish and develop constructive relationships with others in the workplace. You should think about how positive or negative your behaviour is and how it may help or prevent the team achieving its aims.

Staff team meetings can be effective in stimulating new ideas

Behaviour and characteristics of team members that is positive	
Positive behaviour	**What it includes**
Volunteering information	Offering facts, feelings, views or opinions
Summarising	Helping the group to sort things out, bring things together or round things off
Compromising	Admitting an error or changing your view or position
Confronting	Challenging others if you think they are wrong, but doing this with skill and concern for the feelings of others
Time keeping	Not wasting time and ensuring that the group keeps to time
Working harmoniously	Helping to solve disagreements, relieve tension and explore differences
Encouraging others	Initiating things, getting things going and keeping them going

Behaviour and characteristics of team members that is negative	
Negative behaviour	**What it includes**
Blocking	Preventing the group from getting on with its task
Being aggressive	Attacking others, belittling their contribution or putting them down
Withdrawal	Showing a lack of involvement
Avoidance	Preventing the group from facing issues
Dominating	Asserting authority, interrupting, interfering with the right of others to join in

Assisting others in the team and carrying out instructions

When you work in a team it is important that you:

- offer assistance, that is help, to others in the team when they need it.
- do this willingly in a friendly, positive and helpful way.
- take responsibility for what you do, taking care to do everything you are asked to do, not assuming others will do it for you and understanding your role if you are the person who is in charge of the activity. The activity can be anything from sharpening the pencils to being responsible for taking a child out for a walk alone.

You may need to make a note of instructions you are given to make sure that you are able to follow them accurately. You should then carry out the tasks to the standard required and in the time allocated, making sure that you are aware of the policies and procedures of your workplace for any of these activities.

You may need to ask your line manager or someone in a supervisory role if you do not understand what to do or if you think the task is not your responsibility. You may need to delay some tasks until someone in a supervisory role has shown you what to do or until you have received appropriate training.

If you have any suggestions for changing things, make them to an appropriate person, rather than grumbling or gossiping behind their back. Open communication of positive and negative issues helps staff to develop positive relationships with each other. You should put your point of view, but also be open to the views of other people.

Time management

If you agree to do something within your work team it is very important that you do what you agreed. You need to manage your time well to achieve all the tasks that you are responsible for. This means prioritising them. Prioritising means putting tasks in an order of importance; you should decide which must be done first and allow the right amount of time to get it done. You should arrive at work at the right time and not leave before your finishing time, unless you have permission or have been instructed to.

You may also find the following tips helpful:

- Make lists and add dates/times by which the task needs to be done. If you do this then you should be more able to cope with the busy and stressful times that occur within any work setting.

- Observe and learn from experienced staff. Watch them to see how they manage to do their tasks within the time that is available to them.

- Ask your line manager for feedback about how well he or she thinks you manage your time.

- Avoid interrupting people while they are working with children or talking with parents or other colleagues. This could make them negative in their response to you. Unless it is urgent, choose a time when they are free to speak with you.

- Observe others in your team and, if you can, offer them help and support if they are very busy.

Stress and conflict within teams

Within any team there is likely to be conflict or clashes at some time. Conflict usually happens when people do not understand what each other are doing or why. It is important to deal with conflict constructively and positively rather than try to ignore it. Conflict can also happen when everyone is particularly busy and feeling stressed. Workers should try to be aware of this and be sensitive to other people. You can then avoid causing further stress to others at busy times.

If you disagree with someone you should:

- try to settle differences of opinion in a way that avoids giving offence
- never be rude or impatient
- remain calm, positive and polite.

If you do this you are more likely to maintain respect between you and your colleagues. You may need advice from your line manager about the best way to deal with the problem. Conflicts that are not sorted out become a barrier to good working relationships.

You should also get advice from an appropriate person, such as your line manager if you experience interpersonal problems that include clashes of personality, bullying, harassment and discrimination.

It is important to deal with conflict constructively and positively

The following guidelines for behaviour are likely to help handle and minimise inter-personal conflict:

- Join with the other person so that you can both 'win'. People in conflict often tend to be against rather than with each other. Keep a clear picture of the person and yourself, separate from the issue. The issue causing the conflict may be lost by the strength of bad feeling against the other person. You need to be committed to working towards an outcome that is acceptable to both people.

- Make clear 'I' statements. Take responsibility for yourself and avoid blaming the other person for how you feel and what you think.

- Be clear and specific about your view of the conflict and what you want. Listen to the other person's view.

● Pool your ideas for ways of sorting out the conflict: make a list of all the possible solutions and go through them together.

● Deal with one issue at a time. Avoid confusing one issue with another and using examples from the past to illustrate your point. Using the past or only telling part of the story to make your own point can lead to a biased version of what happened. The other person is likely to have forgotten or may remember the incident very differently.

● Look at and listen to each other: deal directly with each other and the difficulty.

● Ensure that you understand each other: if you are unclear and confused about the issue, ask open questions and paraphrase back what you think you hear.

● Choose a mutually convenient time and place. It is useful to agree on the amount of time you will spend.

● Acknowledge and appreciate one another. Think of the other person's attributes separately from the conflict issue and acknowledge and appreciate them.

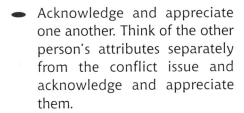

Element
CU10.1 Are you ready for assessment?

Contribute to effective team working

You need to show that you can competently contribute to effective team working. To do this you will need to be directly observed by your assessor and present other types of evidence.

Direct observation by your assessor

Your assessor will need to see you carry out these performance criteria (PCs)

CU10.1 PCs 1, 2, 3, 4, 5, 6, 7

During these observations your assessor must see you cover at least ONE aspect in each range category listed in this element.

Remember the range categories listed for this element are:

1. The worker's behaviour
2. Problems

Preparing to be observed

Your assessor may observe you working with other people in a team while she or he is observing and assessing another unit. While working in a team you should show that you are keeping the team informed about what you are doing. This may be through face-to-face contact with an individual person, during a small team meeting or a whole staff meeting; or it might be through making effective records that can be shared with others.

You should make sure that you behave positively and are supportive towards others in the team. In this way you will help the team to work well. When you can, you should offer team members ideas and information that will help them.

If others offer you suggestions and information you should show that you accept these positively and make use of them to improve what you do. Your assessor should also be able to observe you offering to help others in the team in a friendly and helpful way.

You must show that you do something you have previously agreed to do, unless something else becomes a priority, such as dealing with a distressed or injured child. You must also think of some improvement to the way the team works and tell a relevant team member. For example, you may want to suggest to your line manager that she encourages you and other junior staff to give some feedback about an activity at a staff meeting rather than making senior staff responsible for this.

Read the performance criteria and range carefully before your assessment. Try to cover as much as you can.

Element CU10.2 _Develop oneself in own work role_

KUS
2, 3, 15, 16, 17, 18, 22, 23, 24

 ## Personal and professional development

As a professional worker you must take responsibility for your own development and performance; others can help and guide you but you will only make good professional progress if you:

- become aware of your strengths and weaknesses
- are committed to improving your skills
- take responsibility for doing this.

However, we all find it difficult to evaluate our own performance. To evaluate our performance means that we try to understand how good or bad we are at something, and identify our strengths and weaknesses. Most people need the help of others to do this.

To work out your strengths and weaknesses, to evaluate your professional performance and to improve your skills, you must:

- want to do this
- take responsibility for it
- identify what your needs are
- be realistic about what you can achieve
- take responsibility for your own development and learning
- take feedback from others in a positive way in order to improve.

It can be very difficult to do this on your own. You could try to write down what you think are six of your strengths and six weaknesses. We often find it easier to see our weaknesses rather than our strengths. Help and feedback from others is very important to get a clear and balanced picture. You should try to:

- listen to others
- understand what they say to you
- be open to suggestions about how you can change and improve how you work.

This will help to improve your future work performance. Supervision by a line manager or an experienced worker will increase your self-awareness. It is helpful if you and your supervisor can arrange a set time to see each other alone. In-service staff development training will also help to keep you up to date with new developments and improve your working practice.

Supervision by a line manager or an experienced worker will increase your self-awareness

It is important that those working on their own also find ways of getting feedback on their practice. They also need support and professional development. Discussion with parents and with others in a similar role can be very supportive. Advice may be available locally. There are many local childminder networks. Opportunities for updating and further training and advice may also be available through your local Early Years Development and Childcare Partnership (EYDCP) and National Childminding Association (NCMA).

Professional development and further training

As a professional child care worker you should aim to identify your own needs for development. You can do this and review your progress when you have supervision time with your line manager. You may decide to take further training in order to do your job better. You should also think about your personal career aims and whether your current work is helping you to move towards them.

You will have to decide what further training you are able to do and the time that is available to you.

There may be personal and professional obstacles to your development. You should think clearly about what these are and go through each of them with your manager. These could be:

- your educational achievement so far
- your domestic situation
- skills that you have not yet achieved
- changes in practice of which you are not aware, for example, health and safety procedures.

There may be ways you can deal with some or every one of these obstacles and make them less of a barrier.

Types of professional development

The government encourages us all to continue to learn throughout our lives. There are a wide range of opportunities.

These opportunities include:

- Training for appropriate early years care and education qualifications on the Qualifications and Curriculum Authority (QCA) framework. This framework is available on-line.
- Short courses to gain specific skills to meet the National Standards for Under Eights' Day Care and Child Minding, e.g. First Aid, Basic Food Hygiene, Child Protection.
- Short courses to increase your professional skills in meeting the developmental needs of children.
- Training and development opportunities to understand new developments, e.g. the Foundation Stage, Assessment, Inspection and Regulation, Quality Assurance.
- General educational opportunities, e.g. Key Skills.

Trade unions and professional organisations

You may wish to consider joining a union and/or a professional association. Trade unions and professional associations may offer the following to their members:

- access to legal protection
- negotiation of pay and conditions
- inexpensive insurance cover
- collective efforts to improve working conditions
- protection of its members through health and safety practices, pension and entitlements issues.

Aisha's personal development

KUS
2, 16, 17, 18, 22

Aisha was pleased to get the job as a nursery assistant at Tall Trees Day Nursery. Although it was two bus rides from where she lived and the wages were low, it was what she wanted to do. She knew she wanted a career in child care. Aisha worked hard in the first few months, making sure she arrived on time and letting the nursery know if she had missed the bus and would be late. She observed how the more experienced staff worked and asked them questions.

Aisha offered to plan an activity. She prepared it and carried it out with the children. She asked for feedback and her line manager gave her ideas about how to improve it.

After a while, however, she began to feel 'put upon'. She felt she was being asked to do too many jobs for other members of staff. This was reinforced by one of the other nursery assistants, who was always moaning and was pleased to have someone else to criticise the other staff in the team with.

In one of Aisha's supervision sessions, her line manager asked her what she thought about her progress. The line manager said that Aisha seemed less enthusiastic than when she started and had been late a lot in the last month.

Aisha opened up and explained how she was feeling. Her line manager told her that she thought she worked very well with the children and suggested Aisha could work towards NVQ Level 2 in Early Years Care and Education. This would mean attending college once a week and training and gathering evidence in the work setting. Aisha thought about it and decided to have a go. It was hard work gaining the skills and producing the evidence. However, the other staff supported and encouraged her. She enjoyed the purpose and focus it gave to what she was doing. She kept going and was eventually successful. She became a qualified member of staff and her wages went up. Aisha is now a full team member in a nursery room and enjoys helping other students in the nursery.

At a recent supervision session she discussed her progress and talked about the future when she might have gained sufficient skill and confidence to register for a Level 3 award.

➤ *Why do you think Aisha's performance was poorer after a time in the nursery. What helped and what hindered Aisha's professional development?* **KUS 17, 18**

➤ *How was Aisha helped to identify her own competence and progress?* **KUS 22**

➤ *Describe the things Aisha did to take responsibility for her own development and performance and why this was important.* **KUS 2**

➤ *What career goals did she achieve and how relevant to her work were they?* **KUS 16**

➤ *How might it help Aisha to talk about her progress with her supervisor? What are Aisha's future aims?*

Element CU10.2

Are you ready for assessment?

Develop oneself in own work role

You need to show that you can develop yourself in your own work role. To do this you will need to be directly observed by your assessor and present other types of evidence.

Direct observation by your assessor

Your assessor will need to see you carry out these performance criteria (PCs)

CU10.2 PCs 1, 2, 3, 4

During these observations your assessor must see you cover at least ONE aspect in each range category listed in this element.

Remember the range category listed for this element is:

1. Feedback from others

Preparing to be observed

You need to show your assessor that you have identified your own development needs against the demands of your work role. For this you need to be clear about your work role before you are observed. You may have a printed job description. If you do not have one you should work one out with your supervisor and record it if possible.

To be observed for this element you could invite your assessor to observe you during a supervision session (with the prior agreement of your workplace supervisor.)

You should plan with your supervisor to discuss:

- your personal development objectives – what you are aiming to achieve in the short and longer term

- which of these aims are achievable and realistic
- how they might be achieved
- whether the way you want to do this is at the right level for you and gives you the right level of challenge (if it is too easy or too difficult you will be wasting time and achieve very little)
- your recent performance while carrying out an activity with children including the strengths and weaknesses of your performance
- any training and development needs that you have.

During this discussion with your supervisor, your assessor will be able to see you taking responsibility for your own development, learning and performance.

She will also be able to see you taking feedback from your supervisor, discussing your performance constructively and positively, and showing that you understand how you will use this in the future to improve your work performance.

This will cover the 'Verbal feedback from others' part of the range.

Your assessor may also observe you receiving feedback from others at other times while she is observing you carrying out activities and routines as part of the nursery team.

Read the performance criteria and range carefully before your assessment. Try to cover as much as you can. ▶▶

Other types of evidence

You may need to present different types of evidence in order to:

- cover criteria not observed by your assessor
- show that you have the required knowledge, understanding and skills
- cover other parts of the range.

The amount and type of evidence you need to present will vary. You should plan this with your assessor.

Check your knowledge

- What do you need in order to contribute to effective team work? **KUS 20, 21**
- What are the things you need to do in order to develop yourself in your own work role? **KUS 2, 22, 24**

Appendix

Legislation in the four countries of the United Kingdom relating to the care and education of children has differences. You should ensure that you know about the regulations that apply to the area where you are working. Your supervisor or assessor will be able to advise you about this.

The information below is a brief overview of some of the legislation concerning children in each of the four countries.

England

The Children Act 1989 came into force in England and Wales in 1991. It aims to protect children in every situation, whether in their own homes, in day care or full-time care. It provides extensive guidance on the regulation of services for children and their families.

The National Standards for Under Eights' Day Care and Child Minding (2001) apply to all child care providers in England. The standards relate to the Children Act 1989. They are regulated by the **Early Years Directorate within the Office for Standards in Education** (Ofsted). The 14 standards include staffing, organisation, care, learning and play, physical environment, equipment, safety, health, food and drink, equal opportunities, behaviour, working in partnership with parents and carers, child protection and documentation.

The standards have been revised in 2003.

Wales

The Child Minding and Day Care (Wales) Regulations 2002 arise from the Children Act 1989. Regulations and national minimum standards cover such matters as planning for individual needs and preferences, quality of life, staffing, management, concerns, complaints and protection and the physical environment.

The Care Standards Inspectorate for Wales (CSIW) inspects and aims to ensure that services meet the standards set out in the regulations.

Scotland

The Children (Scotland) Act 1995 is the major piece of legislation relating to children in Scotland. It provides guidance on the regulation of services for children and their families.

National Care Standards for child care cover services for children and young people up to the age of 16 years. These standards are regulated under the **Regulation of Care (Scotland) Act 2001** and are inspected by the **Scottish Commission for the Regulation of Care**. The range of services covered includes nursery classes, creches, childminders, after school clubs and playgroups. The main principles of the standards are dignity, privacy, choice, safety, realising potential, and equality and diversity.

These standards are currently being revised.

Northern Ireland

Northern Ireland operates a separate jurisdiction to England, Wales and Scotland.

The Children (Northern Ireland) Order 1995 is the major piece of legislation relating to children. It provides extensive guidance on the regulation of services for children and their families.

The detailed regulations and standards relating to day care services for children under 12 are contained in the **Children Northern Ireland Order 1995: Regulations and Guidance Volume 2: Family Support, Childminding and Day Care**. The standards set the regulations for services in day care in nurseries, play groups and with childminders. The standards include regulations relating to the management of settings and to the safety, protection, health and well-being of children.

The standards are regulated and inspected by local Social Services teams.

Index

Note: Page references in italics indicate figures, tables or illustrations

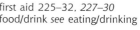